PACING TO PEACE

**The autobiography of MARGARET FROST, Australia's first
champion reinswoman, and her search for answers.**

Dual Gaited Publications
New Gisborne, Vic. 3438

Published 1999

Distributed by Dennis Jones & Associates
Bayswater, Vic.

Printed by Brougham Press,
Bayswater, Vic.

National Library Of Australia
Cataloguing in Publication data

ISBN 0 9577804 0 0

Dedication

**To my son, Garry David Frost, whose loss
precipitated my search for answers, leading me into
a stronger faith and allowing me to accept more
readily those things I cannot change.**

To Dear Vivien and Bob,

Thank you so much for all
you have done for me, I loved
being with you.

I hope you enjoy my story.

love & best wishes,

Margaret Frost.

4-10-2009.

CONTENTS

ACKNOWLEDGEMENTS

It was never my intention to write my life story. If my racing career had not been cut short by a serious race smash, I would still be training and driving pacers with no time to even consider writing. While recuperating from the smash, my friend John Cushan suggested I write what I could remember to stimulate my impaired memory, which led to extending this to be a record of my life for my grandchildren. I mentioned all this to an elderly friend, Bant Iliff, who has written four books herself. She rang me one day and said, 'Margaret, bring me the first chapter'.

Well, I was committed, and started writing. Between Bant and John, the die was cast. Without their help and encouragement, there would never have been a book. Thanks to Bant for the early corrections and for helping to 'polish' it up for me, making my rough writing so much smoother, *and* to them both for the 'pushing'. As I wrote, it occurred to me that perhaps I could share my experiences and my search for answers with others who also may be searching and struggling to come to grips with the loss of a loved one and to come to an understanding of their life's purpose.

I give my special thanks to George MacDonald Paterson, my father, and to my mother, Annie Paterson. Firstly for being my parents, and for their decision to leave England, their family and friends to come to Australia where I was privileged to have my life's experiences. And secondly, for the hardships they endured to make it all possible.

To Vic, for introducing me to the wonderful world of pacing and for sharing the highs and lows of our lives together. To Glenn, Toni, Susan and Brett, for their love and support. To my sister Neena, for her fount of knowledge of family history and for always being there and giving me sustenance whenever I needed it, thus allowing me time to write.

To Marshall Dobson for his assistance and encouragement. To Max Agnew for his enthusiastic assistance, contributions, and helping to make it all happen in book form. To John Tapp for his generous Foreword.

To Alan Parker from the WATA for his assistance and photos of our visits to Perth with Westburn Grant. From Harold Park HRC, Peter V'landys, John Dumesny, Camille Hodder, John Ponsonby, Liam Farell, Chipps and Mary Lette, who helped with dates, information and photos. To Ken Dyer and Rod Pollock from the Australian Harness Racing Council, and Bob Cain. To Harry Pearce for his advice, and Bill Whittaker for the cover photo. To Margaret Davies for her helpful contribution. Thanks to those people who asked for the first copy of my book, because they kept my nose to the grindstone, and to Michael Cross for his expertise on computers.

To Rev. Gordon Bradbury and the ladies at KYB for their help with my search for answers. My friends Janet and Ron, Kevin and Ruby, Joan and Ron (Ron is now deceased), Peter and Doreen, Dianne and Rod, Ken and Cynthia, and Jan, who have encouraged me, not only with this story, but all through my trials and tribulations. We have shared many tears together and upheld one another through our hard times. True friendship is just one of the beautiful blessings in life. I apologise to those friends I have missed.

Thanks to the RBC Ministries for allowing me to copy some of their very inspirational quotes, which are prefaced by an *.

Margaret Frost

FOREWORD
By John Tapp

I witnessed dozens of trackside presentations during my 13 years as a harness racing commentator at Harold Park Paceway, but one stands alone in my memory. It was June 2nd 1978. As I looked down from the broadcasting box, I was full of admiration for the petite fair-haired lass wearing a set of famous racing colours, flanked by her husband and three young children.

Judge Alf Goran, Chairman of the New South Wales Trotting Authority (as it was then known) acknowledged how history was about to be made at this famous track. In just a few minutes, Margaret Frost, wife of legendary trainer-driver Vic Frost, would become the first woman to compete against men since night trotting began there in 1949.

The night didn't have a fairytale ending because her horse (Welcome Imp) struck trouble and was beaten, but the first stone had been laid on a path that was to see female drivers take their rightful place at the headquarters of New South Wales harness racing. How prophetic it was that Margaret would soon be the first reinswoman to win there, driving the pacer Pretty Tough—something this remarkable lady proved to be as her life unfolded. Her talents in the sulky blossomed rapidly over the next few years, driving with judgement, determination and flair.

There would be doubles, trebles, feature race wins, the first sub-2:00 mile race won by a reinswoman in Australia, and the honour of being the first to represent Australia in a world driving championship for women. Behind these bright lights and the glory, Margaret never once lost sight of her duties as a wife and mother. How this little dynamo could work, raising a family and helping Vic with their big team of horses. It seems so unfair that anyone who has given so much could have so much taken away. The tragic death of a son, a marriage breakdown, a horrifying race fall that almost claimed her life and prevented her from ever driving horses again. Her resilience was also recently put to the test when almost losing her other son in a boating mishap that claimed the life of his best mate.

When you read through the following chapters you will understand how she came to put her life back on track, drawing great strength from the love of her family and beloved grandchildren, and in no small measure thanks to the chiropractic skills of her new partner, John. Her new soulmate is now God, to whom she turned when at her lowest ebb. She hasn't been disappointed with his response. I don't know whether or not the Good Lord gives preferential treatment to the right kind of people. If he does, I'm not surprised he reached out to help Margaret Frost. In my book, this lady is a saint!

John Jaffy

INTRODUCTION

By Max Agnew

Probably more than any other sport, harness racing is a world of its own, allowing families and women to participate at a closer level with their horses than is usually possible with thoroughbreds. Harness racing's classification as a family sport was well established in a bygone era and it has never lost this appeal. It may be narrow at times, but it does involves people from all walks of life, and it is the people who help make it such a popular sport. It also remains one of the few areas where you can rub shoulders with the rich and the poor, jokers and villains, and experience triumph and disaster, hope and despair.

Australia may have been among the first countries in the world to allow women a vote at elections, but the support of women participating on a level playing field in a male-dominated sport such as trotting was not so forthcoming. For years the belief was that women were too fragile and so could not be considered equal in a sport where betting was so important. In the days before the Australian Harness Racing Council was formed in 1962 and brought uniformity to the sport's rules, the states went their own way. What may have been accepted by authorities in one state might not have been in another.

During an extended visit to Perth during the First World War, Victorian Pearl Kelly's expertise with standardbreds impressed WA Trotting Association president James Brennan. He held the view that drivers (and riders) should be licensed on their ability. Brennan allowed the recently married Mrs Kelly to become Australia's first licensed reinswoman. Harness racing in Perth then took place around the famous WA cricket ground, the WACA, across the road from where Brennan would later begin the construction of Gloucester Park.

When Pearl Kelly returned to Melbourne her licence was recognised by Victorian authorities, a little surprising for the staid old Victoria Trotting & Racing Association. She underlined her competence and ability with both pacers and trotters by finishing third on the 1923 Melbourne metropolitan driving premiership, when the sport raced at the old Richmond track. Lil Welsh and Alice Laidlaw were other reinswomen to follow in her footsteps. Despite the success of this trio, the general prejudice against women continued to simmer. The main fear was that the sport would receive adverse publicity, should one of the fairer sex be badly hurt in a racetrack smash. The VT&RA decided that this prejudice was correct, and in 1931 banned all women from registered competition.

Women could train and be stablehands working behind the scenes, with their extremely good ability as strappers being widely accepted because of their patience and love for horses. No doubt in this male-dominated sport there were times when some chauvinist males would put these girls down by reminding them a woman's place was in the home and raising kids. (New South Wales did make a brief exception to this ban when allowing the mother of noted trainer Lawrie Moulds to drive in races during the war years, though this too was ended when Harold Park began planning for night meetings.)

The first woman licensed to drive on metropolitan tracks was Margaret Frost, who became the first champion reinswoman of Australia. She was the first woman to win at Harold Park, the first of her sex to drive 50 winners, the first to represent Australia on the world stage and the first to break two minutes in a race, among many other records.

The success she and other reinswomen came to enjoy in the early eighties helped pave the way for others to follow. It was never easy then, as there still lingered the prejudice that women were not as strong as men, so they could not match the men when it came to brute strength. But coaxing the best out of a horse and having it want to do its best for you has never had anything to do with brute strength. In business and politics, both men and women can put on a few airs and graces to make them look like a winner—but not on a racetrack. You either have it or you don't!

If Margaret is remembered as our first champion reinswoman, she is also remembered for being the first to suffer the hell of the very thing that years earlier officials had feared—the time when a reinswoman would be badly injured in a race-fall. But times had changed, and society had come to accept women as equals. Despite the fact that horses were now travelling much faster than before, and risks were even higher, as she lay in hospital seriously injured no-one publicly slapped officials over the wrist for permitting women to be exposed to what can be a dangerous sport.

When some months later a reinswoman did die from serious injuries suffered in a race smash at Northam, WA, there was no public outcry, either, only the sad loss of Veronica Hayes, a young woman of 26 who had accepted the dangers of racing as an occupational hazard. The best reinswomen today are accepted as equals. If they prove their ability at trials (as men must also do) they no longer have to take on the establishment as Margaret Frost and her colleagues first did.

When viewed from a distance, it probably seems that Margaret's career was one of glamour, as no other reinswoman since has been so sought-after by the media as she was. In the following pages she tells it like it really was. Margaret's whole life has been a book lying open, and somebody with the power of life and death was reading the pages.

ONE

The End of a Career

There was the usual race-day flurry of activity around the stables, a ritual I had been involved in so many times with my husband Vic, and in recent times with our trainer-driver son Glenn. Even after years of going through this familiar routine on race day, competing at your state headquarters can still give you a thrill, whether it be Melbourne, Brisbane, Perth, Adelaide, or our oldest metropolitan track, Sydney's Harold Park Paceway.

The men were putting the gear on the truck and would soon be loading the horses engaged that night. I glanced briefly at the clock on the kitchen wall. It was almost three o'clock. As I leaned over to turn on the kettle, I could see Glenn through the window, making his way towards his house. I opened the window and shouted to him, 'Hey Glennie, how long before we leave?'

'You be ready to leave in half an hour, Mum,' he called back.

'I'm just making some sandwiches to eat on the way.'

'Don't worry about me today,' he shouted, pausing to make certain he was heard. 'I have to leave early and Packy will be driving the truck. I'll meet you at the track.'

'Packy' was Graeme Gunther. For years Packy had been helping to transport our horses to the races. A half-hour would give me time to have that cup of tea and finish making a couple of sandwiches and fill the flask. I'm sure there are some women in harness racing families who can identify with this chore. If you haven't had time for much lunch and have a couple of hours' drive ahead of you, you need something in your stomach. I still had to pack my colours, including my wet weather gear, because there had been a great deal of rain that day.

Packy was already in the driver's seat and the International motor burst into life as John and I hauled ourselves into the passenger seats next to him. John Cushan, a chiropractor from Wollongong (the major provincial city in our district) was a good friend who enjoyed coming out to the farm at weekends. So keen was Packy to get started that the truck was moving before the passenger door was shut. Two loud blasts from the air horns, our usual signal to Glenn's wife Toni announcing our departure, and we were on our way to Harold Park. It was a trip I had made hundreds of times, only this journey would end up vastly different from all of the others. I would not be returning with them.

It was the night of June 16th 1995. Glenn had already won two earlier races with Cuckoos Nest and stable newcomer The Collegian. This increased his lead on the metropolitan driving premiership for the season, an honour his father had known on five occasions. He was to drive Just Baz in the last race of the night, and I had taken the drive on the stable-mate Westburn Fella. It was raining and extremely cold.

I ran up the ramp to the stables to carry out those last-minute preparations, as I had done so often at Harold Park, totally unaware that this was to be the last time I would wear the distinctive colours of white with black stars, that this was to be my very last race—and that I was only precious minutes away from walking a tightrope with death

On the last lap, just turning into the straight for that final one hundred metres to the winning post, I was caught between the lead horse and a horse outside of me. My pacer broke his stride, due to interference, falling heavily. This brought down two others in a tangle of horses, harness and sulkies. I was catapulted out of my sulky, face down into the hard, wet track. The other drivers scrambled to their feet and walked away from the wreckage, as is often the case. But this time, it was not my turn to walk away.

Of the ten days that I spent in the Royal Prince Alfred hospital, my clearest recollection is of standing at the nurses' station just outside my ward, with my bag between my feet, saying my farewells to the nurses there. It was early evening and I was waiting for John. Any other memories of those ten days were kaleidoscopic pictures of faces and events. Any detailed knowledge of that period that I have at all was related to me later by friends and members of my family, who were my constant visitors.

Apparently ambulances were unavailable on this day and John was transferring me in his car to the Lawrence Hargreave Rehabilitation Hospital at Thirroul, near Wollongong. A trip that would normally take about an hour took decidedly longer, due to the pain I was in and the need to stop frequently, sometimes inconveniently, to allow me to vomit.

Eventually we arrived at our destination and I was admitted at about 9pm. I had a right eye that would not open, a numb, swollen lower lip, a stiff and painful jaw, pain in both shoulders, pain in my back and in my chest, as well as being nauseous, not to mention having an impaired memory. I just wanted to lie down.

My stay in Thirroul hospital was for a further six weeks, during which time I was given neurological tests, mental assessments, X-rays of my jaw (revealing a double fracture), and the diagnosis and removal of my gall bladder. Pain was still with me and my right eye remained closed. My memory was a disaster. But I had lots of time to think, as I was going nowhere. I spent much time trying to make sense out of what had happened to me and get some sort of focus on the recent events.

As I lay there in my bed during the times between various treatments and assessments, my mind, as it was, wandered through many aspects of my life, from the very early impressions to the more recent. There were large gaps where I could not recall events that I should have known. With so much time on my hands, I began writing down the things I could remember, using this as a kind of stimulant to my mind. Perhaps later I would be able to fill in those gaps. In spite of everything, there emerged one very clear and irrefutable fact: my accident had turned my life upside down, leaving me to cope with some daunting decisions.

At first I held on to the hope that I would recover from my injuries enough to drive again, but as time went on it became evident that I was in for a long haul. I didn't accept the seriousness of my injuries at first.

As more and more notes on the past were jotted down, it was mentioned how my grandchildren may be interested to read them and learn a little of the life and times of their grandmother. It was not so surprising to find, as I began to write, that there was some difficulty in getting any first-hand information to fill in gaps about my early life. The generation who could have helped were deceased or unable to due to their respective ailments. It would need time and effort to chase up many important items from the past that I now had little recollection about.

TWO

My Life in England

I was born on July 26th 1943, in Bedworth (near Coventry), England, the third daughter of George MacDonald Paterson and Annie Paterson. They christened me Margaret. Mum's father was Henry Blacker and her mother Agnes (nee Carter). They were, as my mother would say, 'real English'. Mum had been born in Stonehouse in the county of Lanark on December 28th 1914.

My father was born on January 3rd 1910, in the United States at Pittsburgh, Pennsylvania, of Scottish parents who returned to Scotland when Dad was six years old. Mum was still living in Stonehouse when she met and married my father. It was there that my two sisters, Agnes Neena and Catherine, were born. Agnes, seven years older than me, would always be known as Neena. Catherine was a year younger than Neena.

Dad was a coalminer in Scotland and later moved down to Bedworth for better wages and conditions. This was before the outbreak of World War II. During the war Coventry became a centre for major industries for the war effort and as a result was bombed heavily by the Germans. Because Bedworth was so close to Coventry, it too received its share of bombing. Quite often, when everyone was required to rush off to the shelters during the air-raids, my mother would shepherd the family into safety like a mother hen looking after her brood. This also included rounding up her brother and his family who lived nearby, as they were often too terrified to move without help. It was always Mum who organised tea and sandwiches and kept everyone calm during the air raids.

My father was an avid gardener and grew his own vegetables, along with raising ducks and chickens. This proved very beneficial to the family when food was not plentiful during the war. We always had fresh duck eggs, an abundance of green vegetables and fruit. We were more fortunate than a lot of people in those dreadful years. It was compulsory to have coupons to buy groceries and, as Dad was a coalminer whose work was essential for the war effort, he was provided with extra coupons. Because of the produce gained from his garden and the poultry, Mum would often swap the extras with the neighbours for tea coupons. There was no acceptable substitute for tea, which the English deemed to be an absolute necessity.

Dad was also involved with the home guard, and because of the additional duties, he was often away from home. There was a story Mum recounted about her brother George. One night when the sirens had sounded, announcing another air-raid, Mum was urging her brother to move as fast as he could to the nearest shelter when his braces caught on a door handle as he was passing. George screamed out in alarm, 'The Germans have got me. The Germans have got me!' Her comment to us about this incident was, 'I don't think your Uncle George was all that brave.' It took a lot of Mum's patience to calm him down enough to get him to the shelter!

On one occasion when my sisters, on seeing the bombed homes, asked Mum, 'Why are the houses down on the ground?', Mum told them the houses had become tired of standing, and lay down. The closest our house came to being bombed was when the Germans dropped a landmine by parachute, obviously meant for Coventry, but which had drifted off target and become entangled in the branches of a tree in a field nearby. Thank goodness it had failed to explode, as detonation would have created much devastation within a radius of two kilometres.

Memories of much of my early life in England are almost for-gotten. But there is one memory that comes to mind now and then. This is of Julie, my little cocker spaniel, which I had been given for my first birthday and still had when we were preparing to move to Australia seven years later. I remember that, instead of taking her for a walk, I preferred placing her in my doll's pram and covering her up with my doll's blanket. Usually she was quite content to stay there as I pushed the pram along. There were times when Julie and I would be out strolling and someone would stop us and ask me for a peep at my dolly, and be most surprised when they pulled back the blanket to be greeted not by the painted face of a doll, but by a little dog's face peeping back with her big brown eyes.

As sad as it was to leave our close friends and relatives, my greatest sense of loss when we migrated was when I understood that Julie would not be able to come with us. Having to leave my little cocker spaniel behind was a most notable regret. Many tears were shed during the trip from England to Australia whenever my thoughts turned to her.

The memories of my little friend from next door, Susan Hart, came back to me relatively easily. We had enjoyed each other's company and played together almost every day. I am afraid that the memories of her family do not come as easily, but what recollection I do have is that her father was a coalminer, just as my father was. We used to skate on a pond near our home with my sisters, and would make slides on the pathway at the side of our house when it was frozen. It was good fun until the day came when Dad was wheeling his bicycle along on his way to work at about six in the morning and did a spectacular somersault, landing heavily on the icy path.

Most of our relatives lived in Scotland and I enjoyed my visits with them. Because these stays were only once a year, there was always great excitement when the time came for us to take the trip. Travelling from place to place was not as easy then as it is nowadays. In fact, travelling any distance then was considered a luxury. Staying with my father's parents, Catherine and James Paterson, was a delightful experience, but the high point of the holiday was being allowed to sleep in a bed that was built into their sitting room wall.

Grandmother's cottage was one of a number built side by side and separated by a wide pathway known as a 'close'. Their house was occupied by eight members of the family. Uncle James, Dad's younger brother, and my Aunt Mary lived next door. The cottage was rectangular in shape with one narrow wall, with its garden facing a small main road to the front. The back wall was bordered by another close. The longer walls were each bordered by a 'close', while there were four rooms leading off a hallway which ran the length of one long wall.

The room at the front of the cottage was the largest, being a sitting room-dining room-bedroom. It was in there that two double beds were built into one wall. These were concealed during the day by large curtains. This was a common occurrence in the small Scottish houses because of limited space. To be privileged to sleep in one of these special beds was the high point of my holiday. The next room off the hall was the main room. This was the kitchen-family-dining-guest and second bedroom. The beds in this room were sofa lounges and in one corner was an open fire. The third room was the

IT'S ALL OVER FOR MARGARET

A week after being seriously injured in an horrific race fall at Harold Park, M...
didn't...

Margaret Frost i... in serious acc...

End of driving career of top reinswoman

Margaret Frost is unlikely to ever drive again following a serious racesmash last Friday night at Sydney's Harold Park Paceway.

Top reinswoman seriously injured

Margaret Frost, Australia's first top reinswoman, was taken unconscious to hospital on Friday night after a bad racesmash at Harold Park.

0 The Sydney Morning Herald

Pioneer Margaret Fros... comeback a tough tr...

Glenn Frost came around the hometurn on Just Baz in the last race at Harold Park on June 16, with wheels only centimetres apart and the usual screaming ... around him, and ... being

Vic, and some friends bolted out of the trainers' stand and jumped the fence on to the track.

As he got back to the sce... and jumped out of his own ...

THE LAS...

with Noel Ovi...

THE Frost's experienced the highs and lows of harness racing at Harold Park last Friday night. Glenn scored a winning
double with Cuckoos Nest and stable newcomer The Collegian
however when Margaret Frost wa...
in the final event.
...at the top of the home straight th...
shed heavily - catapulting Margare...
...s propelled through the air and land...
...here was concern as she lay motion...
lose range. In fact, Hezour Grant an...
...e ground, their gear entangled, an...
...t the frightened horses could fall bac...
...lage.
...the ambulance and taken the Roya...
...amperdown, while Greg Turnbull an...
...re treated on the track with both bein...

Margaret Frost involved in serious accident

POPULAR rein-
swoman Margaret
Frost suffered serious
injuries in a horrific
race fall at Harold
Park last Friday
night.

this stage.
"We're just hoping it
will be all right."
Margaret was rushed to
nearby Royal Prince Alford
Hospital, unconscious
after being tipped out
from Welburn Fella in
the last race.
Family and friends

David Hope and stewards
continued their inquiry into
the accident into the early
hours of Saturday morning.
Margaret Frost was one

of the pioneer
reinswomen to make
impact on the sport.
She retired in the
'80s, however, to dev...
her time to charity wo...

...eing released from hospital before th...
...undergo a series of tests to determin...
...I am pleased to report that Margar...

Newspapers carried the story of the near fatal crash

The Paterson family in 1945 when they lived in England at Bedworth. From left they are Catherine, Father, me when just two, Mother, and Neena.

The war was still on when this picture was taken of Neena, me and Catherine. There were many bombing raids in our district being so close to the important area of Coventry.

That's me riding in the Novice Lady Rider 17 years and over at the 1961 Royal Easter Show in Sydney, the major show in the land. That was a thrill of a lifetime, winning against some very good competition.

Royal Agricultural Society
OF
NEW SOUTH WALES

GRAND EASTER
DAY & NIGHT EXHIBITION
24TH MAR.-4TH APRIL, 1961

FIRST PRIZE

RIDING COMPETITIONS

CATALOGUE REFERENCE

Section   1
Horses
Class Nº   170
Cat.gue Nº   467

Awarded to MISS M. PATERSON
Exhibited by
NOVICE LADY RIDER, ON
FLAT, 17 YEARS AND
OVER.

DIRECTOR

Our official wedding
photo. That's my Mother
and Father on the left, and
Vic's Mother and Father to
the right. The year was
1963.

Vic made a handsome
groom. He earlier had
impressed Dad, as he
sought Father's permission
before proposing to me.

10

LUCKY CREED, 2.1 2/5
(King Creed (imp.) - Overdrive (N.Z.)
ER - TRAINER: M. WANLESS.   DRIVER: V. FROST

Vic won many races driving the Queensland owned Lucky Creed, a winner of 24 races in succession, and only beaten in a photo in a major Sydney race after being off-colour leading up to the race. He was a real tough horse, and invited to the US for the International Pace.

Vic pictured after being the first Australian reinsman to drive more than 100 winners in a season. That was in the season 1969-70. He went on to win five Sydney driving premierships.

11

Even in the cold of mid-winter the horses had to be worked. We would rug ourself up pretty good on those cold mornings. I am following Vic in this training picture, taken shortly after we moved to our farm at Exeter.

Vic on our three-wheeler motor bike to get around the farm, with our three children Garry, Susan and Glenn. Behind them is our brand new two-storied home at Exeter.

With Friday night's racing at Harold Park behind us, the family go out to a local restaurant for Saturday evening's dinner. With Vic and myself are Glenn, Susan and Garry. Such outings were a great way to counter the long hours we set ourselves in maintaing such a large team of horses.

John Tapp looking dapper in his Channel 9 sports jacket. I am proud to say he and the Frosts have been friends for many years. A real enthusiast of harness racing, John even drove at gymkhanas on a Frost-trained pacer. In recent years he has trained his own pacers. John also wrote the Foreword for this book.

When the two boys were a little older, Vic would take them on fishing and hunting trips. This one was up to the Gulf where they each enjoyed a good catch. That's Glenn on the left with Garry and their father. The two boys were very much outdoor types, with both having a passion for adventure from an early age. Such adventures twice went close to claiming the life of Glenn in incidents that made headlines.

laundry-bathroom, and then there was the toilet. Entry into the cottage was via two doors off the close—one at each end of the hall.

A horse and cart was used in those days to deliver the milk right to my grandparents' front door. I recall pleading for permission to take the milk container and be allowed to collect the ration for the day. The milkman, bless him, graciously gave me permission to pat his horse and talk to it while I waited for him to fill the milk container.

My maternal grandmother was a horse lover who looked forward eagerly to the local agricultural shows. She would sit with her rug around her knees and watch the horses perform all day, usually staying until the very end of these events. This is my first recollected association with horses, which was strengthened by the sight of beautiful horses ridden by magnificently dressed riders with their hounds going to the hunt. The riders with their lovely red jackets, black boots and caps, and the horses with their glistening coats and plaited manes were a great sight. Even though circumstances would not allow it, I constantly begged my parents for a horse from then on. It was only after we migrated to Australia that I was to discover just how good my father was with horses.

In the boom years that followed the Second World War, Australia required migrants for the rebuilding of its young nation at a time when the Government had a 'White Australia' policy in place. English migrants were welcomed with open arms. My father had been there before and spoke in glowing terms about this big country that then needed migrants. My family were among many who signed up to join thousands of others keen to start a new life.

We left Dover in 1951 on the ship the *Ranchi*, a trip not easy to forget. It proved to be the ship's last official voyage, breaking down for a week in the Suez Canal, leaving passengers and crew with no fresh drinking water. The boiled water we had to drink was intolerable.

While the ship was anchored in the Suez, traders from either side of the canal would come out in small boats to offer their goods to the passengers. The trader's customers would lean over the railing of the boat and lower down baskets by rope to receive what goods were on offer. The customer would peruse the items for sale, take what they wanted, then return the basket to the trader after having negotiated a price. Perhaps the only time a trader came off second best occurred when a passenger might purloin some of the goodies, but this rarely was the case. How things have changed since Australia was first settled as a penal colony with convicts banished to the other side of the world for such minor indiscretions. Now here we were, along with many others aboard, looking forward to Australia as a land of hope.

My journey to our new country is largely remembered as being fun and games. As an eight-year-old, curly-headed, blue-eyed blond girl, I was spoiled by some of the older sailors. They taught me to play cards and gave me treats from their meals from time to time, such as fruit, cakes and biscuits. Aided by their tuition, it was rumored at the time that I had become something of a cardsharp. They would usually let me win and I learned some card games quite well. I was considered hard to beat at Sevens and Donkey, and super at Snap. I would graduate to the game of Five Hundred in my teens and often played with Dad and other members of our family and friends. My son Glenn today enjoys playing Five Hundred when time permits.

On my journey to a new and exciting life in Australia, I was totally oblivious as to what lay ahead, of the fortunes and misfortunes that I would encounter. I could not in my wildest dreams have possibly imagined the exhilaration and excitement that followed the triumphs, or the deep despair and sadness that followed tragedy in my life. I know this to be a useless mental exercise, but I have wondered: if given the opportunity, would I do it all again?

THREE

George Paterson, my Father

Some years ago, Dad was asked by members of his family to jot down the recollections of his youth. This he did. I knew these notes existed, but they have only recently come into my possession. I was so moved after reading his handwritten pages, I felt compelled to share his experiences here, with some extracts from that letter written to his grandson Alexander Paterson, my brother Eddie's son.

Dear Alexander,

... I was born in Lawrence, a town on the outskirts of Pittsburgh, in Pennsylvania, USA. It wasn't my fault, Alex, I just happened to be there on the 3rd day of January 1910. My parents were Scots, as Scottish as the heather on Ben Lomond. My mother was a MacDonald from Edinburgh, a descendant of the MacDonalds of Glencoe. My father, was Jim Paterson, the Patersons are a branch of the MacLaren clan, whose lands were in Perthshire. My parents lived in America for about 20 years, and had four children there, my sisters, Margaret, Jessie, and my brother Walter. We all returned to Scotland in 1916, where my sisters Jeanette and Rina and brother James were born. ...

We lived with my Grandpa and Grandma MacDonald at 52 Burnhead St, Lanarkshire in Scotland and we started school at the Taskhall Academy. ... I was named after My Grandpa. My Grandmother's maiden name was Tudehope. She was almost deaf but had a love for music and played a mouth organ and a jew's harp beautifully, and often played old Scot's songs for us. My favourite was 'Flowers of the Florist'. She died when I was about ten years of age. ...

I came home from school at lunch time to find a house full of people in tears. My Pa had been seriously injured in the mine and had been taken to Glasgow infirmary. I was sent back to school, but was called out for punishment by the teacher for inattention. He was just preparing to bring the strap down on my outstretched hand, when my school-mate, Jimmy Graham, called, 'Please sir, Geordie's faither has just been hurt in the pit.' The teacher then sent me home with Jimmy. ... Ma could only afford to go to Glasgow once a week to see Pa, who was in plaster from the waist down. Six months later, Pa came home, but was unable to move his legs. Ma would fill the bath with boiling water and place lumps of rock salt in it. She would rub Pa with oil, put the towel in the tub, lift it out quickly and lay it on Pa's back and legs. His groans haunted us for a long time afterwards, but soon, he could move his legs and gradually he learned to stand. Sometime later, he was doing his usual work at the coal face. How much he suffered doing it, God only knows—No-one could have had better parents.

Sister Jeanette had just started work at the co-op when the 26 weeks miners' strike began. Miners never have achieved any improvements in their conditions, without having to starve themselves and their wives and children. Miners wives suffer most, I think. We lived on potatoes and turnips we stole from the farmers' fields at night, and the shilling a week we got from the Russian miners. Children were falling off their seats at school and some had their head or face cut from the sharp corners of the desks. The teacher gave permission for children who felt faint, to lay on the floor. Sometimes there were more children on the floor than on the seats. ...

Ma carried the greatest burden, as she had to conserve and divide the little food we had. Ma's long auburn hair turned white during those 26 weeks. The only time I saw Ma in tears was when my sister Margaret went out of our house with a slice of unbuttered bread, and a neighbour, whose husband was working, put some jam on it. Margaret came running back into the house and cut it into eight pieces so we could all have a taste. It was too much for Ma and it was a long time before she could eat her piece. ...

I remember one instance, when it was my turn to fetch coal from the railway wagons, which the railway men refused to move. The trucks were about a mile from our house, through the woods and I stopped for a rest when nearly home. I must have slept with my head on the bag. I awoke with a start, looking up into the face of a policeman. He asked for my name and address, and what was in the bag. He picked it up and said, 'This is too heavy for a wee boy like you, come and I'll carry it for you.' He did, and when leaving, told me 'Next time, get home before two o'clock in the morning.' ... The miners went back to work gaining nothing. ... I was working in the mine along side Pa, at age fourteen years and six months. ... I decided to emigrate to Australia. There were glowing accounts of British boys who had made good in Australia, in the papers and the British Government were subsidising the boat fare. For ten pounds, we could get to Sydney in New South Wales. From here we would be sent to be trained as farmers and guaranteed a job. ... So, on the 22nd of December 1926, I left London for Sydney on the P&O liner 'Barrabool'. ... Jimmy Weeks from Glasgow, 'Lofty' from Inverness, Bill Thorbourn from Aberdeen, Oliver Evans from Shropshire, arrived in Sydney in February 1927. We were marched to the YMCA to have dinner and receive a lecture from an Australian politician, who mentioned how happy the Australian people were to have British boys in their country. We were too hungry to mention our experience, both in Melbourne and on our way to the YMCA in Sydney, where we were greeted by the usual, 'go home you shower of pommy bastards.' ...

My friends and I volunteered to be sent to Cowra for training. We were met at the station and taken to our training farm outside Cowra. ... I had heard that there was no class distinction in Australia, but it was soon to prove otherwise. ... After a time a Mr McKye came to the training centre, and chose me to go with him to his farm. ... Joe had 24 plough horses and worked two teams of 10 horses abreast in each plough. He harnessed one team to a four furrow plough and I sat beside him on the plough and watched him work. Soon I was able to drive the team myself and we were able to use both teams together, with Joe in front and me following. ... By August, Joe told me that he had no more work for me until harvest and to try to get another job until then. I decided to return to the training farm at Cowra. The manager of the centre was none too pleased to see me and this earned me the name 'Boomerang'. ...

Since it had not rained for sometime, I was given the job of cleaning out three large galvanised iron tanks, each about 30 feet high and nine feet in diameter, to earn my keep. There was a steel ladder up the outside of each tank and I was given a rope ladder to lower down on the inside, and two buckets. When I returned to the tanks, there was a lad standing at the base of one with a big grin on his face. This was Jim Ferguson from Belfast. Jim was soon re-christened 'Paddy'. He said he had just arrived back at the farm, and been told to help the other 'bloody boomerang'. I volunteered to go down first, with a bucket on a rope and a stick to test the depth of the mud. As I descended, the ladder started swinging and my elbows and knees started bumping on the side of the tank. Paddy said later I was like a toy monkey on a string. We changed places when it got too hot to bear and soon became expert rope climbers and bucket handlers. ...

As I mentioned, it hadn't rained for some time and the trainees could not use the toilets, so had been going behind a row of pepper trees a short distance from the farm house. We were told to get a horse and dray and take the manure to the paddocks. We knew it wouldn't be a pleasant job, but it was worse than we dreamed. We were both sick repeatedly. I said to Paddy, 'Enough is enough. I'm rolling my swag tonight and Paddy said he would come with me. ... We set off at about 3 o'clock in the morning, and headed for Lithgow. The night was quite warm and we moved fast as we thought someone would come after us. We needn't have worried—'Boomerangs' are expendable!

We travelled a long way before seeing a house. Paddy volunteered to go and ask for food and offer to work while I waited behind a tree on the road. Paddy returned after a long time, with a parcel under his arm. His payment for chopping wood was some sugar, tea, flour, salt, a small amount of fat and half a loaf of bread. We did this turn about. ... Even on the track, Paddy and I kept ourselves clean. We washed ourselves and our clothes regularly, at the windmills and clean sheep troughs. Late one afternoon, we arrived at a farm and was given a job for both of us, cutting thistles. The thistles stood shoulder to shoulder, from three to six feet high, and as thick as they could grow, with the bulbs ready to burst and *scatter their seed to the four winds. They stood in ranks like soldiers on parade, out of sight in every direction. We were to begin cutting them the following day.*

We slept in a bed made of wool packs in the shed. The mosquitoes had a birthday and our faces and arms were covered in small blotches like measles the next morning. After breakfast, we were taken to the paddocks, given two scythes, a sharpening stone and a pitchfork. We had to cut the thistles, stack them in heaps and burn them on the open ground. Lunch was brought to us with a billy of tea and we were taken home at sundown for dinner. The tucker was the best ever. Paddy had a crop of blisters on his hands the second day and from then on, I did the cutting. The job lasted eight days and the boss gave us one pound each.

Joe McKye later moved to a holding of about 2000 acres, just outside the little village of Carrol, 20 kilometres from Gunnedah. Work was hard to find in the Great Depression. After carrying his swag, Dad again worked for Joe at Carrol before he left Australia to return to Scotland. Obviously, he had made a good impression on Mr McKye, as the grazier had expressed an offer that, should Dad ever return to these shores, there would always be a job for him there.

Dad had always wanted to return to Australia and farm life. He adored the wide open spaces and the different style of living 'down under'. For a coalminer, he was most comfortable and right at home with the lifestyle of country living: the sheep, cattle, farm dogs and horses, and the laid-back atmosphere of a small country town, so vastly different from the villages of England. He had painted a glamorous picture for the family of a vibrant and exciting new land.

FOUR

Australia, Land of Opportunity

Our ship docked at Sydney and we were taken to a Migrant Hostel at Bathurst for a few weeks until transferred to the hostels at Fairy Meadow. It was an era when many migrants were coming to this land of opportunity for those prepared to work. From Fairy Meadow we later journeyed to the little village of Carrol and Joe McKye's farm. Dad found there was a great deal of work for him to do as so much during the 1940s had been put off 'until tomorrow'.

The challenge of restoring the farm to its full potential was not an easy one. From the day Dad started, he seemed never to have a minute to spare. This became the main contributing cause to my mother's eventual dislike and even loathing of the lonely existence she found on an Australian farm, distanced from cities and towns. Dad's love of country life surely rubbed off on me. I was never happy cooped up inside the house, and was in my glory helping out around the property. I enjoyed riding behind him on horseback, droving the sheep and cattle to market. The only thing that would have made me happier then was to have had my very own pony.

There were six dogs on the farm and I enjoyed going rabbiting with them. I would carry a long piece of wire with a hook on the end. If a poor rabbit was unfortunate enough to run into a hollow log, the exercise was to manoeuvre the hook around the rabbit's neck and then pull it out from the log. I then killed it with a blow to the back of its neck and cut it up for the dogs to eat. Times have certainly changed, as years later it revolts me even to think about doing this. But it was the way of country life then and the accepted means of supplementing the diet of the farm dogs.

Because of the distance we lived from the nearest school, my lessons were done by correspondence. This I found a splendid idea, as I was able to do most of the allotted work on the first morning the assignments arrived, then have the rest of the week free to be outside helping Dad, or just making a nuisance of myself, believing I was helping.

The most frightening things I had ever seen in England had been spiders, so I was totally unprepared for the surprises that the Australian bush had in store. The shock I felt from one such surprise was almost too much for a little 'Pommy girl' to handle. This particular day when I went to feed the hens I was confronted by a huge goanna, about a metre long, trying to climb the wire around the hen house.

Immediately, from somewhere deep within the recesses of my mind, came the description—Alligator! Somehow I was able to jump over the large dog kennels outside the pen and flee back to the house, screaming 'Alligator! Alligator!' This triggered off instant consternation for the family, who rushed out to the hen house as fast as they could to investigate the source of my terror. Dad was most relieved to see that it was only a goanna, which he killed, because goannas were constantly visiting the fowl yard and eating the hen's eggs. They were a threat to the chickens as well. Dad cut open the stomach of the goanna, revealing the shells neatly separated from the yolks of the eggs it had eaten.

What an experience! I wanted to go back to England and my mother wanted to get off the farm and move to some place more civilised! This wish was strengthened when my sister Catherine killed a snake in the garden. My mother's growing hatred of the bush was reinforced when Joe McKye had to reduce an over-proliferation of resident cats by shooting some of them. The cats would keep us awake at night with their fighting and squabbling on our corrugated iron roof. To a family of English people who had lived in a little town close to every convenience and had never come in contact with reptiles or any other dangerous species, it was proving to be a real shock to the system!

The isolation of farm life made mixing with townspeople difficult for me. When I did go into town with my parents, I would avoid communication with people as much as possible. My interests were centered on farm life. I'm sure those who find the bush fascinating will understand this, just as others who prefer being closer to shops and people will find being isolated unacceptable. My mother became increasingly aware of the isolation and the consequences it might have on her three daughters, missing out on playing and mixing with other children of similar age. With this in mind she urged Dad to seek employment closer to a town.

We had been on the farm at Carrol for two years. After much insistence by my mother, who believed moving would be in the best interests of the family, Dad applied for work in the coalmines. He was offered one position near Gunnedah, but Mum refused to go to another isolated area. He finally accepted work at Cessnock, much to my disappointment at the time. I was later told that Joe McKye, who had become fond of the youngest of the Paterson girls, surprisingly conveyed a wish to adopt me on learning the family was preparing to leave. Of course, I had no say in the matter, and my parents would not have even considered it.

Our new home in Cessnock was nothing more than a Nissan hut. These huts had been built during the war to help house troops at the army camps. After the war they were converted to migrant hostels to provide short-term accommodation. They were just like tin huts and looked like large, galvanised, corrugated iron tanks cut in half lengthwise. But they were large enough for the family to be comfortable. I started school at the local primary school. When laughed at so much for my English accent, my mother enrolled me in elocution classes to soften the tone of my speech. This did alter my accent and I persevered with the classes for three years, but never achieved the art of speaking with a plum in my mouth.

It was in Cessnock that Neena met her future husband, Barry Broadley. It was Barry's home-town and he was an electrician in the coalmines when they met. The Broadleys were a family of bookmakers. Barry's father Phillip, his Grandfather Bill and his Uncle Harry were all bookmakers, and Barry would pencil for his father at the various district tracks. His grandfather had also been a professional boxer at one time and had trained thoroughbred racehorses as well.

My greatest dream was realised when my parents bought my first pony, for the grand sum of twelve pounds. Trixie was a sixteen-year-old mare so quiet in disposition that I had no fear of being hurt. We both enjoyed our daily workouts and I was able to gain a lot of riding experience with real confidence. Before long I was riding her to school and taking my school friends to see her at lunchtime, often giving some of them rides. This made me quite popular and gave me a lot more confidence mixing with other children.

It wasn't long before I had most of the class at school converted

to horse lovers, and it pleased me when so many of them later introduced horses to their compositions and drawings. A few of them even
had me illustrating their stories, as I had found a raw talent for sketch-
ing horses. It was something I loved doing. This experience I'm sure
was instrumental in the gradual development of my confidence in
mixing with others, and especially in laying the foundations for relat-
ing to my peers.

My young brother Edward George, or 'Eddie' as we all came to
call him, was born in Cessnock on July 16th 1953. Eddie would be
the only boy in the family of four children my parents raised.

Eventually I outgrew Trixie. She had become too slow for what
was required if I was to take the next step that would lead me into
some form of competition. It was then that Neena and Barry bought
me a new pony named 'Bonnie', a most beautiful little brown mare.
Bonnie cost 35 pounds. I was in seventh heaven because she was able
to appease my adventurous spirit, and she seemed to revel in displaying a burst of speed. My sister's future father-in-law, Phillip, bought
me a very good bridle so that I would have some dressy equipment,
and my sister then bought me a saddle. I suppose, on reflection, all
this could be construed as me having become one rather spoiled teenager.

My father was a good worker, but we found the coalmines at
Cessnock were often calling strikes, so his wages were not always
adequate or consistent. This was something my parents said had not
occurred back in England for a long time. Mum had a hard time meeting basic needs, let alone the extra ones, had they tried meeting my
requests for riding equipment. It wasn't until I became a working girl
that I was able to purchase the good gear and trappings one needed to
succeed in horse shows. But it did take a lot of saving and sacrifice. I
then joined a pony club and was eager to learn as much as I could
about the intricacies of horse riding and management.

Meanwhile, because of the strikes in the mines at Cessnock, my
family once again moved, this time to New Berrima, a little town in
the Southern Highlands of New South Wales and about a two-hour
drive from Sydney. My father worked at Medway coalmine, which
proved to be a more reliable job for him, which meant we were quite
comfortable living there. I started school at Moss Vale Primary and
graduated to Bowral High School at the age of twelve, making new

friends along the way.

Unfortunately, my parents could not afford the transport required to take Bonnie with us, so I had another tearful parting when Bonnie was sold before we left for Berrima. However, I wasn't without a pony for long. I was lucky to meet a girl at school whose father had a pony that was not being ridden. He wanted someone to look after it and give it exercise, and he found a very willing volunteer in me, only too glad to oblige.

This piebald (black and white) pony I named 'Amigo' really became a great friend to me, being quiet, good-natured and safe to ride on the roads. I rode Amigo on the road between Old Berrima and New Berrima frequently, with my dog Nipper tagging along. In no time I became a familiar sight to the truck drivers from the area travelling the same road, and they would often wave to me as they drove past.

Del Throsby conducted a riding school in Moss Vale. After joining, I rode Amigo to the meetings there once a fortnight, a trip of about 20 kilometres. It snows occasionally in the Southern Highlands and in the winters it was so cold that by the time I got home I was almost numb, especially if it rained. There were occasions when my parents had to help me put Amigo away because my hands just would not function until they had thawed out.

As good a temperament as Amigo had, he did have a trick of getting out of the paddock Dad had made next to our home. Amigo would lay down by the fence and pull the bottom rail with his teeth until it came out of the keeper, then wriggle underneath the fence and head straight for the cement works, a little distance away. Their lawns were always so green and well kept, and this grass was lush, a great temptation for Amigo once having discovered it was there. A banquet not to be ignored! The irate manager would be on the telephone immediately to my mother and we had to rush over in the car and lead him home.

When going through this ritual one day, with Dad driving and Mum holding the lead rope from inside the car, which was clipped to the halter of Amigo's headstall, the horse pulled back. The pressure on the rope was enough to pull the top off Mum's finger and make it quite painful for weeks. Amigo and I were not too popular for a while, at least until her finger had healed. I should have been leading the horse, I suppose, since he was my responsibility. Horses were not her favourite animals, now even more so.

Occasionally, when feed was scarce close to home, it was necessary to look elsewhere for good pickings. When a suitable spot was found, I would tie Amigo up in the grassy patch, so he could move around in a limited area. One afternoon, while leading the horse by the side of the road from a paddock I had found not far from home, I carelessly slung his lead rope over my arm. My sisters Neena and Catherine had caught the bus home from Moss Vale after work and were standing in the aisle ready to alight when they saw Amigo take fright at the noise from the bus and bolt, dragging me along the stony road. They jumped off the bus and ran after me. When they caught up to where I was lying, still holding on to the horse, covered in dust and dirt and shedding some tears, they picked me up and dusted me off as best they could, before taking me home.

Being in no fit state to take care of my horse myself, Catherine tethered him and gave him water. The dragging on the stony surface by the side of the road left me with large and painful gravel rashes to my lower legs, hips and thighs. The important lesson to be learned from this experience was *never* coil a lead rope around any part of you while the other end is attached to an animal, particularly one as big as a horse. Serious injury can result if you ignore this rule. I never made that mistake again. It was to be a couple of weeks before I could sit comfortably in the saddle once more.

Eddie was about five years old when we moved to New Berrima. The fact that he was the only boy and the baby of the family probably had something to do with him being quite spoiled, and he could be an absolute horror! There were times when out of sheer desperation I was forced to climb onto the roof of our house to do my homework and study. The roof was the one place I was safe, as he had not learned to climb that high as yet, and there seemed no other way of finding a peaceful spot. I recall him throwing a little hammer at me one day, cutting my forehead at the hairline. Years later it would be the first part of my hair to show grey as I aged, and you can rest assured that Eddie got the blame for that. However, as the rest of my hair is now following suit, I can't give him the credit!

One particularly hot summer's day I became so badly sunburned that I was confined to bed, missing a day's work. The toilet then was located outside. Having to negotiate the trip from my bed that day was a chore I had been putting off for as long as possible. When I knew I could not delay any longer, it took immense mental effort to set out, feeling pain and anguish with every step.

With determination, clenched teeth, and moaning with the effort, I was making my painful journey to the toilet where, unbeknown to me, Eddie was waiting in ambush. Clutched in his fist was a huge green frog. Now, he was well aware how I hated frogs. Eddie hid behind the toilet and waited. He waited until I had almost reached the door, then pounced. In that instant any thoughts of discomfort vanished, supplanted by the terror of this huge green frog thrust in my face.

From finding it difficult to even walk with the sunburn, I suddenly found the strength to raise a gallop, while Eddie chased me around the house with the frog in his outstretched hand. I was too terrified to stop, until my mother heard my frantic screams and came to the rescue. I was so grateful for her intervention, even though she was laughing so much she could not chastise Eddie. I would gladly have administered some sort of punishment right there and then, which would certainly have been excessive for the crime committed. Strangulation then seemed appropriate, but Eddie escaped with his life that day!

Not long after, a day came to exact retribution on Eddie for his many impish pranks. I had been teaching him to ride, and on this particular day I was leading him on his pony behind the horse I was riding. He kept insisting that I let him ride by himself. I knew he was not able to handle the pony just yet, but he continued with his harping.

'I can ride by myself, let me go,' he repeated several times.

I tried explaining that he had not yet mastered the basics of keeping his pony under control. He kept up his chatter and, in youthful frustration, I did it! I let him go. Many a pony can be quite cunning when not under control, and when this one realised she was free, she took off, heading for home. Horse and rider did make the trip intact, and the fright put into Eddie that day was well worth the price I was to pay when Mum found out what had happened. For one who had been such a prankster and spoilt rotten as a young boy, what Eddie successfully became later in life, in a profession that demands considerable discipline and responsibility, was a paradox.

FIVE

From the Highlands to the Coast

Yet another move was decided upon by my parents for the convenience of the family. This time it was to Berrima. It too would be only temporary. Not long after, my sister Neena returned to Cessnock for her marriage to Barry. After their wedding they went to live in Sydney at Waverley, then moved to Bronte, where Barry joined the Fire Brigade and Neena was employed by Grace Bros at Bondi Junction.

Meanwhile, Catherine had been working at Toose's general store in Moss Vale, travelling to and fro each day from Berrima by bus. Both my father and I were some ten miles away from our daily destination, me going to school in Bowral (made famous because Sir Donald Bradman had lived there as a child), and Dad to his work in the Medway coalmines. Buses were then few and far between during the day.

Veterinary Science had been my chosen career, and I had taken Latin at school for this purpose, but when my parents agreed to move on from Berrima, I decided to take a job instead of continuing my education. I had completed my Intermediate Year at Berrima High and it was not my wish to start at another school and have to make new friends all over again.

This time when we moved it would be out of the area altogether, to Albion Park Rail, a little town situated on the Princes Highway about a 20-minute drive south of Wollongong. In hindsight, it seems the move was taking me closer to my life with horses. My parents had purchased a home close to the shores of Lake Illawarra, a delightful part of the world, and I soon discovered how much I enjoyed being near water. It was here that I had my first experience catching prawns.

Wading in the water at night with a net (not unlike a butterfly net) dangling in one hand and clutching a torch in the other, I would thrust the net toward any prawn that would appear in the light. It was all good fun, though perhaps not for the prawn. Having to peer through the water, muddied a little by wading and the ripples on the water's surface, the poor light given off by the torch did give the prawn a better-than-even chance of survival. Many a time I came home with nothing but a wet bottom and sore eyes. After Mum saw that the prawns we did manage to catch had to be dumped alive into boiling water to be cooked, she vowed never to eat another prawn again. I can't say the same. I love fresh prawns even though I don't like seeing them cooked either.

Catherine left her job in Moss Vale to come and live with us at Albion Park. She was vivacious, pretty and very popular with the opposite sex. She would accompany Dad and me prawning or fishing if she had not made arrangements to go out with the current boyfriend. Dad had the patience of a fisherman, which we would test to the limit, when he was introducing the pair of us to the art of fishing. He took us to the Lake and we would fish from the foreshores.

Poor Dad, he watched in frustration as we threw our lines in, seeing the line and the hook going one way, and the bait going the other. 'I think you had better put another bait on,' he would patiently suggest, 'don't you?' We wasted his worms, drowned his prawns and tangled his lines, but he never gave up on us. I can't remember ever catching any fish during those times when Dad was with us. But I do remember his gentle patience as he pushed the bait onto the hook, and with a twinkle in his eyes as he handed me the line, he would say, 'There you are, see what you can do with that one.' Dad was a glutton for punishment, because he took on teaching all of his grandchildren the art of fishing and gardening, as they came along. His patience was rewarded by the outcome years later, when those youngsters became adults.

While we were living at Albion Park, Catherine met and married Roy Sherriff, a baker and pastry cook with a bakery at Unanderra. Roy excelled at tennis and at one time was selected to train with a squad that included Ken Rosewall, but his mother had refused him permission to leave home for the city. He was also a talented hockey player. When Catherine and Roy were married they lived at first in a home adjoining the bakery, where their three daughters, Karen, Sandra and Janette, were born. They later moved back to Crookwell, where Roy had grown up.

Quite a few weekends were spent at Crookwell with Roy and

Catherine, where I enjoyed going off to the local dance on a Saturday night. Roy escorted me there and, come time for the last dance, he would not be far away, waiting to drive me home. Looking back to those Saturday nights, which I enjoyed very much, I may have dressed a little provocatively at age seventeen and was considered quite attractive, confirmed by the glint in the eyes of the local lads, which 'Blind Freddy' couldn't miss.

Those dances were truly fun evenings. At no time did I have to ponder the meaning of 'wallflower'. Like most young girls of that age who might be somewhat naive, I was flattered by this attention and the offers to be taken home after the dance. But Roy was always there to escort me back to their home. Eventually, there was one young man for whom I developed a crush, and these weekends could not come soon enough. He and I were allowed to date a few times and he became my escort to and from the dances, though Catherine later confided that Roy still kept a concerned eye on me as a big brother might. The memory of those teenage dances are treasured and still bring with them a smile and a warm glow. What enjoyable times they were. The exuberance, excitement and innocence of a seventeen-year-old. Oh! What fun!

Elaine and Faye Smallman became my closest friends when living at Albion Park. Elaine and I both loved horse riding, and we had many enjoyable outings together. I then had a grey mare named 'Rebel'. She was an average-looking horse, with some class, but unfortunately she was not a good show horse. By now I was working at the telephone exchange in Wollongong and had to catch the train from Albion Park Rail to town each morning during the week.

Equestrian show days usually fell on Fridays and Saturdays. To compete on these days meant trying to juggle my shifts at the telephone exchange, which was not always possible, so the occasional 'sicky' was taken. If one was able to work on a Sunday, it was possible to have another day off in lieu, though because the shift with the Friday off was the most popular, Friday was not always available. This went well until a friend came across a photograph in the local paper of me competing in a show and pinned the picture on the notice board at work. From then on I was allowed to take the time off, for which I was most grateful, though it was without pay. This was a sacrifice I had to make if I was to continue my association with show riding.

Dad was working at Wongawilli coalmine, near Dapto. To be closer to his work and for me to be a little nearer to mine at the exchange, the family shifted house once again, this time to Brownsville, a suburb of Dapto on the Wollongong side.

Horses did not occupy all of my spare time—just most of it. When the show season was over, I was able to indulge in other sporting activities. Earlier, at school, I had some experience at competitive swimming, after learning to swim when we lived in Cessnock. I had also played netball at Bowral High School and was a member of the team which competed against other schools, earning myself a 'pocket' (an award for an outstanding player).

When we lived at Brownsville, I played competition basketball against women of all ages during the break from the show season. I was five feet three inches tall and had always been a lightweight (skinny, some might have called it), but I was fast on my feet, playing attack wing. One match I played while living at Berrima was against a team that included our next-door neighbour Jan Ethridge, who happened to be playing defence wing. Jan towered over me by almost twelve inches, and was responsible for 'marking' me and vice-versa. My mother had come to watch this particular game and, in the midst of a scuffle for possession of the ball, out of frustration for not being able to cover my movements, she called out to Mum, 'Hey, Patto, bring me a ribbon to tie on this cyclone's hair'. Funnily enough, the name 'cyclone' has been used to describe me quite often.

In Wollongong, I was actually able to play basketball for a few seasons in a team made up of telephonists from the exchange, which we named the 'Dialtones'. We practiced one night each week and played competition on the Saturday. I was able to fit in some social life; I would get together with girlfriends that I had made from the exchange for coffee or lunch, and we would go to the occasional dance together. From time to time I went out on dates and even had a steady boyfriend for a couple of years. But whenever my time with my horses was threatened, my social activities and my dates were curtailed. I lost a few boyfriends this way.

My parents rented a small paddock near our home and Dad built a stable in our yard to ensure that my new horse was well housed. It was from here that I began to compete more seriously in shows, even though my progress was markedly hindered by not having transport. I had friends who had transport and attended shows, and I was greatly indebted to them when they offered to take my horse with theirs whenever they could. Managing to compete so often with the assistance of kind friends may well appear to suggest I was using people, but I always helped out as much as possible in an effort to repay them for their generosity. I was never afraid of work on these trips and was quick to hop in and help. I'm sure this was evident to my friends, because they never seemed unwilling to have me with them.

Riding in hack events demonstrated the ability and conformation of a horse, and competing in riding events demonstrated the ability of the rider. There were other events, such as flag and bending races. These were held in a flurry of activity which I enjoyed immensely. I became quite successful in the sporting events and moderately successful in the others.

Allan Costa was a friend who lived in Dapto. He had two mares he competed with in the novelty events—a mother and daughter. He would ride them both in the heats of the flag and bending races. One day he won qualifying heats with both horses, which meant he could only ride one of them in the final. I gladly accepted his offer to ride his older mare, not sparing myself in the effort. Much to the surprise of some (including myself), the older mare and I managed to beat Allan by a nose. It was a tremendous thrill for me and it was great to see him being just as pleased as he would have been if the result had gone the other way.

From then on Allan would never hesitate to allow me to ride his ponies in the ladies events at the shows on the South Coast circuit, and even some shows in the southern outskirts of Sydney. We made a successful combination, winning numerous events, including one season in which we won every flag and bending event at the shows in which we took part on the Coast from Wollongong to Nowra, and some of the shows in the Campbelltown area as well. Horses that I owned allowed me to enter many events, but they were not suited for the higher class venues. Entering these events was totally dependent on being able to borrow horses, while nominating for sporting events was never a problem, as thanks to Allan there were usually suitable horses for my use.

SIX

A Dream Comes True

In 1961 it was suggested by friends that I enter the Ladies Novice and the Open Class riding events for competitors aged 17 to 21 at the Sydney Royal Easter Show. The Sydney Royal is, I'm sure, the ambition of every budding equestrian rider. It has long been the most prestigious show on the calendar, with the best horses and riders from all points of the compass competing.

The event that year attracted over 140 riders. I was riding a very nice hack named 'Gladwyn', owned by the Baker family from Bowral. The Bakers had employed me to exercise the horses they had competing in Sydney that year. I slept in a rack built for gear that was above the ponies and loved every minute of those two weeks—up at the crack of dawn, cleaning out stables, then taking horses over to Centennial Park to be exercised.

Competing in your first Royal is something any rider does not forget, and I had another reason to remember this one. There were so many competitors in this class that we were separated into several groups for the first stage. From here they picked out the best riders and sent the others from the ring. I could hardly believe it when I was selected in the first group. As the judging continued, Gladwyn and I were called in each time until the finalists were decided.

Each finalist had to ride individually, doing a figure eight and a hand gallop (a gallop under total control of the rider). It was this manoeuvre, which I was so confident in doing, that pulled off the biggest achievement in all of my 18 years. At the completion of my turn, I was placed next to the 'Red Coat' (a ring marshal). One by one, others were forming a line next to me. I thought it was great making the final, and simply accepted that the others were being placed ahead of me

'Gee,' I said, rather softly, to the nearby marshal, 'he's putting a lot in front of me.'

'They're not in front of you, lass. You're at the winning end.'

To have won the Blue Rosette at my first Sydney Royal, aged 18, was a wonderful thrill. After riding around the ring to the applause of the large crowd I was on cloud nine, and back at our stables I found it difficult to dismount. A policeman we had come to know during that show was kind enough to step forward and lift me down. Even then it felt as though I was still floating on air, and it took a little time to come down to earth. Just making it to the Sydney Royal had been a moment to cherish, but actually winning such a prestigious event was a thrill beyond my wildest dreams.

To this day, I don't know whether I can make a reasonable comparison between the elation of this event and some of the most notable races won during my career as a harness racing driver.

Gladwyn had a reputation for possessing a mean streak. I was told it surfaced only on rare occasions. One of those times was during the Open Lady Rider class several days later. The judge called me in again, and when it came time for my workout, Gladwyn just refused to go out for my effort. When she finally condescended to do my bidding, she cut the corners of her turns short, despite all my efforts to control her. The judge was very patient and waited for me to finish. I was awarded sixth place, but under the circumstances I was well satisfied with the outcome. I had gone to my first Sydney Royal not expecting to win any ribbons or gain any recognition at all. But I did call Gladwyn a few names under my breath for her piggish attitude in our second attempt together.

Life slowly returned to normal. I went back to work and continued to ride in those shows to which I was able to hitch a ride. My father was very supportive and often came to watch, but Mum seldom came, as she thought it more of a nuisance than an enjoyment.

SEVEN

My Introduction to Pacing

When looking back over your life there is usually a particular year that stands out from those around it; a year that on reflection was significant. Perhaps a turning point in your life or one that brings back fond memories of several events that helped shape your future. For me, one such year was 1961. It was early that year that I enjoyed my success at the Sydney Royal, then only a couple of months later I was introduced to harness racing, and the man I was to marry.

During my regular outings on horseback around Dapto, I happened to ride out to the Kembla Grange trotting track one day and there meet farrier Arthur Frew. This was the day that would change my life forever. Apart from working as a blacksmith for the mines, Arthur trained a few horses in his spare time. We got talking and he pointed out that he could do with some help around the stables working his horses. When I showed interest, though quick to point out I had never had any experience with pacers, he offered to teach me. It was a challenge I found difficult to reject.

My work at the exchange at that time began after lunch. I was able to ride my horse out to Kembla Grange in the morning, spend several hours helping Arthur work his team, then be back home in time to prepare to leave for the Wollongong Telephone Exchange. Arthur initially taught me how to train his horses under saddle to condition them, putting mileage into their legs. He would carry out the fast work in a sulky. While my days had suddenly become extremely busy, it did allow my horse to have its daily exercise, and me to learn a little about pacers. Maintaining this schedule meant having to do some smart talking with my work-mates to continue with the afternoon shift at the exchange.

It was my involvement with Arthur Frew's horses that brought me into contact with trainer George Frost. Years before, he had made his income from supplying pit ponies for the coalmines and cutting timber, becoming a trainer of pacers after much encouragement from horseman Bob Murray. George and his wife Joyce, their daughter Pauline and sons Vic and Peter, lived in a house with stables on 18 acres near Wongawilli. The Frosts had their own training track, but would often come over to Kembla Grange to do their fast work. This was where I first met the young Victor William Frost, known to all simply as 'Vic'. He was working in the Wongawilli coalmine, where Dad also worked. He was already well involved with his father's horses, with firm ambitions to be a top driver and one day train his own team.

George Frost had seen me riding track-work for Arthur, and remarked to me one day that this was how his son had first experienced the sport. As a lad, Vic had pestered his father for a horse of his own, as his asthma greatly restricted him from playing most of the competitive sports. George paid fifteen pounds for the pacing-bred Darkie's Last and presented it to his son when Vic was twelve years old. This opened the door for him to ride this horse at the South Coast shows, where they were successful in several events when he was still only twelve. One day Vic was keen to see what his pacer might do with hopples on and, with assistance from Bob Murray, they set out with curiosity and hope. Obviously the result was positive, as Murray suggested to George Frost he should give this horse a try racing in a gig.

Placed in full work, Darkie's Last won its first race at the Dapto Show. It may not have been too successful when competing at registered meetings, but it did go on to win further races at shows and gymkhanas and became important in laying the foundations for Vic becoming a trainer and driver.

The Frosts had quite a few horses in their team when I first met them. It required a pacer of considerable ability to be competitive at Harold Park in the era of such the big-name stables such as Jack Watts, Bert Alley, Perc Hall, Jim Cafynn, Sutton McMillan and Alf Phillis, to mention just a few. When Vic was in his 16th year, his father obtained the pacer Galway Bay. It responded so well to the Frost polish that soon the stable considered it might be competitive at Harold Park. George was very happy with the enthusiasm shown by Vic to obtain his licence so he could drive Galway Bay at headquarters. He recognised that here was a boy with those qualities necessary to make the grade as a reinsman, and age should be no bar.

The mandatory age to secure a metropolitan licence was seventeen. When George Frost fronted up in Sydney with an application for his son's licence, it seems Vic had suddenly become a year older. Unaware of this, the stewards could find no valid reason for not granting the licence, as Vic had won four races on country tracks, then the minimum to be permitted to drive at Harold Park. Galway Bay did not let him down, and in March of 1957 the pair duly saluted in their Sydney debut when the pacer started at 14/1. It was the first of many wins and premierships at this venue for Vic.

The Frosts had enjoyed a reputation for their honesty, and it seems as the months became years, the manner of securing an early licence for Vic had weighed on George's conscience. He informed officials of how there had been an 'unintentional' mistake with his son's birth date, claiming the confusion actually occurred during the war years when Vic was just a boy. The authorities accepted this statement and amended their records. Because it is no longer legally possible to alter a junior's age when applying for a permit to drive, it is reasonable to assume that Vic Frost will remain the youngest reinsman ever to drive a winner at night trotting in Sydney.

One day George was fast working horses at Kembla Grange and took me by surprise when he asked if I would like to help work their horses. I talked this over with Arthur Frew, who pointed out that it would be an opportunity for advancement, so I jumped at this invitation. As Arthur mixed his training duties with his work as a farrier and shod the horses in the Frost stables, I was able to see him from time-to-time and talk trotting with him. After I joined the Frosts, George went to some trouble to teach me about pacers and trotters and how they should be driven. He was a good tutor, clearly demonstrated by the ability of his son, although Vic did seem to have a natural flair.

Placing horses in races suitable for their handicap is what it is all about with average pacers, and before I came to know the Frosts they had made several annual trips up north to Southport, campaigning a team of horses at this southern Queensland track for several weeks at a time. The team one year was headed by the trotter Rangfield and the pacers Yes Please, Reg Again, Mustard, Square, Galway Bay and Lumack, among others.

At one of these meetings Vic drove every winner on the program, to become the youngest reinsman in Australia to achieve such a feat, and the following week almost repeated the effort, losing in a photo finish in the only race he did not win. In the previous campaign there, the stable had won a total of 24 races, with George driving eight of these and Vic the other 16. The grey trotter Rangfield won at Southport at one meeting when handicapped off 84 yards.

George's wife Joyce would accompany them on these trips and on race day was the strapper, and she was a most dedicated worker around the stables. Her favourite horse was the mare Yes Please, a notoriously slow beginner who went on to win 22 races when campaigning in Queensland. One of these wins was off a handicap of 120 yards. By the time I first met Vic, he was well known around Dapto for his horsemanship but, despite his early success, he was still a long way from being a household name, and no doubt an unknown in the sport in the southern states. This situation would change before the end of that year.

One of the first rules George Frost impressed on me was to secure the reins. This was done by tucking the loose ends under your bottom when sitting on the seat, making sure no more than a foot or so of them was protruding. If the reins are left dangling, the horse following could tread on them or, if loose in front, they could well flip and become tangled in a wheel, the result of which I will leave to your imagination.

Harnessing a pacer is also important. Much care has to be taken as any small failure could cause an accident, injuring your horse, yourself, or another driver. The harness consists of a breastplate, which goes around the chest of the horse and connects the gig to the saddle by straps. A harness saddle supports the weight of the cart and is fitted on the back behind the withers. A crupper is a loop fitted under the tail and connected to the back of the saddle to prevent the saddle edging forward.

The all-important hopples are hung over the back on each side of the horse, with each leg placed through a hopple hoop, positioned above their knees. These give the pacer confidence to remain at their gait when under speed and pressure. Occasionally you will see an unhoppled pacer, though this is extremely rare at the speed races are conducted these days. The bridle goes over the head, and we usually left it until last, so the steel bit was not in their mouth any longer than necessary. The reins are then connected from the bit and back through steel rings on the saddle to the driver to control and steer the horse. There are a variety of bridles available, all with special traits that suit the habits of different pacers. Boots are usually worn to protect the tendons and knees and, if necessary, plastic 'bell-boots' are worn around the feet.

During the time George Frost was teaching me to drive, I was carrying out pace work behind one horse when it suddenly bolted and I just could not pull it up. As I went flying past Vic's father, he immediately saw my plight and calmly called out, 'Keep him on the track, just keep him on the track, he will stop when he is tired,' he urged. Right then this was very hard to believe; I thought he was never going to stop, he was pulling so hard that he felt as if he wanted to go forever. No-one counted the laps that day, but each time I passed the Frosts they just shouted out some encouragement to me without appearing to be overly concerned about what, to me, was more than a little frightening.

Later I realised that, had they tried stopping the animal and it veered away sharply, I could have been injured. The horse did slow down of its own accord. For some time after my arms felt weak from the strain. Not to panic was a valuable lesson I learned that day, and I was then more diligent with my choice of horses. The horses that did not pull hard and had good soft mouths were my choice after this; it was one sure way for me to know that they would be more easily controlled. Gradually, my arms strengthened and I was able to work and control most of the horses in the stables.

When I began helping out at the Frost stables, Vic was 21 years old. He was then rather slim and quite good-looking. What really impressed me at first was his dedication in placing the interests of the horses first, a trait that would become his trademark over the years as a trainer. He always seemed calm and well controlled in what he did. He also had a quietly spoken demeanor around the stables, a kind of confidence likely to impress both race officials and the public, as well as owners who would come to meet him later, when he had branched out on his own. I also came to respect his honesty, even after his father had told me about the 'confusion' with his age when Vic had first been licensed to drive at Harold Park.

Each morning during the week I would ride my horse out to the Frost's farm and help with track-work, initially driving the quieter pacers. To say I thoroughly enjoyed this would be an understatement. During the show season I still managed to do the rounds of the district circuit, all adding up to an extremely busy schedule. With the benefit of hindsight, I came to realise that I should have been more considerate of my mother. There were the occasions when I did spend a couple of hours cleaning the house when still a teenager, but such mundane things as this were given a low priority behind the horses, an attitude I regret when looking back on those times.

Vic began taking me to harness racing gymkhanas on Sundays when the stable had horses to trial and educate, and from this it seemed natural for us to start dating. Dancing was never one of his interests, and if my memory is correct, I can only recall him ever taking me to one dance. To say that we were both horse mad is no exaggeration, so there was never a lack of a subject for conversation. We both worked afternoon shifts that extended well into the evenings—Vic at the mine, and me at the exchange. The time for developing any romantic notions was extremely limited.

Towards the end of the year George nominated the current star of the stable for the Tasmanian Championship. The club at Hobart then raced at Elwick, the home of the local thoroughbred club. The horse was the smart Tacloban, owned by Allan McMahon. By modern-day standards the prize money of $6,000 might not seem anything flash. In 1961 it was an amount not to be sneezed at. The previous season, Kevin Newman had won this race with Koala Lawn, to be the first New South Wales pacer to take out a Tasmanian Championship. Vic and Tacloban made it back-to-back successes for New South Wales. Harness racing was later transferred across the road to the showgrounds, with this event still the major pacing race in Tasmania. It was the first of many major races to be claimed by Vic on his way to reaching the very top rung on the ladder of success.

EIGHT

Marriage to Vic, and Harness Racing

The first Dapto Show I missed for some years was on January 18th 1964. There was a good reason for my absence that day; Vic and I were married at the Dapto Presbyterian Church. The horses for once had to take a back seat in my life. I was then 20 years old and had been going out with Vic for more than two years. When he decided he wanted to marry me, he was quite the gentleman, going to see my father first to ask for his approval.

The wedding went off without a hitch, except for one small problem. My Aunt Ethel burnt a hole in the tulle material at the front of my wedding dress, when using an iron that was a little too hot. With a little dexterity and ruffling of the material here and there, the damage was obscured. For our honeymoon, we set out for Queensland towing a caravan. When some of his racing mates up there learned the base of the caravan bed had broken and needed fixing, Vic was heckled relentlessly as none of our excuses were accepted. Harness racing friends can be merciless when taking the mickey out of mates.

We were still on our honeymoon when Vic was asked to drive Red Adios in the Melbourne Inter Dominion in February. We had our trip to Queensland cut short, which gave one newspaper the opportunity to print a story under the heading: 'Honeymoon loses to Trots'. Vic had mixed fortunes in that championship, with Red Adios winning its opening night heat with the fastest time of the round, then several nights later winning its second heat. On the third and final night of heats, the horse lost all chance at the start when it came out galloping.

His trainer worked Red Adios hard during the week leading up to the final, in the hope that this would settle the pacer at the start. Following three hard runs the previous week, it settled him all right, with Red Adios standing flat-footed when the strands flew back. It had been a vintage year for my first visit to an Inter Dominion, with a record crowd for the Melbourne Showgrounds of 45,788 attending the final, to see Minuteman beat Angelique and Tactile. Among the unplaced brigade were Cardigan Bay, Smoke Cloud and Pipiriki, with the highly successful Waitaki Hanover, Future Raider and Rising Flood fighting out the Consolation.

Vic and I lived in a flat in Dapto when we were first married, until we were able to buy an attractive three-bedroom brick home close to the Dapto showground. Vic was still working afternoon shifts at the mine, so he was able to work the horses with his father in the morning. I was still with the Wollongong Telephone Exchange. Because of his chronic asthma, Vic had been moved to an outdoor job as a blacksmith's striker, but still had to do the occasional shift underground. It was not that he was afraid of being underground and working at the face, it was the damp and heavy atmosphere below that brought him a great deal of discomfort with his breathing.

The big picks and hammers used for chipping the coal underground would often need to be straightened out or 'hard-faced'. The shuttle cars were also in need of regular repair, and it was the blacksmith shop that was responsible for this maintenance, along with maintaining the steel silos built to hold the coal extracted from two seams that were a hundred feet apart and four miles down.

One part of Vic's work each afternoon was to walk down the mine and turn off the pump. He would collect his lamp and walk half an hour to the pump, turn it off and then walk out again. One night when working overtime his lamp failed when he was preparing to return. He was left in complete blackness. The only way to find his way back was to follow the conveyor belt, and to do this meant walking sideways so he could keep one hand on the belt. Vic was extremely relieved when he finally made it out into the night air.

The wife of any miner who spends time underground lives with the fear of accidents. Dad had been injured in the mines in England when I was a child and I can still remember the ambulance bringing him home. In that accident an artery in his leg had been cut and it was only the quick action of others that prevented it from being extremely serious. My sister Neena had good reason to remember Dad's accident as well, for not long after he was back on his feet, she was running away from a duck carrying a worm, which she hates. Not looking where she was going, she collided heavily with Dad, leaving him clutching his injured leg in great pain.

These experiences gave me a dread of coalmines, and with Vic's asthma being aggravated by his working in the mine, it was not so difficult to persuade him to leave. I was still at the telephone exchange, but gained a transfer from the Wollongong Exchange to Dapto, and as such I was still able to help a little with the horses. The harness always needed cleaning and this was a job that I could count on every time I went out to the Frosts. It was never Vic's favourite chore, and one he never seemed to have time to do.

It was after Vic and I were married and moved to Bong Bong Road, Dapto, that I met and became friends with Marie and Ken Swan. They lived about half a mile from where we were. Ken and Marie now live at Dapto in a delightfully situated residence, presenting some outstanding views of Lake Illawarra, the surrounding escarpment and beautiful valleys. On the occasion of my last visit with them, some interesting stories came to light.

Ken and Vic had grown up together, living in the same street near the Dapto Railway Station. Ken also was interested in horses and became a trainer-driver, while earning his main living driving cattle trucks. In the days before I had met the Frosts, Ken would usually accompany George and Vic to the various race meetings.

He recounted a time when, returning from Newcastle races, they were driving through the northern Wollongong suburb of Fairy Meadow at about four o'clock in the morning when there was a bump, and suddenly a large wheel went hurtling ahead of them. The thumping of the front axle of the truck on the road left no guesswork required as to what had happened. The jarring awoke Vic from a deep sleep and, without thinking, he grabbed for the handle of the door to jump from the cabin. Ken grabbed him just in time to stop him from making an unwise decision.

Meanwhile, the wheel had careered on down the road before veering wildly off course over a footpath and demolishing the front fence of a house. No sooner had the trio arrived to inspect the wreckage, when the angry owner emerged in his dressing gown with smoke pouring from his ears at the sight of what had happened to his lovely fence. He too had probably been abruptly woken from sleep, and began hurling abuse at the sheepish trio, even calling into question the legitimacy of their births. George Frost was a dry old soul at any time, and watching the man storming up to them he said quietly to Ken, 'Gee whizz Ken, I think this fellow is upset.' When the angry owner let forth with another round of abuse for what had been done, George, with his sharp wit, added apologetically, 'Look, I'm really sorry mate, I did my best but just couldn't catch it.'

It seems that when Ken and Vic were young teenagers they had been impressed with the deeds of Roy Rogers and Gene Autry in those cowboy movies, as they took their games of cowboys and Indians quite seriously in the scrub around Dapto. Chasing each other on horseback and jumping over logs might have been one thing, but then Vic took to riding his horse under overhanging tree branches and standing up on the saddle of the moving horse to make a grab for a branch, before hauling himself up to hide from the 'posse' or the 'crooks' chasing him. When this was done in the movies, it was never shown how many takes it might have been before the stuntman got it right. If Roy or Gene could do it on the screen then, to a young impressionable Vic, he too reasoned it was all part of the hero's repertoire. However, the day would come not far down the track when he was able to achieve the feat when under real pressure.

George, Ken and Vic were returning to Wollongong after an afternoon's racing at Goulburn. The horses were tied up in the back of a small cattle truck that had high sides but no top. As they were making their way with great care down the notorious Macquarie Pass, there suddenly came a series of loud scrambling noises on the roof of their cabin, followed by loud banging, as though someone had taken a hammer and was giving it a real thrashing. 'What the hell is going on?' yelled Vic, as George looked frantically ahead, trying to find a safe area where he could bring the truck to a stop.

When they finally were able to pull up on the side of this narrow road and get out, they were amazed to find that Darkie's Last had got loose and had not only its front legs right up on the cabin's roof, but half its body as well. The horse had become well and truly stuck and its fear had turned to panic. Vic climbed quickly up to take stock of the situation, when the truck began moving forward. On the downward slope, the handbrake was not holding.

With the truck moving towards a steep drop and the end seeming only moments away for them all, Vic suddenly reached up and grabbed an overhanging branch to pull himself clear of the stricken vehicle. A tragedy was only averted thanks to the quick action of Ken Swan. He had sized up the situation immediately he saw the truck move and, with little thought for his own safety, frantically hauled himself into the cabin to bring the truck back to the road and apply the brake. With Vic left hanging from the high tree branch, he probably looked more like Tarzan than Roy or Gene!

The other horses on board had become really stirred up as the two boys worked to get Darkie's Last down from its perch and then out on the road to examine it for injury. Ken had an uncle who lived at the foot of the pass. It was decided that he would ride Darkie's Last down to his uncle's place and leave the upset horse there for the night. Ken settled the horse in and waited to be picked up by the truck as arranged. He waited and waited, and finally hitched a ride back up to where the truck had stopped, to find that the repairs to the truck and the securing of the horses had just been completed. They arrived home well into the sleepy side of midnight, bringing to a close a very long day.

NINE

The Time Was Right

One of the major decisions for many a fully professional sportsman is deciding when it is the right time to retire. It is an even
bigger decision in harness racing deciding when is the right
time to branch out on your own if your only income is likely to be
generated by training and driving. Very few young harness horsemen
have become established without the income of a part-time job to fall
back on.

Vic's growing success as a driver was now making him well
known. But when I suggested he was ready to concentrate on training
and driving for a living, he would hesitate and point out the pitfalls
that had befallen other young horsemen. 'It's not so much finding
horses to train,' he would explain, 'it is finding good owners who pay
their way through the bad times as well as the good.' We finally decided the safest way to success was hard work, so we purchased a
van and began a 'bread run' for Buttercup Bakeries, while Vic continued taking more and more responsibility in helping his father train
their team.

The bread had to be delivered in the morning, so we were forced
to train our team of horses in the afternoon. Getting up bright and
early, Vic had to deliver the bread as quickly as possible, then rush
back to the stables to train the horses. Training the number of horses
the Frosts then had in work was really a full-time job. It did not take
us long to realise that the bread run was also a full-time effort in
normal circumstances. That period of our life meant maintaining a
daily schedule that would test our endurance to the utmost. You can
well imagine what it was like on race days, especially when taking
horses to Harold Park on Friday nights.

Friday was also debt-collecting day for the bread run and it could
develop into a real nightmare trying to get it done in time. Some of
our customers had difficulty speaking English, but on debt-collecting day the number would greatly escalate. It was amazing just how
many would fall back on, 'No speaka de English' when you turned up

to collect their money. Others would hold you up by making the most fanciful excuses imaginable as to why they could not pay on that particular day. It was so frustrating, keeping one eye on the clock as you frantically rushed around to get the job done in time to prepare for the drive to Sydney, on the old road.

There was a ladies tennis team that played once a week at the local club, which I joined. On the days that I had planned to play tennis—and there weren't that many fulfilled—I could almost bank on Vic phoning that morning saying, 'I've broken down again Margy, could you bring the wagon, please?' Out I would go to find him, wherever he was, then we would transfer the bread to the wagon before rushing off to finish the run. Another day's tennis down the chute!

As the months went by, Vic finally realised how difficult it was to do a really professional job with the horses while being run ragged with the bread run. After a year or so, Vic took little persuading to decide it was time to retire from delivering bread. He could now devote his full energy and enthusiasm to the horses. Until then, the horses had been trained in his father's name, with Vic taking an ever increasing role in their training and doing all the driving on race days. We knew that branching out on his own was a risk, though I had full confidence in him succeeding. You couldn't work around the stables with Vic without being impressed at the knowledge he had already gained, and the ability that he had to coax the best out of the horses.

When he first started to train on his own we had a few mediocre pacers, which gained places and had the occasional win. Our income from training fees and his driving percentage was always welcome, though there were times early on when this threatened not to be enough, and some bills did start to mount up before they could be paid. However, it was not too long before things improved and Vic and I found that we could well have taken on full-time training even earlier.

Perhaps his first break came when a syndicate formed by Jack Weir gave him the mare Fountain to train. This performer was well known as a most unreliable pacer at the barrier. In those days it was all standing starts, and while there seemed a real risk that she was capable of making a fool out of her new trainer, as she had with others, Vic felt he could not knock back the chance to train a handy mare.

Obviously he found the secret to Fountain's problems, as she went on to win 17 races, some of these at Harold Park. Her success did much for Vic in earning the respect of other trainers, who would no doubt have sacked her.

Some of the stake money won by the syndicate with Fountain went to purchase a horse named Ringo. I was sorry that, due to some problem with one of the other members, Jack Weir did not remain in the group. Ringo turned out to be another problem horse—a chronic knee-knocker. (This is when a forefoot swings in and hits the opposite knee.) Vic would not have had the necessary time to devote to Ringo if he had still been on the bread run.

Spreaders were tried on this horse with little success. Sometimes this piece of gear can assist knee-knockers, often at the expense of speed. Vic began tackling the problem from another direction by making dramatic changes to the way the horse had previously been shod. He was able to improve Ringo so much that among the many wins this horse had for us were a number of metropolitan successes. Harold Park has long been a difficult track for knee-knockers to handle, so again there were some eyebrows raised when Vic and Ringo did so well at headquarters.

The syndicate eventually took the horse from our stable without giving any reason for this decision. This was a disappointment, as both Vic and I had become fond of him. The trainer that took him had no success with Ringo. Vic was quite sure that this was because the trainer had changed his shoeing. When the syndicate finally came back and asked Vic to take Ringo back, he agreed, because he had taken such a liking to the horse. Vic's conclusion about the horse's poor performance was correct, as Ringo had been banging his knee so much that it had enlarged to a point where I had to spend a great deal of time working on it to reduce the swelling. After much effort with the knee and the shoeing pattern Vic again used, Ringo returned to racing and went on to win more races.

We were delighted when Jack Weir and his friend, Arthur McKenzie, bought the chestnut colt Adios Doug and gave him to us to train. This youngster gave the two owners a lot of enjoyment as they always got a 'run for their money' (a saying we have when a horse gives its best in its races). These two men remained with us as owners for as long as we lived at Dapto. Jack is now in his eighties, and I am proud to say he is still a good friend. I see him now and again and enjoy chatting with him, and he delights in filling the gaps that I have forgotten.

TEN

Life at Wongawilli

Six months before the birth of my first baby, I resigned from the telephone exchange. My work then was confined to keeping house, being the resident bookkeeper and harness polisher extraordinaire. The hopples and gear, then made of leather, had to be cleaned and polished after each use, a lot harder to look after than the plastic hopples of later years. One of Vic's additional skills was being able to skip this chore, though I guess it was a team effort and in my condition it was one job that I was still able to do. He would bring the gear home for me to polish and dump all of it in a place where it couldn't be ignored. What a great relief it was for me (and every harness cleaner) when plastic harness came into vogue.

There was one other who was helping out around the stables— my father George, then in his mid-fifties. My parents were living only three miles away at Brownsville, and Dad was still working in the nearby Wongawilli mine. This gave Dad the opportunity to work with horses again. Dad was well acquainted with horses, his experience gained the hard way, as a farm worker, in his youth, shortly after his arrival in Australia.

Glenn Victor Frost was born on October 23rd 1965, a 6lb 13oz son. The joyful experience of first setting eyes on him after his delivery is hard to put into words. What can I say, other than that it was sheer bliss. Through his Mum and Dad's eyes he was a beautiful little boy and I guess we spoiled him some. Often he would not go to sleep unless I sang lullabies to him. Being our first child, we may have been a mite overindulgent with Glenn.

Some 18 months later I gave birth to Garry David Frost, who weighed 8lb12 oz. He was so much bigger at birth than Glenn and my first impression of him was that he was not as beautiful, but he was perfect in every other way and healthy. This first impression was soon to change as I watched him develop into one gorgeous baby. Biased, you think? Well, I was his mother. Being the second child he may not have been as spoiled as Glenn. But then, most parents I'm sure are likely to be this way and be inclined to spoil their children a smidgen. I found it hard to differentiate between being indulgent and doing what was best for their upbringing. On balance, I believe we did our best, and we could take them anywhere and not have to apologise for their behaviour.

It was inconvenient not living on the training complex. The opportunity came to remedy this situation when Vic's parents decided they would sell the farm and move to Dubbo to be near their daughter Pauline and her family. With our stable now winning more and more races, we were in a position to take the plunge and buy our own property. So, with the help of the bank, we took advantage of George and Joyce moving to Dubbo and purchased the farm and stables.

George Frost maintained his interest in the sport at Dubbo by continuing to train on a greatly reduced scale, usually having only two or three horses in work at any one time. At the sprightly age of 67, he and Joyce made a trip to Harold Park, leaving home at 2.30am where George won with Lehigh Grattan and Colourala, two horses he trained. They were both legs of the daily double, and for a $1 investment the return was a handsome $180.80. My in-laws had not bothered taking a double, but winning a double at Harold Park would have been reward enough for them both.

Vic and I had been living at his parents' former property for two years when our daughter Susan Deborah was born. We both felt that a daughter had made our little family complete. Vic was away in Queensland to contest an important race when it came time for me to go to hospital for the birth of Susan. My sister Neena, then living with her family at Dapto, came in response to my frantic call to drive me to the Wollongong Hospital. I was the one who should have been nervous, but Neena was so on edge that she dumped me at the entrance and drove off before I fully realised what was happening. There I was, no husband present, having contractions, my water breaking, a bag in my hand and I had to find my way to the maternity ward. What an embarrassing predicament!

We still have a good laugh about it now, but it was certainly no laughing matter then. I could have throttled her. Right then, I was in no fit condition to carry out my threat. Neena walked into a 'telling off' from her husband Barry when she arrived home and told him what had happened. Somehow, I managed to find the office in time and was ushered up to the labour ward and settled in, not all that long before the baby arrived.

Susan was a little under six pounds when born, and seemed so small that my mother made special doll-sized nighties for her in the first few weeks. Initially, Vic was too afraid to pick her up, and when he did, he claimed she was no heavier than a pound of butter. Like her older brothers, she received much tender loving care; her baby charm was too difficult to resist.

Susan was only several months old when I went back to driving track-work, and almost two when I began going to the races again. It was great having my parents living so close, as Mum would come over and help with the house and also look after our three children when we were required to travel with the horses.

The first ever Ladies Race scheduled was at a Kembla Grange gymkhana, and about 5000 people attended. This race had created much interest, and I was delighted when my horse, Blacken, took me over the line. The trophy was presented to me by John Tapp, the well-known racing and television personality and a real enthusiast of harness racing. It was not surprising that I became keen on these exhibition races for women, and looked forward to the next one with pleasure.

It was about this time that Vic became associated with one of Australia's leading pacers, Lucky Creed, bred by Bill Picken in 1964. It was very well bred, being by King Creed from Overdrive, a winner of the New Zealand Oaks, whose sister Correction produced the very smart Scottish Fusilier. Passed in at the yearling sales for $1200, the colt was later sold for $1400 to Merv Wanless, a car wrecker in Queensland. It was one of the best investments he ever made.

Lucky Creed was an immature two-year-old who showed erratic behaviour in his only start that season when unplaced at Bathurst. A hairline fracture of a pedal bone restricted him to just four starts the following season, winning the last three of these. He won both of his four-year-old starts and came to Sydney at five, as a promising and lightly raced performer. The horse quickly settled into our stable routine, with Merv still recognised as the trainer. Vic did most of the pacework on our track and they swam Lucky Creed in the pool we had established for the horses. Lucky Creed was most impressive in winning his heat of the Carousel and seemed certain to be sent out a short-priced favourite in the final, held at Bankstown.

How could anyone associated with this horse forget that night. Merv and his wife Dulcie, Vic, his father George and I with Lucky Creed arrived at Bankstown for the final, only to discover that one of the most important parts of the horse's gear, the hopples, were missing. How this could have happened seemed incredible. The bottom line was it had happened, and what could be done about it? Because hopples are adjusted exactly to each pacer's stride, you cannot borrow a set from another horse.

Among the visitors that night to see the big final was Merv's son Ron Wanless, then one of the best known speedway drivers in Queensland. Ron offered to take one of us all the way back home to get the hopples, claiming he would be back in time for the race. He did not know the way, so asked for one of us to go with him. No-one put their hand up and I suddenly found a little job that needed doing. Finally Vic's father said to the speedway driver, 'I'll take you back, but I am not looking forward to the trip.'

He then went with Ron to Wongawilli to get those blasted hopples. They 'drove' into the stables, grabbed the hopples, jumped back into the 'rocket', and returned to Bankstown in the same manner. A trip that normally took about an hour and a half took just forty minutes that night. He said on his return, 'What an experience! I have done some fast travelling in my time, I thought, in cars and behind horses, but never, I repeat never, at that speed.' Ron had to drive on the Old Prince's Highway, which was just two lanes wide, between Bankstown and Wongawilli. There was no freeway then and George didn't know whether Ron knew the road or not. George said that in all the years that he had negotiated that same road, this was the first time that he had noticed that the centre line was unbroken, all the way from Bankstown to Wongawilli. Ron never turned a hair. As George thought about the drive later, he didn't remember seeing another car on the road. The hopples were hastily put on Lucky Creed, just in time for him to go onto the track for his warm up, prior to the race. Lucky Creed won the final convincingly, and the hopples looked just fine! George felt that the hair-raising trip to and from home had been worth enduring. Funnily enough, in a newspaper report later, Vic was quoted as saying about his drive on Lucky Creed that night, 'Driving Lucky Creed is like handling a high-powered deluxe car; he accelerated easily and did nothing wrong.' I wondered if it had any reference to the experience his father had had that night.

The stallion and Vic won the Menangle Cup, and a little later after winning his first race at Harold Park, won at Penrith on November 10, and the following day made light of a 36-yard handicap by winning at Menangle. December was almost as hectic as November, when he won all six starts in the month. His 17th successive win was at Harold Park, and the following day he raced again in a Kembla Grange Free-For-All. Three nights later, when attempting to equal Aachen's Australian record of 20 successive wins, he dislodged a shoe and twisted a knee boot, yet still went on to victory. If that sounds like being kept busy, there had been a day in Queensland previously, at the Dalby Show, when he had contested eight races on a track as small as the Melbourne Showgrounds!

Aachen had taken 34 months to achieve the record of 20 straight wins. After being so lightly raced early, most of Lucky Creed's victories were recorded in double-quick time. His win in the 1970 Miracle Mile was in March, beating Bold David and Imatoff, followed in by Deep Court, Dainty's Daughter and Tara Meadow.

With Vic in the sulky, this horse extended his winning sequence to 24 before attempting the Australia Day Cup at Harold Park. When Vic was working the stallion in preparation for its 25th straight success, Vic found him listless. Quite out of character. He had worked so poorly that Vic strongly recommended to Merv not to start the horse in the Cup. Merv loved watching his horse race and by now probably felt it to be almost invincible, and wouldn't scratch him. Its winning run finally came to an end when beaten in a photo finish by Cocky Raider.

We had earlier discovered that Merv was superstitious with his champion. After a few wins with Lucky Creed, he came to insist on wearing his lucky socks every time his horse raced. If these socks had been washed and were still wet, he would hold them out of the car window to dry on the way to the races before putting them on. He was of course wearing them in 1970 when Vic and Lucky Creed won that Miracle Mile at Harold Park. The horse and Vic won 11 races in Sydney on the way to creating that new Australian record of 24 successive victories. His record then stood at 47 victories from 49 starts. What a horse!

Merv was later invited by the US track of Yonkers to take his stallion there to contest the International Pace, promoted in New York as a world championship featuring the best horses available. Merv accompanied the horse on the flight to the US, where 'Lucky' was to be looked after by noted horseman Stanley Dancer, and Vic flew over in time to drive. Lucky Creed injured a knee during the flight, and on arrival this caused much concern. The horse was given one start to see how it coped, but when attempting its second outing on US soil, it broke down, aggravating the knee problem. Lucky Creed did not race again in the US.

Merv Wanless died in 1973, at 52 years of age, from a heart attack at his home in Queensland. His stallion was then standing at stud in its home state, but had limited opportunities. I found it rather sad to see Australian breeders bypass such a great and tough horse over all distances, preferring to support imported stallions from North America that would never have been considered good enough there for an invitation to an International Pace. Perhaps breeders here have placed too much importance on race records created in the US on much faster tracks than we had down under, which tends to place our best-performing stallions on the racetrack at a great disadvantage at stud.

It was in 1970, when Vic was 29, that he became the leading reinsman in Australia and the first in this country to drive more than 100 winners in a season. It was also the year that he won the first of his five driving premierships at Harold Park, dethroning Kevin Newman, a most talented horseman, who until then had been dominating this premiership.

My sister Neena and her husband Barry, who had earlier conducted a milk-run at Lismore, were living on a few acres at Dapto. They owned and operated the cordial manufacturing business at Fairy Meadow known as Collin's Cordials. They also kept a few milking goats as there was some demand for this kind of milk in assisting conditions such as asthma. Neena gave us some milk from their goats when Vic was having trouble with his breathing. I was so pleased with the help it seemed to give both Vic and Susan, and also for Garry's bronchitis, that I bought a goat of our own and learned to milk it. This experience became very handy later on, when we bought a Jersey cow. The Jersey's milk was so creamy and rich; we always had a supply of cream on hand, and there seemed to be a frequent need for this commodity to go with pancakes (pikelets is the Australian name, but I still use the 'Pommy' one).

There was one very notable occasion when the amazing properties of goat's milk were demonstrated. We had a horse called Sir George, which was purchased in New Zealand for quite a large sum of money. We understood this horse to have good potential and as such had great expectations for him to become a top racehorse. However, while he was still in training and before he was able to start in a race in Australia, he developed the scours. This is a disease very similar to gastroenteritis in human beings and, apart from being a very serious impediment to training, is also difficult to manage. This condition was one that we had managed to avoid up until now.

It was our practice to allow our milking goats to roam freely among the horses, in the belief that the presence of goats among other animals reduced the possibility of various diseases in those animals. The absence of disease among the horses on our property, through the years, strengthened this belief.

It became virtually impossible to give the horse any work, with its condition worsening as the days turned into weeks. Everything Vic tried to prevent the horse scouring seemed to fail.

While speaking with my brother-in-law Barry one day, I just happened to mention the problems Sir George had. Barry in a quiet, matter-of-fact tone suggested, 'Why don't you try a mixture of eggs and goats' milk? We know this has helped a lot of babies with gastrointestinal troubles,' he explained, and added, 'It's supposed to put a lining on their stomachs.' Barry said if everything else we had tried was failing, then this was well worth giving a go.

After discussing Barry's suggestion with Vic, his reply was sharp and to the point. 'All the bloody treatments we've already tried have been useless and he's no good to us as he is; so give it a go.' I heard him mumble as he walked away. 'Gees! a bloody egg flip for a bloody horse.' Without turning his head to make sure I heard, he added, 'I don't have the time to spare, stuffing around with all that, its up to you.' So I was the volunteer.

We just happened to have two goats at this time, and it required the milk from both and a little extra from Neena to get enough for a daily preparation. It was no good doing things in half measures, so I went regularly to the Egg Marketing Board in Wollongong to buy large quantities of eggs to help make the 'egg flip'. I started Sir George on a weak mixture at first and, naturally, he turned his nose up at it the first time. Taking his water away for a day seemed to help, and before long the horse was taking to the concoction, while the volume he drank increased. After three weeks he was receiving three dozen eggs and a gallon of milk twice a day.

My perseverance was rewarded after a week. I was amazed to watch the horse acquire a taste for his special milkshake. Sir George would spot me walking down the lane with the bucket, and come up at a canter, whinnying all the way. Sir George would drink it down in no time, and then, I swear, would walk away licking his lips. This treatment finally did the trick, with the scouring completely overcome. Vic gave the horse a spell in the paddock and when Sir George was brought back into work, the pacer responded very well, going on to win many races. I was delighted that this concoction had worked, and I was awfully glad that we had no further signs of scours in the stable.

Our daughter Susan was four years old when she contracted an acute bout of gastroenteritis and was hospitalised in Wollongong. I stayed at the hospital for most of the first day and night. The following day I became distressed by Susan's excessive listlessness. I rang my mother and told her that I was going home to get Vic and bring him back immediately to the hospital. I felt that not enough was being done for her, and needed Vic for support in insisting on a closer investigation of her condition from the hospital authorities.

Mum caught a bus and came straight to the hospital, and I am eternally grateful to her for this as, when she picked Susan up, the child went limp in her arms. Mum screamed, and nursing staff came running from everywhere. A doctor was summoned, who immediately issued instructions to have an intravenous drip inserted. To our great relief, Susan began to respond soon after, and we were able to take her home later in the week.

It was while Susan was in the Wollongong hospital that an observant doctor noticed ugly stitch marks on her right index finger as a result of a deep wound. This had occurred one night, months earlier, while I was under the shower. She had picked up a sharp knife from the drawer. Her brother Garry, who was always protective of his little sister, believed she would cut herself, and grabbed it from her. Unfortunately, Susan had been holding the blade end at the time and, when pulled by the handle, the blade went well into her finger, cutting it deeply.

On hearing the screams and shouts, I grabbed a towel to wrap around me as I dashed dripping from the bathroom to see what was happening. Susan was rushed to the local hospital where a number of stitches were quickly inserted. Evidently, the stitches had been inserted in such a way that she would have been left with a permanently stiff index finger; not a pretty sight for a girl and such an inconvenience. The doctor advised that it would require surgery as soon as possible, to have her finger repaired.

It was a rather traumatic time in our lives, as Vic had been booked into a Sydney hospital to have a sinusitis operation the same week Susan's finger was to be operated on. To be more convenient for me, we arranged for both operations to be done as close together as possible. Unfortunately, they could not be done at the same hospital, so I had to sneak out from Susan's room when she fell asleep, then drive over to visit Vic each day at his hospital. It was exhausting. I did not get much rest, especially since I was sleeping at night in an armchair in Susan's room. It was a great relief when the time came to take them both home.

Susan still had her hand in plaster to protect the necessary work done on the finger, and Vic was too weak to be out training horses, when he graciously volunteered to milk the family, goat, a chore I usually did each day. He said he felt well enough and it would give me a break from my workload. This particular day was windy and dusty. Perhaps he rubbed his nose with a dirty sleeve, or maybe it was just some dust that got up his nose. Whatever was the cause, he quickly developed badly infected sinuses, leading to a more serious condition called cellulitis, which can have some very nasty complications if not treated quickly.

Our local doctor arranged an ambulance to take Vic to Royal North Shore hospital in Sydney, and I accompanied him on the journey. About halfway there his nose started to bleed rather badly. An ambulance officer soaked cotton buds in adrenaline and inserted them as high as possible into Vic's nose, eventually stopping the bleeding.

Half an hour from the hospital, the haemorrhaging started again, only more profusely this time. I tried to stop it the way I had been shown, while the driver continued on to the hospital, but the flow was too rapid and pushed the cotton buds out as fast as I was inserting them. On being alerted to Vic's worsening condition, the driver immediately switched on the ambulance sirens. Those last few minutes it took to reach the hospital seemed an eternity. Vic, who was barely conscious when we arrived, was quickly offloaded to a waiting trolley and wheeled off smartly by the orderlies to the emergency room. It is almost indescribable to think how I felt, though it must have been worse for him in the operating theatre when they removed the offending clots to stop the haemorrhaging.

While Vic was in hospital, I was able to stay with some friends nearby. All seemed to be going well until the night before he was due to be discharged. Close to midnight I felt a strong compulsion to ring the hospital. This desire was finally dismissed since he was considered well enough to go home the following day. I later discovered that at the moment I had that dreadful feeling, Vic was suffering a serious relapse.

The young intern on duty refused Vic's plea to ring the doctor who had performed the operation, assuring him that he would be all right. The specialist was coming to see Vic early in the morning and the young trainee said this would be soon enough. As Vic became worse and blood just poured out, he had to sit there catching the blood in a bowl. He told me later that he really thought he was going to die.

When the specialist did come, he said to Vic, 'It will be okay. We will take you back to theatre and remove the clot we missed.' He tried to get Vic to relax by telling him he would be fine in a few days. Vic wasn't so sure, feeling his days were numbered. After the surgery, Vic would not let me leave his side for any length of time, having me there holding his hand until staff asked me to leave around 10.30 at night.

In the following weeks there can be no doubt that he did lose confidence both in himself and in some medical staff. The experience also had a profound and long-term effect, causing him to be nervous and emotional. He had never been a man to cry easily, but later, something as simple as having to discipline the children would bring him to tears. A change in his outlook on life became obvious, including a desire to seek more time for relaxation.

One of the first things he did when feeling well again was to buy a six-metre boat to enable him to go fishing. These expeditions with Glenn and Garry were instrumental in cementing their interest in the sport. Vic had been pushing himself on the racetrack leading up to his spell in hospital, and was at the top of the premiership table. It was now obvious that driving on dusty tracks presented a definite risk to his health, and he wanted to avoid anything that was in any way a threat of further infection. As a result of this fear, a special mask to cover his nose was made for him to wear.

The first drive Vic had after his operation was on War Stamp, a horse owned by Marie and Tom Bullen of Newcastle, and it raced very successfully at Harold Park. Vic had lost a lot of blood while in hospital and was still feeling weak and, as subsequent actions revealed, he should not have been driving at all so soon after his discharge from hospital. He won the race all right, but on returning to scale with War Stamp he was so dizzy he almost fell out of the gig.

There was an occasion when I developed a cyst in a very sensitive area of my groin, and required a minor operation to have it removed. The act of sitting down was most painful and resulted in much grimacing and gritting of teeth. The discomfort lasted several days, but I still drove at Harold Park two nights after the operation (making my specialist groan), sitting a little to the side of the gig. I must admit I can't remember if I won a race or even ran a place, to convince myself that the pain was worth enduring, but as always in our line of work, the show must go on. We Frosts are probably a little crazy when it comes to harness racing. I'm not sure whether it runs in the family or if it just develops with the profession.

Vic wore the special mask made for him until his doctor finally deemed he was safe and free of infection. The spectacle of the leading reinsman wearing a mask was not missed by the media. Several reports were published, with more than one claiming how much he looked like a parrot. On reflection, he probably did. But it did wonders for his confidence at a time when he was extremely worried about his health. He also went on to win another driving premiership that season.

At Wongawilli we lived in the little fibro home that Vic's parents had built for the first few years of our married life, before we built the much larger brick home. When Garry was about two, he had a habit of taking off all his clothes, and quite often he would walk around wearing nothing but his shoes, as he had not yet mastered the art of undoing his laces. We did not have a childproof fence around the 18 acres and it was almost impossible to watch the two boys every minute of the day.

One day, while I was baking, I heard a knock on the front door. I opened it to find a man standing there, who was quite agitated. He said urgently, 'Excuse me, are those two little boys over there yours?'

Looking across to where he was pointing, I could just see two blond heads bobbing in the long grass. I thanked the man and rushed to the farm over the road, where the boys were creeping along in the grass like Indians, with their pop guns, looking for rabbits. Both boys had the ability to make up their own games, and as they both loved the outdoors, living on a farm was ideal.

On getting closer, I found Garry without a stitch of clothes on, wearing just his shoes. As it was summer and snakes were prevalent in this area, it terrified me to see the boys among the cattle and in the long grass. I marched them home, picking up Garry's clothes on the way. Garry was extremely allergic to bee stings, which we discovered when he was stung for a second time. He became very swollen in the groin area, developing a high temperature, and as from that time I had insisted that he keep his clothes on and be on the alert, whenever bees were around. What a waste of breath!

Each scored a good smacked bottom that day!

The horse training track there was made of coal dust, and the boys loved to play in the large tractor tyres that we had tied together for dragging behind the tractor to smooth the rough surface of the track. They would come up to the stables looking just like their Grandpa, as he surfaced from the mine at the end of a day: absolutely black. Their clothes were as black as their faces. It gave everyone that saw them a good laugh, but me; I often felt like throttling the two of them.

They had an amazing ability to find frogs where you would least expect, and were aware that I was as terrified of them as I was of mice. One day they came into the house with a bucket, and into the bedroom where I was at the end of the hall. They ran up to the bedroom and tipped the bucket upside down, releasing two huge green frogs.

My screams were heard at the stables, where Vic was shoeing a horse. He rushed up, expecting to see me being bashed or something dreadful, and could only laugh when he found me up on the bed screaming at two jumping frogs.

We had added a laundry onto the house, after we had bought it from Vic's parents, and it was downstairs from the boys' bedroom, with their window opening onto the laundry roof. One night, Glenn climbed out of the window and was just about to grab the electric power lines which were above the house, when I found him. If he had held the two at once he would have been killed, and I certainly locked the window securely after that.

One day the boys had broken bottles on the floor of this laundry, so I decided to scrub it after I had picked up the glass. I had made the boys go upstairs to avoid getting cut. I guess I must have taken a long time to finish, because when I tried to get into the house, the boys had barricaded the door.

Managing to enter by another door, what I discovered left me aghast. The terrors had found a tube of blue paint concentrate in the laundry and sneaked it upstairs, where they had applied the paint liberally to the lounge chairs, carpet, the hallway and themselves, and climbed into their beds when they heard me coming. I just stared, at a loss as to what to do.

After giving them a good hiding, I put the boys into a bath, and the water turned almost purple. Even after many scrubs, the lounge and carpets never returned to their natural colours, but from then on carried a definite blue tinge. Their blankets and clothes unfortunately suffered the same fate. This episode taught me never to leave the boys unattended in the home again, if possible, even for a little while.

One night, before we had secured the window, Glenn climbed out of it and hid on the roof. When we discovered him missing, we looked inside, then went outside and looked everywhere we could, leaving no shed or stable overlooked. We even went down to the track to check the tyres and the trees there.

After what seemed like a very long time, he gave himself up. He had been hiding on the roof, just for a prank, listening to us calling out to him, which he was soon to regret after receiving one of the few hidings from his Dad. It was usually me that administered the appropriate punishment to the children, even if it meant a smack on their bottoms. I believe in the old adage, 'spare the rod and spoil the child', and I applied it, when warranted. I also feel that a child feels more secure if their parents love or care for them enough to set boundaries or limits on the child's behaviour.

As I put these memories to paper, I can see that the impression of neglectful parents could be given, but I have the belief (misguided or not) that we were more likely over-protective. But, as it is with children, they manage to foil the best intentions of most parents. I can laugh about these antics now, but I would have been hard pressed to see the humour in some of the boys' escapades at the time.

One afternoon, we caught Susan trying to shoe one of the milking goats, a Saanan, which fortunately had a very gentle temperament. Susan must have been watching the blacksmith very attentively, for she knew, at the tender age of two years, exactly how the job was done. Vic grabbed the video camera and managed to catch the whole episode on film; its viewing has given us stomach cramps from laughing, many times since.

Our little precious had the goat tied, after her fashion, to a toy go-cart. She had a jar of actual shoeing nails and a hammer and was earnestly trying to hammer a make-believe shoe on to the hoof of the poor goat. She pulled the leg of the goat through her knees just as she had seen her father and the blacksmiths do with the horses, enabling her to hold the foot securely during the shoeing process. Susan was poised with a nail in one hand and the hammer in the other, and just at the very moment she was about to hit the nail into the hoof, the goat pulled back. Susan fell over, then jumped up immediately, to grab the goat again.

Susan was not going to be put off by an old goat she tried again and again, but each time, at the crucial moment, when she was about to hit the nail in, the goat would pull back, making Susan fall over once more. This went on for about six times, each time with the same result, with Susan ending up flat on her back in the dust.

At last, she gave up. She turned toward the goat and, bringing her foot up very briskly, she gave the goat a big hard kick in the stomach. She then took the rope, turned around and walked off in disgust. It was then that we got our biggest laugh. Her trousers were light blue and it was obvious that she had wet her pants in frustration.

It looked so funny, her marching away with a large wet patch on her trousers and the goat being dragged angrily along behind.

That goat was so quiet, I was able to train her to jump up onto two drums, with her front legs on one drum and her back legs on the other, thus making it easier for me to milk her. When the next milking was due, she didn't seem too upset by the kick that Susan had given her.

When Susan was three, we were lent a shetland pony for her to learn to ride. I had never liked these ponies, because I knew a lot of them were very bad natured and spoiled. I was wrong in this case, the pony turned out to be very well-behaved and not at all spoiled. It wasn't long before I had taught Susan to steer the pony and pull it up, and she had good natural balance on its back.

We had a fairly long cement ramp built from the laundry of our new house to the lawn, where we lived at Wongawilli. If Susan wanted to go to the toilet, she would ride the pony up the ramp and straight into the laundry, where she looped the reins over the tap and left it there while she went.

This taught her a good lesson. When she had learned to ride well, and was about five, I started to take her to some little shows for her to compete in the tiny tots riding class. This was for children under six years old, and Susan loved to ride in these and won some events and was placed at other times.

She started to do the same at the shows, riding the shetland into the toilet, when she wanted to visit, and tying it up to the tap. It was quite a surprise for ladies and their children, to go in and find a little pony there. It caused quite a lot of humour and laughs; rarely would anyone object. The pony also received a lot of pats and attention, so he didn't mind in the least, waiting for his owner's return.

Swearing was never permitted in the Paterson family as I grew up, and when I married into the Frost family I was introduced to a most colourful and inventive vocabulary, which was added to by exposure to the male drivers during my harness racing career. At one time, a steward asked, 'Margaret how will it affect you, to hear some of the coarse language used on the track, when you don't swear?'

Taking the children to compete at the shows became serious business for us; we eventually owned three horses, and bought a little truck to transport the horses and their gear. For our comfort we pulled a little caravan behind, as well. Our sleeping quarters before had been in the back seat of our car.

We contested a lot of the outback shows, competing in many events, and enjoyed our time together. Susan was not too confident on the big horse, so I resumed riding once again to handle him, and even won some riding classes for over-40-year-old riders, and a reserve champion event at one of the shows. Susan did moderately well, but I am afraid I found out later that she felt as though she could not measure up with me, so I wished I had not taken it up again, and had left it all to her.

One afternoon I was baking in the kitchen, when Garry sneaked into the pantry, and started to look on the shelves. He was hoping I had not seen him, but I had and knew he was up to something. I said, 'What do you want, Garry?'

'Nothing,' he said.

Four or five times, I repeated my question, each time receiving the same answer.

'Garry, I know you are looking for something, what is it that you want? You might as well tell me. I know you are up to something you shouldn't be, so tell me,' I said.

Not being prepared for his answer, it terrified me.

He said, 'Glenn's got a snake down the paddock, and we are going to milk it.'

Demanding to know just where his brother was waiting, I made Garry stay in the house until I got back. I ran to the other side of the track, where Glenn was very studiously watching an area of grass. He had the snake baled up in a section, and was waiting with a stick to try to prevent it from escaping, until Garry came back with a jar.

He got an awful shock when his mother came back instead of his brother! I ordered him to let the snake go and go back to the house. I tried to explain the dangers of what they were about to do and I could only beg them to ask their dad if they ever wanted to do something like this again.

ELEVEN

Mixed Family Fortunes

We had about 30 horses in work now and had a stable foreman, Jack Kelly, and a young lad, Hans Hol, as our stablehand. I would set aside one day a week to carry out the necessary work with our records; because of the heavy workload, I employed a lady to do housework one day each week. On my day in the office I had the responsibility of nominating horses for coming races, allocating the results and prize money won the previous week to those owners, and reconciling the cash books. Then there were the accounts to be monitored. All this was done by hand, as there were no computers or faxes that make today's running of a stable a little smoother.

Jack Kelly was very fond of our two sons, whom he described as little larrikins, always full of beans. One day, Jack entered the feed room to find them both sitting on bins eating powdered glucose, with white powder all over their faces and some on their shirts. Jack bellowed, 'Who has been into the glucose?' Glenn wiped his face furiously and disappeared in a hurry, while Garry looked back at him with the most innocent and somewhat angelic smile and said, 'Not me. Not me.'

My fears about having family working in coalmines were fully realised one day not long before my father was to retire. Dad was badly injured when a prop jammed in the ground. Being the deputy on duty at the time, he went to free it just as the prop came out. It swung around, striking him a severe blow, fracturing both legs in several places.

Until then he had been working part-time in our stables, expressing his enthusiasm to continue when he retired from the mines. I knew just how much he enjoyed being around the horses, and spending time outdoors with him so much reminded me of those earlier happy days on the farm up near Gunnedah. This serious accident ended his involvement with the stables and horses, as his leg never made a satisfactory recovery, often leaving him in much pain.

Sadly, my sister Catherine's marriage to Roy Sherriff's ended after about 15 years, at which time they were both smokers and probably drank a little too much for their own good. During Catherine's unsettled years, Neena and I often had her three daughters, Karen, Sandra and Jeanette, stay with us. This was when I was able to teach the elder girls, Karen and Sandra, to ride on our quiet pony 'Sinbad'. They became good enough to compete in local gymkhanas and, later on, in some shows. Jeanette, the youngest, was not interested in horses, but preferred other activities; she was always an avid reader.

One year Vic and I took our children and the girls with us to Adaminaby. We worked hard at giving them a good time and, in spite of the many tumbles and bruises, it was a happy time for all of us.

Catherine's children didn't have the opportunity to have much contact with my children or Neena's, because she moved about and always seemed to live at an inconvenient distance from us. It was unfortunate for all of us, but Barry and Neena, Vic and I and Mum and Dad did the best we could to make up for this whenever the opportunity arose. Neena lived just a few streets away from me, so our children became good friends and were almost inseparable.

After her divorce, Catherine found another partner, George Adams, a travelling salesman, and took her three children to live in Adelaide with him. Sometime later the family moved again, this time to Canberra. Because Catherine was in a state of 'confusion' and not managing well at all during George's absence, Mum and Dad went down and brought the girls home to Dapto, for a holiday. This 'holiday' lasted about two and a half years; the girls were happy there and did not want to go back to live with their mother until she had settled down in a permanent home.

Catherine and George Adams had two daughters, Neena and Dianne. Tragically, George was run down by a motor vehicle and was killed at Fairy Meadow. Catherine was left with two babies, no money and nowhere to live, so Mum and Dad took the family to live with them, thus reuniting them with the elder girls. Karen, the eldest, was still a schoolgirl herself and, to her great credit, played a large part in taking care of her younger sisters.

Vic and I had moved into our new home on the Wongawilli farm, leaving our little fibro home vacant, and we agreed to let Catherine and her children live in it. This proved to be most opportune, both for our parents and for Catherine. Mum and Dad were feeling the pressure of the large family and inadequate space.

Later, Catherine met Brian Scholey, who was a loving and very caring person. He became a firm and stable influence on the whole family. Mark, the only boy, was born out of this relationship. Catherine, Brian and the three younger children moved several times and finally settled at Mt Warrigal after living in various places, including caravans on occasion. Until then, the three elder girls lived with Neena and Barry on their small farm at Albion Park. Rather than start a new school, Karen decided to stay with Neena until she had completed her high school education at Dapto High; she was happy in the country environment.

Brian took good care of the family, and was particularly loving and supportive to Catherine. Mount Warrigal was not far from Neena and Barry's home, and this was the first time since they each left home as young women that Neena and Catherine lived close enough to visit regularly. They were in contact with each other by telephone every day and shared dinner at each other's homes on a weekly basis. Catherine and Neena enjoyed each other's company and, during those years, developed a very close friendship. Barry and Brian became good friends as well.

The two sisters had much in common. They both had a talent for knitting and sewing, but Neena has often remarked that Catherine's work was exceptional. Catherine demonstrated this talent many times, by knitting or sewing baby clothes for her friends and family. She and Neena also spent many hours together sharing a common interest in gardening.

Vic and I were living on 'Glen-Garry', our farm at Exeter, by this time, and I could only make visits to the family when our busy schedule permitted. Vic begrudged my having days off to visit them. I found myself inventing excuses to go and was made to feel guilty for leaving him with the extra work in the afternoon.

Meanwhile, my brother Eddie, who had been so horrible to me when he was little, was proving to be somewhat of a surprise packet. He had been quite clever at school and matriculated with the ability to pursue a career in the arts, sciences or engineering. Instead, he chose the military, enrolling at the Royal Military College at Duntroon,

Canberra. He left home at 18 to pursue his dream, living at the college for the next four years.

I must admit he did look distinguished and good looking that day we attended his Graduation when he received his Bachelor of Arts at the college. I had to pinch myself to make sure I wasn't dreaming, as Eddie had grown into quite a man. The girl he would later marry he met when his fellow student and friend at Duntroon, Mark Haas, introduced Eddie to his sister Terri. After his graduation, Eddie was stationed in Adelaide, and it was here he and Terri were married in the Mt Barker Chapel in 1978. The family all went over for the wedding.

At a time when my family were having mixed fortunes with Dad's bad injury and Catherine's concerns, Vic and the horses continued enjoying wonderful success on the racetrack. One horse that went through our stable and left fond memories for us both was Local Ayr, from the little town of Uralla, in the New England area of New South Wales.

Local Ayr had won a district two-year-old race before being given to Vic to train. He possessed great speed on our track, and we took him to Harold Park to race in a quality event with the champion Victorian colt Nicotine Prince, considered unbeatable. That night Local Ayr sent the TAB in Uralla broke. He beat Nicotine Prince, starting at 33/1. They claimed back in Uralla you could have heard the local supporters yelling from one end of town to the other. The tote soon ran out of money when it began paying out. The TAB manager got their local bank manager out of bed to get more money for it to satisfy those still holding winning tickets. One newspaper ran the story under the heading: 'TAB sent up in Ayr'.

Further two-year-old wins followed at Harold Park, including one off 36 yards behind, over a sprint distance. This son of Scottish Brigade won further races at three, and when four, won no less than eight races at Harold Park. Among the horses he beat was Hondo Grattan, who went on to be the first to win two Inter Dominions. Local Ayr too, would have matured into a truly outstanding horse, had arthritis not seriously troubled him. As it was, he won 23 races for us with 26 placings. I have always felt that some of those placings may well have been wins, if he had been sound. When making it through to an Inter Dominion Grand Final, he pulled up quite sore after the heats and it was only his big heart and spirit that got him through the Grand Final, even though we knew he was unable to show his best. Later as a sire he left more than one two-minute pacer.

After we first discovered his arthritis, I spent many hours a week standing Local Ayr in a tub of water that included dissolved bicarbonate of soda, using the nozzle of an old vacuum cleaner to create air bubbles, thus giving his legs a gentle massage in the water. After drying off each leg with a towel, it would be gently massaged with olive oil. This was a remedy given to me by my mother, who had declared that it worked well on her arthritic fingers.

Noel McMillan, a pleasant elderly gentleman who part-owned the horse, came to stay with us for several weeks during one campaign. He suffered from arthritis also, and his fingers were so badly swollen that he had trouble even trying to straighten them. I was able to coerce him into putting his hands in the tub and helping out with the treatment of his pacer. Noel seemed amazed at how well his fingers responded to this daily routine, and he found he could use his fingers better than he had in years. Sadly, when returning home he did not maintain this remedy, and within several weeks his arthritic problems returned. He could make the time to help his horse with the treatment, but not himself after settling back into his routine at home. We were not the only ones who took a liking to Local Ayr. Our milking goat 'Lisa' was able to get under a rail into his yard, and there she would enjoy the horse sniffing her and gently nibbling and nuzzling her back. It actually got to the stage where the horse demonstrated a reluctance to be separated from Lisa, and this concerned Vic so much that he was tempted to take the goat to the races with Local Ayr to help the pacer settle down. Vic decided he was not prepared to take the risk of exposing himself to the ribbing he was sure to receive from the other drivers when they saw him leading a goat up the ramp to the stable area, and therefore resisted the temptation. Lisa never made it to Harold Park!

TWELVE

Glen-Garry Lodge

It was about this time that we finally admitted the climate around Dapto was not beneficial to Vic's asthma. We inspected a number of properties before deciding to buy land in the Southern Highlands at Exeter.

This 100 acres was about midway between Canberra and Sydney. It provided a climate and air we thought likely to be better for an asthmatic, but it did get cold in the winter. Well before selling up the property at Wongawilli, each weekend we headed off to Exeter to build the stables and yards we would need before making our move. On our old property we had built a cottage with two small bedrooms, a lounge, a kitchen and bathroom. This was for the staff's quarters. We were able to have this transported to the new property on an average-sized truck; anything as large as a semi-trailer would have been an over-reaction.

Vic and I rolled up our sleeves and went to work establishing a training track, stables and day yards for the horses, along with cattle yards we thought would be a handy investment. We were fortunate in having a friend in Ray Critcher and his wife Beverley, from Wollongong, who often came up at weekends with their family, to lend a hand.

Those cattle yards were erected in midwinter, and to this day I can vividly remember the intense cold that bit into me as I stood there holding the piping in place while Vic did the welding. There were days when I felt almost frozen to the spot, since I was not able to move about to keep warm. The road into the property was so bad after rain that our cars had to be towed by a small tractor to make it through the mud; a situation made worse because one of the men had to walk the half-mile through the cold and mud to get the tractor. We went to the farm at night to enable us to get an early start the following day. It was often late when we arrived and miserably cold and, apart from our noses and hands being blue, so too was the air around us at times, when the men would let fly with a swear word or two. I saw no point in arguing over it, as I knew how they felt.

The children had no trouble finding interesting games to play in the new environment. They were used to playing outdoors, but this was a new farm and much bigger, so there was a lot of exploring to be done. The big difficulty I had was keeping them in view to be sure they were in no danger. Of course the mud made the boys games so much fun, but I dreaded bathtime at the end of the day.

When it came to giving our new property a name, we settled on combining the names of our two sons—and so we established 'Glen-Garry Lodge'. We were later able to purchase 100 acres next door, and a little further down the track another neighbouring 130 acres, to extend 'Glen-Garry' into a very nice standardbred farm.

In our first year at Exeter we had a great deal of work to do establishing the half-mile sand and gravel track, along with the other facilities. The stables were built in a large concrete brick barn with a concrete floor and an iron corrugated roof, with adjoining yards enabling the horses to walk in and out. When horses are kept boxed in stables for any length of time they become bored, so this design worked extremely well, and also prevented swollen legs. It included a spacious feed room, blacksmith shop, wash bay and harness room next to the stables. The sand roll was built alongside, just outside. The wash bay being under cover really came in handy in the cold climate of the Southern Highlands, where the temperature on some occasions can be as low as minus 6 degrees, and you almost freeze if you get wet. I was unable to talk Vic into installing a combustion heater in the stables, as he thought we may have been tempted to spend too much time around it, at the expense of the horses.

The hard work involved establishing the property from scratch, along with the solid workload Vic went through earlier with the bread run, later left their legacy, and he was hospitalised for the repair of a double hernia. We were fortunate in our first year at Exeter in having Barry Goesch come to work for us. He was a tower of strength, being a dedicated and good worker, and his efforts were most appreciated. Vic and I were both disappointed when Barry decided, after some months, to move on to greener pastures, or in this case, perhaps warmer pastures. Finding men like him is never easy.

The cottage we had transported to Glen-Garry Lodge was home

to us for several years. The three children shared one small bedroom and had no room for wardrobes for their clothes, while our bedroom was only big enough to have a double bed, and the wardrobes had to be kept in the lounge room. Perhaps as a reaction to having lived in such cramped quarters, we later built a very large two-storey home, with four bedrooms and two bathrooms upstairs, and downstairs a huge lounge, a rumpus room, dining room, office, a shower and toilet, along with two garages beneath two of the bedrooms.

Not long after we had moved into our new home, Jack Kelly (our foreman when back at Dapto) moved to Glen-Garry Lodge with his wife Jean to work for us again and to see what it was like living in the country. They moved into the cottage. Whatever its shortcomings, they found it better than living in a caravan as Barry had done.

Having them living on the property was not only a great help around the stables, it also provided us with good adult company. Jack was also keen to go to the races with Vic and help out with driving our latest truck, capable of carrying six horses. When Jack and Jean later moved back closer to Sydney, he started training at Bankstown and enjoyed some well-earned success. It was sad to learn of his passing only several years later.

THIRTEEN

Racing in America

One of the highlights of Vic's career had been in 1972 when he was selected to represent Australia at the World Driving Championship, hosted that year by the United States and Canada. This was several years before we established Glen-Garry Lodge. The wife of each competing reinsman was also invited. Suddenly, I realised I did not have a passport. When we had migrated from England, I had been included on my mother's passport. Not having been out of Australia since, I had not bothered to seek one of my own, and now I needed one in less than two weeks. It is not usually possible to get an Australian passport in such a short period of time if you are not already an Australian citizen. Barry Rose, a breeder-owner and someone who then had some influence behind the scenes, very obligingly wrote a letter on my behalf requesting the Immigration Department to grant my passport in time for me to accompany Vic to represent his country.

This forced me to make a quick decision—to relinquish my English citizenship and become an Australian citizen, or to forgo the trip to the US? I was proud of my English heritage and reluctant to give it up. But I did so much want to go to the US with Vic. The decision to become naturalised was made and expedited by mail. What I didn't know at the time, nor was I advised, was that I could have held dual citizenship. I have had some regrets about this since. On some later trips overseas, dual passports would have been an advantage at points of entry into certain countries.

After a frantic preparation for the departure, Neena and Barry were happy to look after the children at their place. Our three children and their two always got on well together, so there were not too many tears when we left for Sydney to catch our flight across the Pacific. To our three, it probably seemed like they were taking a holiday as well.

These championships, hosted every two years by various countries, have a number of heats at numerous tracks to try to even out the luck of the random draw for horses. There is probably no fairer method of doing this. Often after each series, you hear claims by some competitors how they fared poorly in the draws, often having to drive horses not quite in the class of others in a heat.

Ken Dyer, long-time Chief Executive of the Australian Harness Racing Council, who has hardly missed a world series, recently stated that at times it might have seemed incredible how a driver or two could have a charmed existence when drawing horses, often coming up with one of the main fancies, while another horseman might continually draw an outsider. No-one could possibly challenge the honesty of these random draws—it was just the luck of the draw, even when the 10 representatives from around the world contested a total of 20 or more heats in these series.

Vic did win a couple of heats driving against horsemen considered to be the best in the world, and on the overall points he finished fourth, behind Giuseppe Guzzinati (Italy), Joe O'Brien (USA) and Herve Filion (Canada). He did not complain about some horses he drove, but I do remember they included more than his share of outsiders on the tote—a rating of their chances made by the betting public who would have known all participating horses quite well.

The Americans never do anything on a small scale and had arranged for daily social events for us. These were most enjoyable, though adding to the already busy schedule; it meant that we were not getting as much sleep as we wished. Each day we would fly to a new venue for the next set of races to be held at night, and another social function. The international drivers and their wives were a wonderful group of people and we all seemed to get on so well together. The United States Trotting Association looked after us very well, and we were accommodated at the most exclusive hotels and taken on exquisite sightseeing tours. Nothing seemed too much trouble for them.

On our way home we flew over the Grand Canyon before landing in Las Vegas, Arizona. As brief as our look at the Canyon was, the sight was truly breathtaking. Our stopover in Las Vegas was for one night only. Both of us were extremely tired and I suppose we should have gone to bed and caught up on lost sleep. But having come this far and being here for just one night, there was no question of staying in.

Vic and I were never gamblers in the true sense, having a trifecta or double here and there and the occasional flutter. That night (or was it morning) we went to a casino and had a little flutter on the pokies, an activity that Vic normally avoids and one in which I seldom indulge. He won a jackpot on the dime (ten cents) machine and hastily stuffed the coins into his pockets and called it quits. From there, we went to a topless nightclub and watched the girls do their routine. Like most men, Vic would probably under normal circumstances have enjoyed this form of entertainment. On this occasion I could see he was struggling to keep his eyes open.

We flew out of Las Vegas a few hours later, bound for Sydney and home, and for the first couple of days we caught up with some much needed sleep. Our hectic lifestyle at Wongawilli took little time to return to normal, after the hurried but wonderful trip we had through numerous US states.

This visit to America must have sown a seed in Vic's mind, because he later took some horses to the USA to race before selling them. The return on the horses was worth the trip. He actually made two trips by himself and a third one with the four of us. When Vic went on his own he stayed in a motel and tried to complete his business as soon as possible to prevent him being away too long from the family and the stables.

Viruses among horses in US racing at that time were epidemic, probably fanned by the system of stabling all horses at the track at which you are racing for the period of that carnival, whether it be weeks or even months. Vic was well aware of the problems so often encountered by imported horses when trying to become acclimatised to the northern hemisphere, and he would wash out all feeding and watering containers before and after use. He never let his horses drink from a communal watering trough.

It was in 1976 that we took the children over for a stay of more than two months, renting a home in a lovely part of Los Angeles, the suburb of West Chester. This was about a 15-minute drive from Hollywood Park racetrack, the main one in California—a track that would attract the rich and famous. Vic had travelled with the horses and had first gone to Sacramento, where he and the horses found it unbearably hot, the temperature rising to 95 degrees Fahrenheit. Having come from the Australian winter, the horses suffered a rapid loss of hair, and took some time before they became acclimatised. He then took them on to Hollywood Park in time for that track to open its new season. Our horses were stabled at the track, where all training facilities were provided, along with all the others to race there. The races were held every night of the week except Sundays.

We later moved on to Florida and were fortunate to lease a very comfortable home, and the owners provided us with all of their facilities. The folk who lived nearby made us very welcome, and we were able to secure the services of a young man to babysit when necessary. He always called Vic 'Sir' and me 'Madam', no matter how much we urged him to use our first names. It was while in Florida that we came to know the phrase 'Have a good day now' so well. The Americans loved our accent, as we did theirs.

Before the children left Australia, they had been given work to do during their absence by their school at Exeter. We arranged the feed room especially to allow them to carry out this homework in the mornings while Vic and I were not far away, working the horses. All of a sudden the kids developed a love for horses and began begging to be taken for drives or be allowed to help out with the chores around the stables. We knew what lay behind this change of attitude: being so far from home and their teachers, they weren't too interested in their homework. After a while, being subjected to the combined and constant lobbying by our three youngsters, Vic and I thought, 'What the hell! this may be a once in a lifetime experience, when we are together as a family, in the United States, so why not?' They could catch up with their studies when they were back at school. As it turned out, it was a decision that we have never regretted. We took the family to Disneyland for two days, and it was fascinating! We loved it so much, but still did not get to see everything in the time we had. It was a wonderful working holiday for Vic and me, and quite an experience for the children. We returned home to New South Wales fully refreshed and keen to get the stable back to winning form with some new pacers that we had brought into work.

FOURTEEN

Women Treated as Equals

The early 1970s had been a busy and successful era for our stables and for Vic as a leading reinsman. Some of the big races he won in the period following his first Miracle Mile success with Lucky Creed came with Kiwi Lad and Atomic Smoke; the first Canberra Derby with First Patch; the 1971 New South Wales Edgar Tatlow Stakes with Local Ayr; the 1972 Youthful Stakes with the smart Tidy James; and Vic's second Australasian Four-Year-Old Championship in 1975 with Willie Rip (his first, in 1969, was on Brand New). Then there were Eenalla, Atomic Adios, Pay Her Way and numerous others.

One of our biggest disappointments in racing was the result of the 1973 Inter Dominion Trotting Championship, one we believed that Vic should have won. Among the few trotters he trained was the smart Finnegan, handicapped off the front that year where it won both its heats impressively. In the Grand Final it was severely checked, losing a great deal of ground. The New Zealand star Precocious (Jack Carmichael) off the backmark of 48 yards won the title from Touch Merchant (12 yards) and Bay Johnny (12 yards). The following week, off level marks, Finnegan turned the tables on Precocious, showing just how unlucky he had been in the Grand Final when off the front, beating the mare on level terms.

In the mid-1970s, successful owner Tony Azzopardi asked Vic to fly to New Zealand and buy him a promising pacer. After trialling several pacers, he selected Double Agent. Bred near Christchurch by Jim Dalgety, it had been unplaced in three starts as a two-year-old during the 1973–74 season. Even though it had finished 16th to Sly Kiwi at its last outing, Vic liked this youngster after driving it in track-work. On Vic's advice, Tony paid the asking price, a figure then considered quite high for a non-winner.

Vic raced Double Agent only three times as a three-year-old because of leg problems, though he did win back some of the outlay for its new owner by winning two of those starts, the second of these victories at Harold Park. The horse was then turned out for a spell. When Double Agent returned to racing it really began showing its class, winning a heat and the final of the Superstars Three- and Four-Year-Old Championship. His Sydney record then was four wins from five starts. The tendon problems that had restricted his racing again flared up the following season, when he was given just three race starts.

Double Agent won the second heat of the 1980 Inter Dominion, with the press claiming it had been a dashing display of horsemanship by Vic. There were tears in my eyes when I took the horse back to the stables that night, though not from its win. Double Agent's head had given me a whack while holding him during the brief presentation ceremony, and for several minutes I saw stars, and I don't mean the stars worn by my husband. Because of the pacer's unsoundness, Vic suggested to Tony that the horse should be given to Joe Ilsley, who conducted much of his training on the beach at Mona Vale, north of Sydney, and had a good record with unsound horses. The pair won a Miracle Mile at an age when most horses had retired. Double Agent would live to a ripe old age, finally leaving this world on the 27th August 1999, aged 27.

Since all three children were at school, I had become more involved with the overall training of the horses. This would often mean attending the races as well. Vic would occasionally comment how competent he thought my standard of driving had become, and it was a personal thrill to know that we had horses in the stable that would respond well to my light touch.

There are pacers that will produce their best effort without excessive or heavy use of the whip. Men generally are more aggressive with its use, and some horses will dig deep with this vigorous approach, but not all. Every horse is an individual and should be treated that way. It can be most satisfying to be successful with horses you know race better when coaxed to achieve their best, without having to use vigorous driving. It is also my belief that many horses react according to how they are treated.

Vic and I were driving track-work every day now, even sharing the fast work as well. My father-in-law had been an excellent teacher, and I never forgot how he and Vic stressed that all horses were different and required more or less work, according to their stamina. Some horses needed to be worked hard to have them race better, and others required less work. A trainer that prepares every horse the same way can expect certain members of the team not to reach their full potential. Each horse has to be carefully assessed and trained according to its capability. This is one reason why some horses, when changing stables, might race better, while others struggle to regain the same form they showed with their former trainer.

On those occasions when we required an outside driver to fill in for Vic, I had become rather apprehensive, as there were times I thought I could have done better. This is not meant to convey that we put up inferior drivers, but more that there was a lack of bonding or communication between the horse and driver. Mind you, there are a handful of 'catch drivers' (freelance) who have that rare quality, when told about the traits of horses they are to drive for the first time, of being able to coax the best from them as though they were old friends.

One of the horses that I drove to a win at those special races for ladies at gymkhanas (often referred to then as 'Powder Puff Derbies') was Jan's Daughter. She was the first pacer we had from New Zealand owner Barney Breen, who years later became very much a part of the stable's biggest successes. John Tapp also won an invitation race for celebrities, at a charity day held in Sydney, driving this mare.

Vic's experience made him aware of the dangers of driving, and he worked hard to teach me how to avoid some of the pitfalls. He stressed how important it was to make sure the head of your horse is directly in line and behind the head of the driver in front, or in line with the middle of his back. He explained that if this was not done, your horse would have its front legs following the wheel of the cart in front, and there was always a chance, if a leg did strike a wheel, that your horse might stumble and fall.

There were other women competing in these exhibition races for reinswomen who felt they could be competitive driving against the men. It was this feeling, which was often discussed amongst the girls, that led to the formation of a movement whose prime aim was to try to bring about equal competition. The 'Reinswomen Association', formed in 1974, had a committee that held regular meetings to promote the cause of reinswomen and to develop a strategy. 1974 being the International Year of Women seemed to provide added inspiration for us to pursue our goal.

The meetings were held at first in the home of the secretary, Karen Pearce, at Richmond, and were chaired by President Margaret Davies. These meetings were later moved to Fairfield and then Penrith. The latter club would become extremely helpful in promoting the cause of reinswomen. Margaret Davies, who would remain association president for ten years, was dedicated and untiring, a clever and energetic worker for the cause. We knew it would not be easy and would involve a real fight, as many officials still viewed women as the 'weaker sex' in a male-dominated sport.

Some of the girls travelled to country tracks whenever exhibition races were programd by a club. These were usually well accepted by the public. I didn't have the time to travel to too many country areas, but when such events were held at venues closer to our district I contested them. A point-score was introduced for the women and Anne Tracey won the first one held.

Anne was the daughter of one of racing's most successful and colourful characters, Tony Turnbull. The family was from The Lagoon, near Bathurst. Ever since the sixties, Tony was one of our most travelled horsemen, usually campaigning a team of horses in Queensland during the winter months. He became the first person in Australia to drive more than 2000 winners. His daughter Anne later married Brian Hancock, whose stables were established in the Albion Park area, not too far from Bulli raceway, south and a little inland from Wollongong.

The fields at Bathurst sometimes consist of various members of the Turnbull family. One race at nearby Blayney once had eight of the nine starters with a Turnbull driver. It was won by daughter Cynthia, who delighted in beating her father. Even today you might find Tony Turnbull in a race where the opposition includes sons or grandsons all hell-bent on beating him. They have been a wonderful family for the sport. Anne Hancock's son from her previous marriage, to Garry Tracey, is Mark, who is now the number two driver for the powerful Brian Hancock stable.

The year 1977 remains one of significance for me, as a filly we had purchased to race ourselves, Cheryl's Delight, won the New South Wales Oaks, the state's major classic for three-year-old fillies. It was also in 1977 that the new anti-discrimination laws came into being. It was that season the New South Wales Trotting Authority was also formed to oversee the sport in our state.

Our president, Margaret Davies, shrewdly used the new Discrimination Act to the advantage of the girls. She really 'threw a cat among the pigeons' by threatening the New South Wales Trotting Club and the newly formed Authority to take matters to the Anti-Discrimination Board if our request to be licensed was again refused because of gender. This really gave the men who administered the industry something to think about.

What was to follow has never been reported before, and I have Ken Dyer, then Secretary of the Australian Trotting Council, to thank for this little story. The inaugural president of the New South Wales Trotting Authority was Judge Alf Goran. He had grown up in England before moving to Australia, where he became greatly interested in harness racing and for years was Council's legal adviser. The judge never lost his image of being the old-style English gentleman and, along with the other members of Council, found it difficult to accept ladies competing as equal to men.

When it was reported to Council's annual meeting that the women's association in New South Wales had threatened to take the matter to court, Council, knowing this would be their last throw of the dice, stubbornly issued a recommendation to the states to 'maintain the status quo'. This was even after Judge Goran explained that, with the new anti-discrimination laws in place, they would soon have to reluctantly end their opposition to women being treated as equals. Margaret Davies had been quite serious, and within weeks Ken Dyer found himself carrying out a hurried postal vote with delegates from all states. Their earlier vote was soon reversed, and the Australian Trotting Council quickly issued a recommendation to all states that they should no longer refuse licences to women on the grounds of gender.

Our president was actually the first to drive in open races, having two drives at a Nowra meeting in late 1977. Debra Wicks shortly after became the one to gain the esteemed recognition of achieving the first win in an open race. This was at Hawkesbury with the pacer Darwin Boy. My debut was forcibly delayed several months due to a stint in hospital, and recuperation, after an operation for varicose veins.

All drivers seeking a licence have to drive competently at gymkhanas or official trials in front of stewards before they are granted a country licence. As soon as I had recovered from my operation, I won several races at some shows. Then, at a gymkhana and the Dapto Show in the same weekend, I drove a total of eight winners for the weekend. This led to my being granted my licence to begin country racing in February 1978, making my open debut at Canberra—the first woman to drive at this venue. The Canberra Trotting Club presented me with a trophy in acknowledgement of this. My drives that night were on Tan Cove in the Canberra Derby (a classic race for three-year-olds) and Pretty Tough in the Free-For-All, finishing second in both events. The crowd gave me a stirring reception and the press were complimentary with their reporting.

After several drives at various venues, I had my first win. This was again at Canberra, driving another of my favourite horses, Welcome Imp. He was a horse born and bred on our farm, and his temperament was such that he became well liked by all who ever handled him. I drove him in most of his races and he won the Dennis Scanes Memorial Trophy for me at Canberra. It was fitting for me to win this memorial race as the Scanes family were friends of ours, sometimes staying overnight at Glen-Garry Lodge and stabling a horse with us on their way to racing at Harold Park.

By coincidence, Margaret Davies and I drove our first winners against the men on the same day, March 4th 1978—hers being at Bulli (her home track) and mine at Canberra. Vic was not really happy about me racing at Canberra if it was a Friday night, the same evening he was competing at Harold Park. He preferred being there to see me compete so he could pass on a tip or two about my opposition, or just be there giving me encouragement. At first, I was not that confident taking the car and float with two horses on my own. Both Vic and I breathed a little easier when 'Packy' (Graeme Gunther), a good friend of ours, not only began driving the car and float for me when Vic was in Sydney, but would also be my strapper.

On March 28th, Vic and I became the first husband and wife ever to drive in the same race on an Australian track. He was behind Challenge Proof and I was on Lagnitook. At the start, my pacer began fast and I was happy to bowl along in the lead, remaining in front around the home-turn the last time. When straightening up for the dash to the post I began smelling victory. Then a horse flashed up on my outside in the familiar colours of white with black stars. With what could have been a smirk or a smile, Vic called to me, 'Sorry, Margy', as he passed, then his horse went on to win by a nose. For the record book, this was the first husband and wife quinella in Australian trotting.

There was an interesting sequel to that race, as when returning back for the 'all clear' signal, a punter with a loud voice was heard to call out, 'Frosty, why don't you stop beating your wife?' I found nothing wrong with this, until it was later pointed out to me how it had upset one elderly lady in the crowd who took it to mean that nice Mr Frost was not so nice after all, being a wife-beater!

My first treble was driven at Bulli on April 4th with Tarport's Luck, Clem's Gift and Welcome Imp. This also went into the records as the first reinswoman in the country to achieve the feat. Victorian women were soon to follow the lead of New South Wales, and several women were granted a licence. Reinswomen were still very much a novelty on the scene, and invitations from clubs for me to be a guest competitor were now arriving in the mail. These included an appearance at Forbes in the state's mid-west, the old Melbourne Showgrounds, Townsville, down at Launceston in Tasmania, and over at Globe Derby Park, Adelaide. Some states were slow to introduce the women, but all eventually came into line. It did not take too long before women could be seen at many tracks, and were eventually accepted by the punting public. The first female quinella was taken out by Margaret Davies and Karen Pearce in June 1978, with Margaret on Pipe Dream and Karen second piloting Queen Victoria.

The first of my falls was at Fairfield, when having my 20th drive. I was making what I believed was a winning run down the outside with Welcome Imp, when Gozo Star interfered with us, and down I went. I was taken by ambulance to Fairfield Hospital and checked over for several hours before being allowed to leave.

On June 2nd 1978, I made my Harold Park debut, being the first woman in the modern era to be licensed to drive on metropolitan tracks. Judge Goran, Chairman of the New South Wales Trotting Authority, made a special presentation to me trackside, with Vic and the three children there. For one who had earlier resisted women being equal in harness racing, he was now generous in his comments. My two drives that night were Welcome Imp and Pretty Tough. Neither won, but this did not prevent it from being a wonderful evening, though it would end on a sour note.

On our return to the farm, Vic and I were attending to the horses, and my mother went over to open the back door. She was shocked to find it had been bashed in with an axe. Mum rushed back to the stables 200 metres away, with the news that our home had been broken into. Because of the pre-race publicity, a great many people would have known that the whole family would be at Harold Park to see me create history. An inspection of the house indicated that nothing had been stolen. Still, it left a bad feeling knowing the sanctity of our home had been invaded, and we never discovered who had left their 'calling card'.

The following night there was an invitational race in Adelaide for well known reinsmen and reinswomen. Vic and I had both been invited to represent NSW. Vic was now not prepared to leave the property unattended, and advised Adelaide he would not be coming, but was insisting I should go. This was the first mixed invitational event to be held in Australia.

The horse I drew was the mare Juanita Belle. Not a quick beginner, I was forced to take a position three back on the rails, but was then lucky enough to get room to push through a gap and go on and win this special race.

It was usual for me to drive the second string from our stable whenever we had two horses engaged, which was quite reasonable, considering there was no better reinsman in the state than Vic, in my opinion. After gaining my licence, several owners offered me horses to train and drive. One of the first was the six-year-old mare Another Marie, still a maiden after being through other stables. When I brought her home after competing one night at Canberra, Vic was not very happy, as he thought little of this pacer. I was determined to prove him wrong, and in the following weeks worked the mare hard, and Vic altered her shoeing. She won for me at Fairfield, setting a race record, then later picked up a couple more wins to make me feel well satisfied.

Before Another Marie was given to me, she was trained and raced in block-eye winkers. These are leather squares attached to the bridle alongside the eyes, thus forcing the horse to look straight ahead, preventing distractions from either side. This type of bridle is used on horses that tend to be skittish, shy easily, or want to look away from the front. This was a practice that Vic and I avoided if we could, because we had found that, in trying to correct one problem, you were presented with another. Our experience was that horses wearing this type of bridle did not give of their best. If they were able to see around them, the horses raced with greater confidence, and their orientation in and during the race seemed much better.

During her training sessions and track-work, Another Marie gave no indication that she possessed any of the traits that required this bridle, so I left it off and worked her without it. She performed very well during her training on our Exeter track and, according to her times, seemed to be giving her best.

At last she was ready. I nominated her for a night race at Menangle and she was accepted. My decision, this night, was to race her without the block-eye winkers. The mare showed great promise and was on her best behaviour. Another Marie moved out onto the track like a lady, and I was feeling the excitement building as we moved easily toward the barrier. We had been given a wide barrier draw, off the front line.

The barrier flipped back and we were away. I was beaten to the lead but settled down, three back on the fence. Then it happened. Another Marie began to pull. Really pull!

At this stage of my racing career I had driven many horses which had various kinds of handling characteristics, successfully. I considered myself to be reasonably strong in the arms, and confidently adjusted my grip on the reins. 'Now I'll show this little upstart who's boss!' I thought. Oh! Was I mistaken. She clamped on the bit like a steel trap and took off, even though there were horses ahead and around us. The force the mare had on the bit, and the pressure I was applying to the reins, had me lifting from my seat. The only message she was sending me was how she was prepared to run over the horse in front of her.

The pressure I was feeling would have tested the skill of most male drivers. We were halfway through the first lap, with two more to go, and if this horse didn't stop pulling and settle down, I knew I was going to be in some serious trouble.

The driver next to me was urging his horse on and his voice did nothing to help the situation. Another Marie never slackened the grip on the bit, and it seemed as if she was pulling harder with each furlong. As I looked up at her head for the faintest clue to my next move, they were not ears I could see, they were horns. I was almost standing in the stirrups. I tried to soothe her down by talking to her, but it didn't help, she just continued to pull, and the driver alongside me continued to shout. At that moment, the whips were being applied. I was thinking, 'If something doesn't happen soon, and I mean real soon, I am going to crack.' My arms were aching, my back was aching, and the risk of coming in contact with the driver in front and falling increased with each stride. The last thing I wanted was to instigate a fall.

The horse made no attempt to slow it's pace, my arms were going numb and had absolutely no idea how much longer I could prevent an accident. I was managing to hold the mare's head in line with the back of the driver in front, but the mare must have been blowing hard, straight down his collar. Most horses will slow when they encounter an obstacle, but not this one. This wretched horse was the boss.

At the precise moment when I was about to shout for a clear passage from the drivers around me, my rescue came. The horse outside of me pulled out for a run; I was lucky that no other horse rushed for that position. With what strength I had left, I managed to pull Another Marie out from the rails and away from behind the horse in front, and let the mare continue her headstrong dash for home. She went on to win the race with ease. She won and I got the credit. The crowd gave me a cheer as I went by. I didn't feel the elation that I had experienced at the beginning of the race, for only moments earlier I felt fear. The colour of my face matched perfectly the colour of my white silks. By the time I had pulled up to weigh in, some colour must have filtered back to my cheeks, because there was not a mention by anyone of the difficulty I was in, and there was no way I was going to tell them. I just put it down to experience. I went straight home and put those damn block-eye winkers back onto the bridle, immediately, ready for her next race. There was no guessing now about the reason for their need; the winkers were the only things that could stop her from pulling, and they sure made a difference to my control. Usually if a horse pulls very hard, most trainers use a different bit, but this mare had only a snaffle bit, which is for horses with good mouths, and I had no reason to expect the ordeal that I experienced that night.

Horses getting too close behind, running right up to my back and so close that their heads are alongside of mine, is one experience I could well do without. It is not a very nice feeling in a race, with horses that close behind you, as all drivers would agree. You don't know if the driver of that horse has it under control. The horses should be kept back, clear of your gig. It only takes a bump on your wheel to bring you down in a field of horses. There have been times in my career when I have bumped the horse's head with my skull cap, when this happened, in an effort to persuade it to pull back. This action may be frowned upon, but when one is desperate one tends to take desperate measures.

After gaining my unrestricted licence I drove most weeks at Harold Park, and gained my first win on the New South Wales main track with a horse called Pretty Tough. Pretty Tough was, as his name suggested, tough, but not gifted with brilliant speed. He was out of a mare called Turbulence, which means commotion and riotousness. This should have been a premonition of what was to come this very night—and how! Pretty Tough needed to lead from the start in a race to be able to win, and had to be drawn on the front line to be able to do this.

His barrier draws in every race so far had always been on the back line. As a result, he had never been given the opportunity to prove his ability.

In several press interviews since I had commenced driving this horse, I had said quite clearly that when he did draw the front line he would be hard to beat. In harness racing, in a standing start race, horses start from the position for which they are eligible, which is governed by the number of races they have won.

The horses with the least wins would start from the front, then further back according to the amount of races won, in increments of five metres. A tape is held in place across the track, in front of each line of horses. A warning is given to be ready and then the tape is released, allowing the horses to begin as fast as they are able. It is quite a skill to be able to train your horse to jump quickly when the tape is released, and one with which we were lucky to have success. Glenn is now as good as we were at training fast beginners.

Trainers are responsible for nominating their horses for races for which their horses are eligible, and where they would be drawn in a position with the best chance of winning.

On August 11th 1978, my fortune changed. Pretty Tough was given a front line draw in the C.H. Obrien Memorial Stakes, in the same race as Vic, who was driving the favourite, Lochinvar Girl.

With a feeling of expectation, I harnessed my horse, and as I placed the number three saddle and head number on him, which was the barrier that I had drawn on the front line, I felt very fortunate and elated, as this was my 'lucky number'.

Vic had drawn barrier five outside of me. At that stage of my career it was a requirement of the club to wear the club colours. These were red and green halves with black sleeves. I wished that I could have worn our own colours, the white silk jacket with black stars on the body and sleeves, and a black skull cap. Later, when I was permitted to wear our own colours, they were modified. To enable the public to distinguish me from Vic, the stars were removed from my sleeves and I wore a white skull cap.

In spite of my predictions of his ability to lead from the front line, my horse started at the long odds of 33/1. Lochinvar Girl was made the short-priced favourite at 11/8, and just had the edge on Koala King, driven by Brian Hancock, which was 6/4. I knew Pretty Tough was a fast beginner, and here was our opportunity to prove my predictions.

My horse was quivering with excitement; we were poised ready to go. When the barrier was released, he sprung forward to lead. Lochinvar Girl was not so fortunate. The horse drawn next to her, toward the inside rail, had jumped sideways and bumped her on the side, making her gallop. She had lost her chance for a good position at the start, and when she resumed pacing, Vic settled her down at the tail of the field. Vic thought his best chance would be to move up to the 'death seat', the position outside of the leader, which he did with a lap and a half to go.

Pretty Tough and Lochinvar Girl were now racing side by side. This was not a pre-planned strategy for the race, but the interference with Lochinvar Girl had given me my chance to lead, and the move by Vic was his only option. I expected further challenge from this horse, but I was not going to give the lead away easily. I believed I was still in control of the race, and 'Tuffy' was still responding strongly.

When drawing the lead position, it is an important tactic to set the pace to an acceptable rate for each horse. I was able to judge the field accurately enough to prevent the other drivers from pushing forward to make me surrender the lead early, or sit outside of my horse to make me go faster.

With the race half run and now having a lap and a half to go, I had the favourite outside of me and I was waiting for Vic to make his run, which didn't come.

My horse felt strong and willing in my hands and was giving me his best. I felt a surge of hope that I had the race in my grasp. Could I maintain this position and hold off any challenges? That was the burning question. Pretty Tough and Lochinvar Girl were pacing well side by side, and the rest of the field was bunched up behind.

The night was cold and most of the drivers wore gloves, but I did not as I felt in better control without them. I couldn't feel the wind on my face or the cold on my hands, or hear the roar of the crowd; I was so intent on winning the race.

At the ringing of the bell, which warns drivers that there is only one lap to go, I was ready for the challenges that must now come. Lochinvar Girl was still battling, making it necessary for any horse that made a run now to go three wide on the track. This made it easier for me, causing the other horses to cover extra ground at the end of a race, when the speed is the fastest.

Brian Hancock, driving Koala King, made a fast run and moved into second place with a furlong to go. Pulling the whip, I placed quite a few strokes on my horse's rump, and he picked up his pace. Pretty Tough pulled out all the strength he possessed and fought on with a tremendous will. His great effort carried us to victory. I went on to win that race by a length, and it was one of the biggest achievements of my racing career.

Immediately on the completion of the race, as we were slowing the horses before the return to scale, Brian Hancock ranged alongside, leaned over and shook my hand, congratulating me on my winning drive at Harold Park. The event would be entered into their book of records as the first woman driver to win there since night racing had commenced.

Due to the mixed reception of the race crowd, the night was like my horse's name: pretty tough! It should have been a happy night for me, but any celebrations had to be postponed. The punters could only acknowledge the fact that the favourite had been beaten, and any historical significance of that night was lost. They could not be blamed in thinking that we had planned the outcome. It was just that the race circumstances fell in my favour, giving me my supreme chance, which I was able to exploit to its fullest. No matter how the circumstances may have appeared (obviously punters thought that Lochinvar Girl wasn't trying), there was no shame to Pretty Tough's win. He won the race on his own merits; the opportunity arose and I took it.

The ugly demonstration at the end of the race was appalling and went on for the rest of the night. Beer cans were thrown onto the track, actually hitting one of the drivers (the late Laurie Moulds) on the head. Vic and I were not allowed to go in front of the crowd up to the stable area; our helpers had to take the horses up, take their harness off, wash them and pack up for home. We were not even allowed to go out into the float area; the truck was brought into the stable area, so that we could load the horses there. Of course I was congratulated by a lot of well-wishers after the race, but the ones that had turned nasty had spoiled what should have been for me a very memorable experience. We managed to drive out of the track and arrived home without any harm, albeit at a very late hour.

Upon arriving home after the two-hour trip, all horses had to be unloaded, another heavy rug put on, as it was the middle of winter, and a leaf of lucerne hay given to each. Quite often a horse that we had not taken to the races, but had eaten all of his food, would whinny for a second helping, which it usually received.

There were often times, when we had taken seven or eight horses to and from the races, that there was an obvious lack of enthusiasm when Vic and I would drag ourselves out of the truck, half asleep, to unload and put them away before we could eventually scramble into bed for the remaining four or five hours left to us.

It was only several weeks later that Vic and I had another unforgettable night that left us feeling uneasy.

Our filly Cheryl's Delight, who had won the 1977 New South Wales Oaks for Vic and me, had come back even better as a four-year-old, and seemed certain to start a short-priced favourite in a four-year-old classic at Harold Park. On the morning of the race, Vic had gone down to the stables to work the first of the horses, but came back in a hurry to say he had found footprints on the track that should not have been there. At the end of each day's track-work, the surface was always dragged to remove any humps or hollows, leaving it almost as smooth as a billiard table. The following morning you could even see the marks of bird claws or a lizard if it had been on the track. Now there were footprints left by a stranger.

While we were discussing this, Laurie Simpson, our stablehand at the time, reported that he had found a man's wristwatch in Cheryl's Delight's stable while cleaning it out. Then I told Vic that at 5.30 that morning I had found the stable door open, even though I felt certain I had closed it the night before. On closer inspection, in and around the stables we found what appeared to be drops of blood in the dust. It seemed that someone may have been in the mare's box, leading us to believe that they could only have been there for one reason: to nobble her with an injection into the neck.

When the police were called in, we explained that this mare was known to bite and was never fond of strangers. It seemed logical to us that, when approached in the dark, she had attempted to bite the intruder's arm, breaking the watchband in the process. By the time the police arrived we even had a suspect in mind. On the evening of the mare's recent win at Menangle, our suspect had arrived at Glen-Garry Lodge with what seemed a senseless explanation for the visit. As we were putting the horses away, he was most interested in which horses were which, taking particular notice of the stall Cheryl's Delight had. The police made it clear they required more evidence to interview this man than just our suggestion that he may have an arm that carried more than a few scratches, and it was never followed through.

On that day Vic and I had a decision to make: whether or not to start the mare that night. The prize money was larger than any previous race won by one of our own horses, and would be extremely welcome. On the negative side, if she raced and a swab later proved positive to any drug, Cheryl's Delight and her trainer would most likely be banned from racing for two years. We concluded that because her disposition was so mean, it would have been difficult for just one stranger to have coped with her. We felt it would have taken two men to catch her in the dark and give her a needle—and we found only one set of footprints. We decided to press on with the race.

Every horse we raced was always given a walk after arriving at the course and before being harnessed. When we walked Cheryl's Delight, she had the annoying habit of having a little buck, and would kick out some dozen times. No matter how we tried to prevent this, she was as regular as clockwork when being walked at the track. As usual, it was me who walked her that night, as most of our strappers avoided this task. If she didn't carry on with her normal habits, then our worst fears would almost certainly be realised. I was holding my breath as we began walking. When she did finally let go, it was the first time I had ever been happy to see these cantankerous actions from her. She later went out and won the race. The next few weeks found us more than a little anxious, chewing our nails waiting for the mail. We were highly delighted when the welcome cheque arrived from the club, and not a letter announcing a positive swab, with a request to appear for an inquiry.

FIFTEEN

Learning to Enjoy Life

Living in our new and spacious two-storey home at Glen-Garry Lodge probably presented the image of success, though I admit there were times when I actually missed living in the small cottage, where it had been easier to keep an eye on the little ones. It was far more difficult to do this in the big house, even for short periods, as they could disappear in a hurry to just about anywhere, upstairs or down. We had a swimming pool built near our house for the family and, before erecting a fence around it, the pool attracted some unusual swimmers.

I was feeding the horses one afternoon when a young boy ran over to me and called, 'Mrs Frost, is that baby horse supposed to be swimming in your pool?' Not waiting to answer, I took to my heels and was shocked to find a two-week-old foal desperately struggling in the water, with its anxious mother standing by whinnying. Someone arrived in time to help, and together we managed to pull the foal out. The little foal was extremely stressed and waterlogged, so we tipped it upside down and I applied what could be mistaken as a form of mouth-to-mouth resuscitation.

Perhaps it did work, as the foal coughed up some water and after a few minutes began to breathe again. It wasn't too long before I had it back on its feet and sucking from its grateful mother. As I stood there very much relieved, watching the mare and foal, the thought struck me of just how death can be only moments away and when one may least expect it. Had I been more than a couple of minutes later getting to the pool, the foal would have surely met its end in a watery grave. Now it was having an early tea.

On another occasion, a particularly freezing night in winter when Vic was away driving, the pool presented me with another drama. I had stayed home from the races to catch up on my bookwork. The children were in bed asleep and I was sitting in our lounge room in front of a blazing open fire, engrossed in my work, when my German Shepherd Dana began barking loudly outside. She had two or three weeks earlier given birth to five beautiful puppies. It was quite out of character for her to be barking at night. I tried to ignore it for a while, but the barking persisted, so I dashed quickly outside into the cold night and to my horror saw that her five puppies were in the pool.

Dana was standing at the pool's edge not knowing what she could do. I was able to grab four of the squirming little bodies out of the freezing water and put each up on the cement apron of the pool. The fifth was floating well out of reach, and not moving. I dashed away to grab a long broom, and pushed the remaining little body towards the edge so I could then pluck it from the water. I held it head down, hoping to drain some of the water out of it, then attempted the same procedure I had adopted previously for the little foal.

Never having applied mouth-to-mouth aid to a human, here I was trying to revive a little puppy that was not moving. Imagine my surprise and relief when, after what seemed an age, but was probably minutes, it unbelievably started to breathe again. All five pups were taken inside, and using several towels, I rubbed each one dry in front of the fire. The little one was the last to recover—but recover he did. I became misty-eyed as I watched the little mite struggle for his very existence, then later have some much-needed milk from his mother. He made slower progress than the other pups in the following weeks. When he was older we gave him to a friend, where he became a very much loved dog, demonstrating his mother's gentle nature.

Then our cow was seen drinking from the pool and the ducks would hop in for a swim. That was it! It could no longer remain a hazard, so up went the fence around the pool, with another fence further out around the house. Never again did I have to worry about what was in the pool at unexpected hours, apart from the water.

The daily schedule for Vic and me was extremely busy after Jack Kelly moved to Bankstown and we decided not to replace him with a full-time assistant, then preferring to make use of casual help. My day began very early, with the first chore being to milk the cow and separate the cream. The horses had to be fed next, before returning to the house to attend to breakfast. Although the climate of the Southern Highlands was better for Vic, he was still unable to feed up for fear of becoming stressed with dust and other particles being stirred up when preparing the feed for each horse. So that task became mine.

Right after breakfast I would cut the kids their lunches, clean shoes, do the dishes, and carry out a quick tidy-up of the house. Then it was time to check over the children, making sure each had their hair done, ties on straight, clean handkerchiefs in their pockets, homework and lunches in their bags, before putting them in the car to drive down to the farm gate to meet the school bus.

Carrying out the track-work with our team of horses would take us both through to lunchtime, when I would dash back to the house and prepare our midday meal. After lunch Vic often headed off into the paddocks to carry out work from the tractor. Sometimes it was ploughing, other times it may have been seeding, slashing, spreading fertiliser, fencing or irrigating to be done. One never has to look far on a farm to see something that requires attention. During this time I had to wash and clean all the harness and then take the horses to their various 'pick' paddocks.

These consisted of quarter-acre enclosures containing natural grasses, which are always a good and necessary supplement for a working horse. While the horses were out, it allowed me the time to clean out the stables, replacing the new wood shavings in each, and have them clean and ready for when it was time to bring each horse back from its paddock. It was our policy to leave some horses out for just over an hour, and others a little longer. If any of the horses had raced the previous night, they had the day off work and would spend a half-day out on the grass.

You can imagine what it was like on a race day, as on normal days during the week it was always a challenge to get through this routine and be down at the front gate to meet the school bus on its return. On occasions when I was running a little late in the warmer weather, there the crew would be, ambling up the dusty road, shirts hanging out, sock tops down, and ties off or askew, with Susan always bringing up the rear with Glenn or Garry carrying her books. While they were changing their clothes, I would prepare a snack for them before they went out to play, and I went back to the stables to give the horses their evening feed.

We knew we were pushing ourselves with the busy and demanding lifestyle we had set ourselves after moving to Exeter, so we tried adding some variety to it by going out to a restaurant or somewhere pleasant for a meal with the family at least once a week. We also made certain to continue taking time off for our annual holiday. When the kids were quite young we travelled to different areas, but as they were growing up we went to Adaminaby in the summer for trout fishing, or in winter we would go there as a stopover for the snow fields.

Sometimes we towed our caravan and went wherever we wished, staying any place that took our fancy. After Vic discovered there was more to life than working and driving horses every day of the week, he began to relax a little, often taking us all on fishing excursions.

When we first started trolling for trout, we caught more snags than fish, but we soon became aware of the hidden trees and shallow spots. We didn't really like the taste of the trout initially, and gave most of our catch away. That was before I learned how to smoke them. From then on we couldn't catch enough. It was really peaceful, going slowly up the lake with the three children in the boat. They were happy and we enjoyed it immensely. We would often have a swim at the local pool and then tea at Shamus's motel to end a perfect day. It was certainly a wonderful break away from the horses and made a tremendous difference to Vic and his asthma, making it another memorable holiday.

Glenn enjoyed his fishing from the moment he wet his first line. He would grow up having a real affinity for getting back to nature— enjoying the experience of sleeping out under the stars, wrapped up in a sleeping bag with a campfire nearby and listening to the sounds of the bush.

Both Glenn and Garry, even as small children, were outdoor types and able to amuse themselves by inventing their own games. At home or wherever we stopped our car when we were travelling, there always seemed to be a spot where they could make an impromptu dirt road on which to push their toy cars and trucks along. I cannot remember my children ever complaining that there was nothing for them to do, or that they were bored, nor did I have to concentrate on entertaining them during the day. They were capable of making their own fun. It was more my looking for them than their looking for me.

One habit I did pass on to Garry was impatience. He became just like me in wanting things to happen 'immediately'. Vic would say that as long as I could get things done straight away it was okay, and that's how it was for Garry too, often going at things like a bull at a gate. He was about five or six when we started fishing, and he quickly learned to love the sport.

Perhaps when he was small he was inclined to be a little meek and mild, being content to follow in his brother's shadow, as he adored Glenn, following him everywhere. This did change as the months became years and Garry developed his confidence. He became a determined and self-willed young man who could make friends easily. But when he made his mind up to do something, nothing could change it. He would laugh often, with a deep, bubbly laugh.

When he was at high school, Garry announced to us one evening that he was going camping to Paddy's River, about a half-hour from the farm. During the night it started to pour with rain and, being a typical mother, I began to worry about him. Just before midnight I said to Vic, 'I'm going to drive down to the river and see if Garry's all right. It's very cold and wet out there, he might even catch pneumonia.' Vic would not hear of it. 'He'll be all right, he will be home in a few hours.'

He returned home quite all right, in fact, very happy with himself. It was only later that I learned he had camped out with one of his friends—a lovely little blonde. Goodness only knows where she told her parents she was going. Even at that age he probably kept quite warm in the small tent during the night. Oh gee! What we mothers don't know is probably the best for us sometimes, I am sure, but I worried about the boy just the same, and pondered the shortcomings in *my* lessons on life.

Soccer became Garry's favourite sport and, after playing for several seasons, he took on the job of coaching his team for one year. He put in a lot of effort and was rewarded, his dedication paying off, when the team went on to win the final.

Almost from the start, Glenn could bait his own line and seemed to catch more fish than the rest of the family, and this would often be the case when he went out camping with his friends. He became a keen pig and kangaroo hunter and a skilled marksman, in those areas where this is permitted.

Having two brothers who were so much into these outdoor activities was not Susan's idea of fun when she was little, although she did prefer ponies and dogs to dolls. When a little older she eventually learned to fish and would catch her fair share. Before long there were occasions when she went rabbiting with her brothers, and did not seem afraid to fetch the rabbits the boys had shot, though I suspect it was to gain the respect of the 'men' more than anything.

One year we had a wonderful holiday together on Norfolk Island. It did not take long to drive across Norfolk Island and we explored it fully, finding it a lovely and peaceful place. I remember one night at the restaurant of the motel where we were staying, I had tried to teach Vic how to rock and roll without much success. A man who had been watching asked if I would mind having a dance with him. Vic watched for a while, then took the children off to bed. I enjoyed dancing so much that night, the next hour just flew by. Another year we went to Fiji, which proved an education to us all, to see the locals go about their daily lives and be so happy without the material things that seem to be so important and necessary for us.

Vic and I always worked hard at ensuring the children were able to experience good and happy times being part of a loving family. He was a good father, no matter how busy he was with the horses, always trying to make some time available to play with the kids. Helping out with homework or reading them stories at bedtime had been my job. When they had been little, I took them to Sunday School while I went to church myself. This was never a regular occurance in those days, for either the children or me, as the horses which were our bread and butter took priority and still had to be worked. They never knew it was Sunday.

SIXTEEN

The Honour of Representing My Country

Other wins soon followed that success at Harold Park with Pretty Tough, and the media was not backward, constantly seeking interviews with the woman the Sydney media found was good news in this still male-dominated sport. The situation developed where Vic was the number one driver in the state, but his wife was now attracting more attention from the media. If he answered the phone in the evenings and it was for me, I often heard him say, 'You want to speak to the boss. Hold on and I'll get her.' Men! Some of them do have a weird sense of humour when women are competing with them.

The people in our district organised a special dinner for Vic and me at the Moss Vale Services Club, in August 1978. It had just become public that I had been selected to represent Australia in a Women's World Driving Championship to be held in the US during October of 1978. Only weeks before, Vic had won both training and driving premierships for the season at Harold Park, and I was about to become the second leg of the only husband and wife team ever to represent any country in the world in harness racing.

The dinner in August was jointly sponsored by the Wingecarribee Shire Council, the Berrima District Trotting Association and the Moss Vale Services Club. Almost 300 people attended, including some officials and stewards from Harold Park, along with some of our training and driving colleagues. Some of the comments made during speeches were extremely flattering to Vic and me. It was claimed that the success our stable was enjoying had really helped put Exeter on the sporting map. We were presented that night with a dinner set, a pencil drawing of us together and a couple of ornamental trees, which we planted on either side of the front gate to Glen-Garry Lodge.

One of the chief organisers behind that dinner was Jack Townsend, a friend we had nicknamed 'Tripecta Jack'. He enjoyed taking trifectas (picking the first three placings in a race) and could never pronounce the name correctly, always referring to it as the 'tripecta'. Jack's wife had died a few years earlier and he lived alone at Sutton Forest, about four miles away from our farm, and proved to be a real friend on many occasions. There were times, when Vic was away interstate or in the US, that I had to transport the horses to the track myself, and Jack would be quick to put his hand up to come along as company. There was one night I'm sure he wished he had stayed home.

On this trip to Harold Park I had two pacers on the float, with which I had enjoyed much success: Marriage Encounter and How Cute. We were about a half-hour from the track when I became aware that something seemed amiss in the float. Vic was always quite strict with the maintenance of all our vehicles, regularly checking the floats, tow bars and anything he thought could go wrong. Yet somehow, to my utter surprise, a hole had been pushed through the floor beneath How Cute's hind leg. Having to be at the races at least half an hour before my race, we had no time to seek repairs at a garage, and I had no alternative but to press on. I persuaded Jack to stand in the float and hold onto the horse's headstall to keep him forward of the hole, and hoped that he would be all right.

Not being very experienced with horses, and well on in years, Jack was terrified. I might add he had little alternative but to stand there after I had closed the door behind him, leaving him in the dark with two horses. It might have been an ordeal for him, but we reached the track with no further problems. Our friend Kevin Wells came to our rescue at Harold Park by taking the float away, repairing it and having it back in time to load up for home. One thing is for sure, Jack had a better ride on the way back from Harold Park than he had coming, and so did I. Jack passed away peacefully at his home about five years later.

That World Driving Championship for women attracted the leading reinswomen from Italy, France, Germany, Finland, Canada and Sweden, with the well-known Bea Farber representing the US. Vic was already in the US, because he had taken another small team of pacers across there at this time. Leaving these with a local trainer, he joined the tour and gave me some helpful advice. I had stayed at home training and driving our racehorses until it was time to leave on this trip, one that I could not refuse. After all, how often in life does one have the thrill of representing one's country and fulfilling a dream?

I was able to get a man to look after the property and train the horses while I was away, and the two week absence from racing did not present any problem.

It took a little time to adjust to the wider gigs, which are also harnessed much closer to the horse than they are down under, thus allowing the animal's tail to hit you in the face if it flicks it about. The sitting position in these wide sulkies was most uncomfortable; because of my short legs, I had to have my feet wide apart and held high. It was quite different from the position that I was used to at home, but I managed reasonably well.

We all gathered for the first function at Batavia Downs on October 2nd, with the first of the heats two nights later at Arlington Park, and finishing 10 days later in California at Hollywood Park. The series was not as busy as the one Vic had taken part in six years earlier, giving us all a little extra time to enjoy racing in that country. In one of the heats, we all drove trotters. This was the only time I can recall driving a trotter in a race, as Vic mostly trained pacers.

The title was won by Bea Farber, who then rated extremely well with the best men in the business. Bea had been a real trendsetter for the girls in North America, having figured prominently in the drivers' premierships. The Italian, Agnese Palagi, finished second on points, and I was third. It was interesting to read an interview with the successful American reinswoman in one magazine, in which Bea stated that the Australian representative had been the hardest to beat in most races. We were well looked after by the US Trotting Association, once again staying in the best hotels and being entertained wherever we went. That series produced an interesting and unexpected surprise for me.

Being English, with parents who had spoken so often about what the Germans had done during the war, I had grown up with an intense dislike of Germans that almost bordered on hatred. Yet during that series I became very friendly with the German reinswoman Irmgard Mueller and her husband, and a friendship developed. I only came to realise during the series that there was a lot of forgiving and releasing of anger for me to do in this area, and it gave me great relief and made me happy to make my first German friends. On a later business trip to Italy, I made the time to visit the Muellers in Villich (near Dusseldorf), and spent a wonderful week in their home and met some of their friends.

An English newspaper, the *Bedworth Echo,* had featured a story under the headline: 'Bedworth Girl Makes History Down Under'. It appears my cousin Jean had passed information on to the local newspaper in the town where I was born, then posted the feature on to me. The article explained how one of their own, who had migrated to Australia, had recently struck a blow for women's lib on the other side of the world with her success in harness racing.

SEVENTEEN

More History-Making Events

Our stable continued to win its share of races. Among our smart performers was the mare Remember Joy, which Vic trained for the McColl family from Newcastle. She won her way through the classes at Harold Park and we nominated her and Chime Bay for the Craven Filter Championship in Brisbane in June 1979. Vic drove them both in the heats, winning with Chime Bay and also qualifying Remember Joy for the final. He had to choose which horse he would drive in the final, and elected Chime Bay, which had drawn barrier 6; Remember Joy had drawn barrier 7.

Vic asked Alan McColl if he had a particular driver in mind for his mare in the final. I was overjoyed when he selected me. I was greatly honoured, as there were several big- name reinsmen who could have been engaged.

This was my first Grand Circuit appearance, but I do recall not being unduly nervous when taking the mare onto the track in a field that included some of the best horses racing in the country, such as Paleface Adios, Koala King and Michael Frost. One angle the sportswriters stated was that this was the most important race any Australian reinswoman had contested up until that time, and no reinswoman had ever won a classic.

Vic and Chime Bay were caught out in the 'death' early, while I angled for a position on the rails, eventually being able to go through and secure the coveted position on the back of the leader. With the mare not having had the same hard run as Chime Bay and one or two others, she was full of running in the final lap as I looked for an opening. When it did finally come, both Joe Ilsley (Michael Frost) and I went for it. The mare might have made it through, but there was no room for the sulky. I went over the line restraining 'Joy' and could have cried with frustration and disappointment. Remember Joy should have been my first classic winner, she really should have.

It was a close finish between the first five pacers; Brian Hancock won with Koala King, from Paleface Adios and Michael Frost. Vic and Chime Bay were fourth, and Remember Joy the closest of fifths. I knew I had been desperately unlucky, a fact reaffirmed later, when I watched the replay on the course video. Also watching next to me was Joe Ilsley, who said, 'Gee Margaret, I cost you that race. You would have surely won but for that interference.'

That's racing, of course.

Joe was a horseman Vic and I respected. Any praise from Vic was always well deserved. Joe Ilsley trained his horses on the Mona Vale beach, north of Sydney, and was very successful with unsound pacers. After sending him Double Agent to train, we later also gave him Tricky One, who needed to be trained on a beach because of leg problems.

Harness racing is not always 'bunny slippers and ear muffs' for reinswomen. In my first year or two of driving, the only change room for me was the ladies toilet, and showering facilities did not exist then for women. Some men gallantly offered to share their shower room, promising to keep their eyes closed. Perhaps they were trying to treat me as an equal then? On winter nights, especially when it was raining, I wore a skivvy, jumper and woolly socks beneath my wet-weather gear, and yet still felt the icy chill out on the track. As water-proofing materials improved, I was able to graduate to a one-piece overall in my colours.

Some drivers wore gloves, but I preferred not to, because I felt I had better control of the reins without them. The only other protection we had in the wet (apart from the splash sheet extending from under the horse's tail to the gig) was a pair of mesh goggles, which I wore over my plastic ones. The mesh goggles became covered with mud, and I got rid of them when it became impossible to see, and quite often the plastic goggles as well. The major problem on cold wet nights wasn't just the cold and the wet, it was the slurry of mud and slop thrown back onto me by the horse's hooves and the wheels of the gigs. This would completely cover me down the front, from my face to my boots. This was one mud-pack facial that I would certainly not recommend; it didn't do anything for my skin. Any of the track that was still in my eyes when I got home was washed out with cold tea, a successful Scottish remedy. When conditions for reinswomen improved, we looked forward eagerly at the end of the meetings to having a hot shower in our own facilities, to thaw out and wash away the part of the track that still covered us.

Another achievement for me was becoming the first woman to drive in an Inter Dominion Championship. We had both Grand Thor and Chime Bay nominated for the 1980 Sydney Inter Dominion. The pre-post favourites were Pure Steel and Grand Thor. Unfortunately, we had to scratch Grand Thor because the navicular disease that troubled him had flared up again. I failed to qualify Chime Bay for the Grand Final, but we finished second in the Consolation. I was probably one of the most inexperienced drivers to drive in this race. I had only thirty-seven country wins and five Harold Park wins before attempting this quite daunting challenge. That championship will be remembered for Koala King giving Brian Hancock his first Inter Dominion success.

On July 18th 1980, Vic and I were driving in the same race at Harold Park. Vic was driving Marriage Encounter and I was driving Blazing Summer. I was on the rails, mainly to give my mare a better chance than if she were on the outside, as that uses them up more in a race and she wasn't too strong. I was hoping for a bit of luck, and to secure a run in the final lap. With less than 400 metres to go, the horse in front of Vic fell, allowing him no chance of avoiding the crash, and bringing Vic down. Luckily, I missed the fall and finished third, then I allowed my horse to continue around the track to see how my husband had fared. He had been slow getting to his feet, but was not badly hurt, just badly bruised and shaken.

That week I had been suffering from a bad case of laryngitis. After crossing the line I called in a croaky voice to a steward to inquire if I had to weigh in immediately. He could see I was anxious about Vic, and he waved me on. But later, stewards thought I had been given such a fright by the accident that I had lost my voice and, to my annoyance, they refused to let me drive the rest of Vic's horses, and engaged another driver.

My impromptu reaction to Vic's fall at the end of the race was later picked up by ABC television, who dispatched a news crew by helicopter to Exeter to film a day in my life. They arrived on a bitterly cold day that was close to snowing, which we get during winter in the Southern Highlands. It took them hours to film, yet they later edited it all down to a 12-minute brief.

The children were overjoyed when the crew took us for a ride in the helicopter, though I was terrified looking down between my feet through the plexiglass floor at the ground so far below. The pilot was amazed that somebody who could sit on the flimsy seat of a gig, being dragged along at high speed in a melee of sweating horses, could be so affected by a little ride in his machine, enclosed safely inside his little bubble. I'm sure the marks from my fingers biting into the armrests would have stayed on for some days after our ride.

Vic and I had become quite well known by now as a 'Sensational Husband and Wife Team'. It was common to see headlines like 'Husband and Wife Team Taking Sydney Pacing by Storm', and 'Frosts Were Far Too Hot' and similar headings. We were written up in gazettes, the Trotguide and our state racing papers, most weeks. It seemed that almost anything we did was newsworthy.

We raised a few sheep at Glen-Garry Lodge. Occasionally I would find a lamb deserted by its mother. Rather than let it die in the cold, I would take it back to the house and place it in the warming drawer of my combustion stove. (Many a cold bottom has been warmed by that stove.) One day, as I was keeping one eye on a little lamb being gently warmed, the chief steward phoned from Sydney. As I answered the phone, the little lamb bleated. The steward asked me what the strange noise was. I told him briefly, thinking no more about the incident. A few days later, an article appeared in one of the Sydney newspapers along the lines, 'Margaret Frost not only races horses, she saves lambs'. This trivial incident on a farm made me realise just how the media could make something out of virtually nothing, and I tried to be a little more circumspect with my comments from then on.

Marriage Encounter was a horse that gave me many wins. It also brought me my worst suspension. I was caught on the fence with this horse one night, behind Les Chant. In the final lap there was just nowhere to go. When Les's horse drifted slightly away from the rails, I was tempted to try and force a passage through. But Les had won the first driving premiership at the Melbourne Showgrounds and was now one of our leading drivers, and I respected him greatly. He would not be careless enough to allow a horse from behind to squeeze through inside him. I elected to maintain my efforts to push off the fence and draw clear outside of him. I did not win the race but went on to finish in a place.

Stewards later suspended me for two months for not attempting this manoeuvre. I greatly resented this, firmly believing I had done everything in my power to win. Later, on appeal, the Authority halved the suspension to one month, but I still felt wrongly done by.

Steward inquiries often lead to a suspension of one's licence for a particular time, be it days or weeks, and these times are dreaded by all drivers. It usually involves being called into the stewards' room after a race, when they feel you have not driven in the best interest of your horse, caused interference to another driver, or your driving ability is drawn into question. Quite often the inquiry goes on during the night, and well after the last race on the program.

Videos taken from every angle of the race are reviewed and evidence is taken from all drivers concerned. The drivers are sent out of the room while the stewards draw their conclusion from the evidence, and make their decision. The drivers are then called back to be given the result of the inquiry. When this happened to either Vic or me, it meant a very late night for us, so we always hoped the problems would be sorted out well before the last race, but we weren't always so lucky.

One night we both waited outside the stewards' room until after midnight, to be given some trivial word of caution and no penalty. We went home fuming about the lateness of the hour and the inconsiderate attitude of the head steward. *He* didn't have to travel two and a half hours, unload and put five horses in their boxes in a temperature of minus six degrees, before scrambling into bed!

One year Marriage Encounter and I won the last race of the New South Wales season at Harold Park, and several days later at Bankstown the first race of the new season.

Among the many successes I had during this period, there was one sad event that removed some of the gloss. I was driving the horse Something Royal at Harold Park on April 28th 1981. This was a pacer which a friend, Stan Weir, Vic and I had bred and raised on our farm from a foal. It had won several races for both Vic and me, and was a popular horse around the stables. That night at the bell lap I felt Something Royal begin to stagger. Knowing something was very much amiss, I began easing him out of the race. Right in front of the main grandstand he staggered again and fell to the ground. I jumped out of the gig and rushed to his head.

The bell lap in the race I would create history by becoming the first reinswoman to drive a winner at Harold Park night trotting. That's me with Pretty Tough running second in the 'death'. This pacer really did live up to his name. Later we won further races together.

This is me with a pacer in New York's famous Madison Square Gardens as part of the build-up to the World Reinswomen's Championship when I represented Australia. At the end of the series I was third on the points table to the local star, Bea Farber.

The competitors in the 1978 World Driving Championship in North America. From left are Elay Bron-Heloner (Switzland), Bea Farbor (USA), Marie-Christine Joney-Weiss (France), Rita Vaisamon (Finland), Irmgard Mueller (Germany), Agnese Palasi Italy), yours truly in the Frost colours, and Donna Degrow (Canada).

112

ABOVE: My victory in the 1981 Inter Dominion Consolation for pacers driving Grand Thor. It was the first win by a reinswoman in any Inter Dominion series. Grand Thor could have been an ever greater horse but for leg problems which restricted his training.

BELOW: A satisfying win for me (on the outside) with Grand Delight, as the horse I beat was No Tie being driven by Vic. When we met in any race, it was an added incentive to beat each other. Any thought of team driving was never an option.

Clem's Gift and I warming up before a race at Harold Park, which we won. Winning at Sydney's major track was always a thrill, as you knew the opposition was tough, and the men never made it any easier for a reinswoman. And that's how it should be.

Trainer Fran Donohue and I pictured during a meeting at Harold Park. Fran concentrated on training and was most successful at it too.

ABOVE: The birth of Glenn's Thunder provided some difficulties for the little colt, and I had to lend some assistance. Not only did he mature into the most wonderful young stallion to handle, but he was truly an outstanding performer until his tragic death.

BELOW: Our son Glenn with a young colt he was breaking-in. He was quick to label it a star of the future. The colt was named Westburn Grant, and went on to win more than $2 million in stakemoney.

ABOVE: I only ever got to drive Glenn's Thunder once in a race, and it was like driving a Rolls Royce. There was plenty of gas in the tank when he cruised to the post for me on October 1st, 1988.

BELOW: This is me winning at Harold Park with Speed Partner. He was a grand pacer as he also won races when driven by Vic and our son Glenn. So he really did live up to his name.

LEFT: Our son Garry with his good friend Lisa Lewis at our special Christmas dinner held on the Wednesday prior to Christmas when Vic and I were flying to Perth the next day for Westburn Grant's big race there. It was the last picture ever taken of Garry.

BELOW: The horse Vic and I owe so much to, Westburn Grant, which we fondly called 'Spot' because as a colt a rain storm left some marks over his body that only hours later were burnt by the hot sun, briefly leaving him 'spotty'.

All Humour carries me to victory at Harold Park in which I became Australia's first reinswomen to win a race inside two minutes. It's a record that can never be taken away and shall always remain in the record books.

This is me in our famous Frost colours of white with black stars. Of course, Vic won countless big races in all States using these colours. But they also proved very lucky for me on many an occasion.

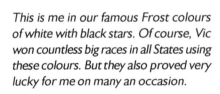

He lay there motionless, at first with his eyes open, then they closed as I sat there with his head cuddled in my lap. I started calling his name and cuddled his beautiful head to my chest. A hand came to rest on my shoulder, and Vic said, 'He's gone Margy, he's dead.' Common sense did not prevail then. I would not accept the fact that he had died, and tried to give him further aid, but my friends and Vic hauled me off the track, away from my stricken animal.

The horse had suffered a massive blood clot. It was then, for the first time, that I experienced such an intense feeling of helplessness It made me realise just how final death is. The crowd present that night amazed the officials, because usually after a race they can't wait to rush off to the betting ring and start betting on the next race. However, this time, no spectator moved until I had been led away from the fallen horse.

One of my more memorable history-making races was on the night of 30th October 1981, when I drove All Humour at Harold Park to win, in the mile rate of 1 minute 59.5 seconds; fast indeed, especially in those times.

At the start, I had no alternative but to settle All Humour back in the field, because I had drawn barrier nine, on the back line. Mobile barrier starts had become the main way of starting races, and this was one such start. A utility pulls a wide, wing-like steel frame, on which six numbers are clearly marked, one for each of the six horses drawn on the front line. As the mobile moves off to start the race, each driver must keep his horse directly behind his drawn number and as close to the barrier as he can. The horses drawn on the back line must follow closely behind the horse they have to follow out of the barrier.

It is easier on the horse, having drawn this wide position, to ease him back rather than to forge forward early in the race. This was especially so this night, as the leader set a very fast first half-mile, with a mile rate of 59.3 seconds, making it virtually impossible to make any forward movements.

This race was over the distance of a mile, and in these shorter races, the closer you can be to the lead the better chance you have. With a lap to go, I moved All Humour up to being three wide, outside the two leaders, on the home turn. He responded well, and just continued to surge forward, winning by a head from the second horse and a head from the third, thus making it a very close and exciting finish.

It felt like just one more winner until several reporters met me coming off the track to ask what it was like to create such a record. Immediately after the race I had not realised the winning time for the mile was inside two minutes. For the first time in Australia a woman had bettered this mark in a race. It was a night to savour as this is one record that can never be taken away.

October and November of 1981 were extremely successful for me, as a flurry of winners in this period enabled me to become the first reinswoman in Australia to drive 50 winners. It was quite a milestone at the time. My first winning double at Harold Park was on October 23rd with All Humour and Chime Bay. It was the second time a reinswoman had achieved this in Sydney, as Kim Moore had chalked up this feat a little earlier. Kim was a pretty blonde, and very photogenic, which helped the reinswomen's cause, earning extra attention from the media. She drove a lot of Charlie Parson's horses and did extremely well. She later married a jockey and switched her allegiance to the thoroughbreds, which she has continued training to this day.

On country tracks, and twice at Menangle, I had driven doubles, but driving two winners at a Harold Park meeting was always special. I was delighted on November 13th when I repeated the effort with Tricky One and All Humour. No doubt my rush of winners in this period was largely because Vic was out of the running, having been given a two-month suspension by Fairfield stewards for making the unforgivable mistake of miscalculating the laps in a race, making his move a lap early. He made certain never to repeat that mistake again.

All Humour, the horse that partnered me in several entries in the record books, was a pleasure to drive. His name, however, was a real misnomer, as he was anything but humorous, being a rather cantankerous horse that would put his ears back when approached. But he did enjoy the rub-downs I gave him without any sign of irritation. Later on, All Humour injured a fetlock that required surgery. An infection developed in the bone that became so bad we were left no alternative but to have this horse, that had given us so much, put down. It was my task to float the horse to the University where this painless procedure was carried out. The drive home was difficult, as it was not easy seeing through a film of tears.

Transporting my horses and equipment to and from the gymkhanas and shows was, at first, difficult for me. It necessitated my being able to put the float on the car, and manoeuvre my car and float into awkward positions at the various venues. I wasn't confident enough then to drive the car and the two-horse float, fully loaded, down the Macquarie Pass, on the road between Exeter and Dapto. I was most grateful to our good friend and supporter, Graeme Gunther, affectionately known to his friends by the nickname 'Packy'.

It was Packy who drove me to Canberra for my first race drives, because they then held their race program on the same nights as Harold Park. Vic was not pleased that I drove without him being present. I was so keen to drive that I wanted to go to the venues with or without Vic, and I was most grateful for Packy's help and support. Now, twenty years later, he still comes to the farm. Packy no longer drives a car and two-horse float for me, but he frequently drives a truck for Glenn.

On June 24th 1981, I was invited to drive in a Ladies Race at Melbourne's Moonee Valley, and drew the pacer Appleack, trained by Henry McDermott. Henry had earlier moved from the western districts of New South Wales to prepare his team at Bendigo. Two mink jackets had been donated by a generous sponsor: one for the winning trainer and the other for the winning driver. Appleack was in a rearward position until I secured a late run to flash home and just win. It was the first and only mink jacket I have owned, and I'm sure Henry's wife was also delighted with hers.

If my impaired memory these days makes it difficult to recall some events of the past, the 1981 Australian Pacing Championship is one that does come to mind readily. Grand Thor was a pacer possessing outstanding ability, when sound. He was raced by Fran and Lionel Bates, and because of his excellent record was handicapped off 10 metres in that championship. Vic drove the stallion in the heats and just failed to make the final, but because of a minor suspension handed out to him that week, he was not able to partner the horse in the Consolation. I was more than thrilled when Fran and Lionel asked me to drive Grand Thor.

Grand Thor began well from his back line handicap, and looked like getting a good position straight away, but the field settled down in single file and I was forced to race without cover. I moved up slowly, as a horse pulled out from the rails to move up into the position outside the leader. This gave me cover and a good position. Kevin Newman made a run with Ardstraw with a lap to go, and I made a run at the last two furlongs, challenging the two leaders around the final turn. Penny Jack, which had led all of the way, tried valiantly to hold on, but I drove Grand Thor vigorously with the whip, and we won by half a head from Penny Jack, with Christmas Adios, driven by Richard Hancock, running third.

The navicular disease that afflicted Grand Thor could be likened to a form of serious arthritis in the feet. Vic used an American treatment, which consisted of packing the stallion's feet with wet clay. It helped relieve the pain, but was not a cure. This condition restricted Grand Thor from ever reaching the full potential we knew he had. Vic used this treatment during the heats of the Hobart Inter Dominion, and he responded well to win a heat, but three races in a week left him sore, giving him no time to recover in time for the Grand Final, which was won by San Simeon.

Vic had become quite gifted in the art of shoeing problem horses, always being prepared to try something different to correct a problem. He even went to the trouble of altering shoes for different types of tracks, using bar shoes when racing on circuits with high-banked turns. Among Grand Thor's major wins was the Breeders Plate as a two-year-old, and later the R.C. Simpson Sprint at three, and in Victoria he won the Four-Year-Old Championship at Moonee Valley and the Cranbourne Cup, and more than $270,000 in stakes.

Grand Thor was by Thor Hanover (11 times leading sire of Australia) and from the mare Party Gossip. This was considered excellent breeding and we believed the horse might make a handy sire with the right opportunities. Luckily for us, we had served several of our own mares by him, between his racing campaigns, which produced two outstanding pacers. Even though the most ardent breeders study the blood lines, I think a lot more champions have been bred by chance than by these methods. It is really a lottery with four-legged tickets!

The breeding season in which we introduced Grand Thor to siring duties was at the time Vic was invited to attend a special function and presentation at Harold Park for having won another metropolitan driving premiership for the season just ended. Unfortunately, on the night of the presentation he was laid up in hospital having a double hernia surgically removed. The hard work involved in establishing Glen-Garry Lodge, which followed the extremely busy workload of that bread run, had finally caught up with him. It was decided that I should accept the trophy. My mother came up to look after the children.

It was a late night, and the following morning I was feeling extremely tired and was faced with working the horses on my own. At the time we had some casual help from an elderly gentleman who was able to assist with the harnessing of the horses. Eight of the pacers were due for jogging, and this was done on the machine Vic himself had built. This left a half-dozen or so others due for fast work. Obviously I failed to check the shoes of one pacer as, when I asked it for top speed in the final stages of its work, it trod on a loose front shoe and came down, sending me sprawling onto the track ahead of it. This happened just as my mother and the children came out to see how the track-work was going.

The impact knocked the wind out of me and I lay there for a moment, then staggered to my feet. It was then that I felt the searing pain in my arm and shoulder, suggesting serious damage done to this region. It appeared the horse had escaped the fall a lot better than me, and was returned to its stable without too much fuss. The wife of our employee drove me to Bowral Hospital. Until that drive between Exeter and Bowral, I was totally unaware of the number of undulations and deformities that were present on the road. The car seemed to hunt up and find every bump, and my shoulder only too readily registered the contact.

An X-ray of my shoulder revealed a broken collarbone. Since I was in the hospital, I decided to visit Vic much earlier than planned. Perhaps someone should have told him about the track accident, as when I walked in on him with my arm in a sling, he was given a severe jolt. When hospital staff took his temperature some minutes later it had shot up to an alarming level, but they were unperturbed when it had returned to normal by the next reading.

Several days later Vic was discharged, and his doctor strongly advised him against doing any work until his operation had had ample time to heal. While we were able to obtain help in maintaining the training workload, it was the breeding season, and we were keen to use Grand Thor when ours and several outside broodmares were in season. Despite the advice of his doctor, Vic held the stallion with a special bit in its mouth, hoping this might help restrain the horse. I held a mare with my one good arm and lead her to the position required for the stallion.

We managed to serve two mares this way. When attempting a third mating, the mare suddenly swung around and lashed out, presumably at the stallion. It missed him, but got a mark—my thigh! I immediately let go of the mare and jumped down the paddock like a kangaroo, in pain. I still had my arm in a sling and now I thought I had a broken leg. The thigh came up like a football and throbbed continuously. A break wasn't suspected, so no X-rays were taken, but some sleepless nights followed. The thigh healed up in a few weeks, but not the shoulder. A year later a pin had to be inserted into the collarbone, because it still hadn't healed. I suppose the progeny from the mares sired by Grand Thor at that time later helped make up for all our pain.

Winning premierships in harness racing over the years has usually meant more in prestige than any real monetary gains, though things are changing. Trophies have long been well received and at times can indeed be quite handsome, thanks to the support of generous sponsors. One year we won a white Ford car, which some imaginative person on the presentation night had decorated with large black stars, to match the stable colours. We drove it home that night with the stars still in place. Driving through the busy streets of Sydney on a Friday night created enough curiosity to draw many stares. It took several washes to finally remove the stars. Twice we won trips to Europe, enabling Vic and myself to enjoy the sights immensely while providing us with a much-needed rest away from the early mornings and late nights.

One horseman who won several premierships at Harold Park was Kevin Newman, a fine horseman and respected by his colleagues. One night at Harold Park in March 1980 he was driving Ashlar Adios and I was driving Little Brett, and we both went over the line in a close finish. As Kevin and I were returning to scale and waiting for the result of the photo, he turned to me with a twinkle in his eye and said, 'I think I have just beaten you, Margaret.' My answer was, 'I think I have beaten you, Kevin'.

When the photo showed my horse had indeed won and beaten him by a nose, I thought he may have been a little miffed, as I'm sure some reinsmen would be in such circumstances. Not Kevin. He just shook my hand and, with a bright smile, admitted that I had been a better judge than he. The win was important to me, as it was the first leg of a winning double. I won the second leg with Darryl Dundee. I have never forgotten the display of his humility and sportsmanship that night.

Kevin was noted for his repertoire of jokes and was often seen surrounded by other men in the stabling area. Attention would be drawn to a group when gales of laughter erupted from time to time with Kevin the centre of attention. On one occasion as I was hurrying by, I remarked, 'That must have been a good one, Kevin'. He only grinned, but funnily enough, he never offered to let me in on it.

Vic and I found his wife Beryl to be a very pleasant and hospitable lady on the occasions we visited their home. As the wife of a successful reinsman, being supportive in his work is not an easy assignment, but it was evident that she coped well with the task. Their daughter Julie is now a competent and successful driver, following in the family tradition, and has her father's likeable disposition.

EIGHTEEN

All in the Game

The year 1984 began on a high for our stable, with Area Code winning the Sydney and Melbourne Derbies and being placed in the Queensland classic. Other members of our team also enjoyed city success, including three horses that Vic and I owned: Tricky One, Grand Delight and True Delight. The latter two pacers were from our mare Cheryl's Delight. We did not know it then, but waiting in the wings was a youngster we had bred with the stamp of greatness about him. Life was good for Vic and me, despite our busy schedule. We were able to provide the necessities for a full and happy upbringing of our three children.

Vic and I were so busy training horses and driving them at meetings that, on reflection, we were usually too tired after a busy day to sit down and enjoy good conversation. Owners realised that we were kept busy during the day, so that, when not away racing at night, the phone would ring constantly with owners asking about their horses. It was impossible to watch television in peace, and eventually I gave up trying. The success we both enjoyed would not be without its price.

We had a lot to be thankful for, establishing Glen-Garry Lodge into a successful operation where there was never a dull moment. One evening when Vic was away, I was preparing a dinner of sausages and vegetables, and remembered that I had to dash over to the stables to check on a horse undergoing veterinary treatment. I asked the boys to keep an eye on the sausages, saying I would be back in a few minutes. The 'few' minutes took longer than I thought, and Glenn and Garry decided in my absence that they would not wait to give our pet budgie Harry his usual evening fly-around, but would let him out then.

Harry fluttered about the kitchen, alighting here and there on his familiar perches. Whatever the reason for it, he must have been attracted to the stove and decided to land on the hot pan and the sausages. His touchdown was brief, but enough for the hot fat to cause permanent damage to his little claws. That night our dog Rover had sausages for his tea. Harry from then on had some difficulty clutching his perch with his claws.

Vic usually raced about three times a week, and again at Sunday's gymkhanas, to help educate young horses. After dinner, on those nights he was home, I would often do some ironing or bookwork— impossible tasks during the day. Vic never left me guessing as to how he felt about me working at night, being quite put out. There were occasions when I would sneak out of bed during the night if I was unable to sleep, and finish off some of this work. I finally realised the futility of this, and employed a lady one-and-a-half days per week for the housework and ironing.

Competition tennis had several years earlier been on my agenda, before those weekly visits to drive at Harold Park increased the intensity of work. It got to the stage where I looked forward to each race day with excitement, and as soon as that came and went, I was eagerly awaiting the next meeting. When this had become a weekly routine for some time, I came to realise that racing and driving was becoming an obsession for me. With this came the thought that both Vic and I should make the time to ensure we were not missing out on having a more normal lifestyle. I decided to return to tennis, joining the ladies A-grade team on a Thursday, where it was a standing rule for the team manager not to put me in the first set.

Without fail, I was always late my arrival was a standing joke within our tennis circle. The team would stand and watch me hopping from one foot to the other, doing up my shoelaces as I hurried to take up my position on the court. Both Vic and I also started playing a Saturday afternoon competition. Tennis gave Vic and me a reprieve from the pressure of everyday work and gave us the opportunity to socialise with our friends.

The pavlovas that I made for these occasions, topped with the fresh cream obtained from our cow, weren't bad. Anyway, if I could rely on the judgement of our friends, with whom we played tennis, I believe the description they gave was 'delectable'. Whether this adjective was fitting or not, there were never any leftovers to take home after our tennis days.

My talent for baking cakes was often called upon, not that I made very fancy cakes, but they were usually nice and tasty. On occasion I made them for the children's schools, and always had a cake on hand for the stables and at home. Our work brought us into contact with many people and, as such, we had frequent visitors. I had been brought up in the Scottish tradition of making all who came welcome, and offering a cup of tea to visitors on arrival, so cake-making was a constant job.

We later built our own tennis court at Glen-Garry Lodge, which became the headquarters for our Exeter team when playing home matches.

Daylight saving was also welcomed, as this gave me extra time in my rather large vegetable garden some 100 metres from our house. This was a legacy from my father.

When the children attended the local primary school at Exeter it was only large enough to sustain one teacher. This was Charlie Moore, and Vic and I were very happy with the way he taught our three children. After primary, Glenn and then Garry went to Chevalier High at Bowral. When it came time for Susan to move on to her secondary education, she steadfastly refused to go to Chevalier. She finally got her way, attending Moss Vale High.

Susan was so small when she commenced school that Mum had to make special uniforms for her. She was a cute little blonde, and pretty, and very spoiled by her Dad! In keeping with the rest of the family, she loved animals, especially horses. Being the only girl, she tended to be left out of many of the boys' games when she was very young, but she grew up tough, to enable her to hold her own with them. They made no concessions for her and treated her as an equal. I always said, because she was born on Anzac Day, that she had to be a real Anzac to survive with her two brothers. They would look after her where other children were concerned and protect her if necessary, but together there were no holds barred.

Susan found it hard to make friends, and this was most noticeable when she went to high school, but the friends she did make remain so. Susan is a most caring and considerate young lady, but I had a few years of doubt, as she was not as easy to guide through her teenage years as the boys. I blamed Vic for spoiling her, although perhaps I did contribute a little of that, but thankfully, all has turned out well to date. I still hold the view that too much love is better than too little.

The horse Area Code came into Vic's hands as a three-year-old.

That season this son of Good Humour Man won 13 of its 19 starts and was voted Australian Three-Year-Old of the Year. Seven of these wins had been in succession. Vic had taken Area Code to Melbourne for the Derby heats, accompanied by owner George Ziade and strapper Kevin Wells. George was a building contractor and was never afraid to have a bet on one of his horses.

Kevin Wells and his wife, along with Kevin's father Jim, had long been friends of ours. When I first began driving at Harold Park, Jim would take my horse around the parade ring and when the drivers came out he would always offer me a leg-up. This was not really necessary, as is the case with riders mounting thoroughbreds, as most days I would be in and out of a cart dozens of times and probably could have done it in my sleep. But it was a gesture that somehow seemed to ease the tension prior to a race, bringing me a sense of calm. His son Kevin never missed a Sydney meeting, and he has long been a dedicated strapper for the Frost stables at almost every meeting in New South Wales and often interstate.

That visit to Melbourne by Vic with Area Code brought satisfying results. The colt handled the spacious Moonee Valley circuit well, winning its heat stylishly. He was going to be very hard to beat in the final. Vic phoned home after the heat to say that on the following Saturday night's program, which featured the final, was a race he thought suitable for Speed Partner, a horse we also trained for Area Code's owner. Vic asked me to find suitable transport to send Speed Partner down for that race, and suggested I catch a plane to Melbourne on the Saturday morning for the Derby final.

Fortunately, I was able to arrange for the horse to travel to Melbourne on an interstate float, and also to make certain that our horses at home would be in good hands. Mum agreed she would come over to look after the kids while I was away. Both Area Code and Speed Partner landed the money that night, with George having a large collect on the two. He was a generous sportsman when his horses won, and he shouted us all to dinner at a well-appointed Chinese restaurant to celebrate the occasion. That night at dinner we met Ken and Cynthia Norton, who were celebrating Cynthia's birthday. It was the start of a long-lasting and treasured friendship with them.

George's generosity was always greatly appreciated, and on one racing agenda he had insisted on Vic and me staying for a week at the

Hyatt hotel in Melbourne. This was 'extravagance plus', white bathrobes and all the trimmings but, in stark contrast, when we had to walk through the foyer of the grand hotel in dirty work clothes and come across Elton John with his entourage, it was 'embarrassment plus'. Vic and I looked at each other nonplussed, and our common thought was to be some place else in a hurry; we both felt like hiding behind the nearest counter, but the lift opened immediately and we rushed in and pressed the button, before they could gather their thoughts.

Area Code's highly successful three-year-old days was about the time our son Glenn decided on making horticulture his career. He joined the local council staff to work in the parks and gardens section.

NINETEEN

Jacky, Our Family Ghost

L ate one summer's night in the 1980s, long after Vic and I had gone to bed, a most incredible sequence of events took place in our home. We awoke with a jolt and were sitting in bed, bolt upright, listening to a tremendous racket taking place in the garage, beneath our bedroom. We sat for a few moments, trying to collect out thoughts, rapidly whispering stupid suggestions to each other while screwing up our courage sufficiently to investigate. There was no jumping out of bed and rushing headlong into the unknown; caution was the order of the day. My heart was thumping high in my chest as I accompanied Vic downstairs. Thinking he would find an intruder, Vic reached into his gun cupboard and took out his rifle, holding it in front of him as we felt our way down to the garage. I was breathing right down his neck.

There wasn't a sound from downstairs now.

We reached the garage door in the dark. Vic reached out, wrenched the door open and switched on the lights. He still had the rifle grasped in his hands and pointed into the garage. There was no-one to be seen. Thinking about the situation later, if there had been someone present in the garage, Vic could not have stepped backwards because I was so close to him we would have been wearing the same pair of slippers. We carried out a thorough search of the garage and the surrounding area and found no evidence of anyone being there or anything being out of place. Vic was able to move about just out of arms reach by this time, making me realise I was feeling a little better. After being satisfied that nothing was disturbed we went back to bed and tried to settle down.

About an hour had elapsed since our first awakening. It was then that the noise began again, but this time *much* louder. There was no possible way we could ignore it. The sound was as though someone was banging on the garage door with closed fists or with a hammer, leaving no doubt that whoever it was, or whatever it was, meant to be heard. The effect was so loud it had to wake the household. The strange thing was that the children, asleep in rooms adjoining our own, remained asleep through the whole procedure.

Down the stairs we went again, taking the same precautions as before. This time we carried out a much wider investigation of the garage, house and it's surrounds, only to find nothing, absolutely *nothing!* During our search outside, Vic's attention was drawn momentarily by a flash of light from the little house which we had lived in previously, just a short distance away from where we lived now, but because the flash was so fleeting, Vic thought it was just his imagination and chose to ignore it.

If the noise had been coming from the stables, we would have gone over there to check, but the banging seemed to be confined to the area of the house and garage, so there was no reason to check in the stable area. The stables were too far away for sound to carry the distance to the house, particularly with the urgency and intensity of that which woke us, so after a cup of tea to settle our nerves, we decided that our only course of action now was to go back to bed.

Next morning, I walked over to the stables to feed the horses and to my absolute horror I discovered True Delight, a half brother to Grand Delight, rolling in agony suffering excruciating pain from a twisted bowel. We called the vet, who did what he could for the animal. He advised Vic to take the horse to the University at Cobbitty, hoping that they might be able to save him.

Susan, our daughter, who loves horses as much as we do, went with her Dad. At Bowral, they heard a loud crash and pulled over to find True Delight dead at the side of the float.

We had pulled the dividers out of our four-horse trailer to enable him to lie down, as he could not stand with the excruciating pain. He had rolled sideways in his dying thrust and forced the side door open, causing him to fall on the road.

Some very kind people helped Susan and Vic carry True Delight on to the float. When they returned home, Vic retired to his room, as he just could not face anyone at that time.

This horse was not a champion, but Vic had recently driven him to victory against much better horses in The Max Treuer Memorial, a Grand Circuit race at Bankstown Paceway. Vic said on that night that he could see the flint flying from the horse's hooves, he was trying so hard. This race gave us the biggest prize money for first prize that we had ever won at that stage of our careers.

True Delight had also given me much pleasure and satisfaction by being able to drive him in many of his winning races. In the two years to the time of his sudden passing, he had won 19 races, with 11 of these at Harold Park.

The irony of the story is that we looked in the wrong place; if we had gone over to the stables to look, instead of in the house, we might have saved this gallant little horse. My mother occasionally gets what she says are insights or premonitions, sometimes as warnings. She says that we have an Aboriginal ghost on our property who once lived there and still wants to protect it.

It is my belief that this was our resident 'spirit' trying to get our attention. I can certainly assure you that he did exactly that! He wanted us to go to the aid of the horse that was in so much trouble, but we failed to understand the warning. Since that time, other incidents have happened on the farm with other horses in trouble.

On the night of the Canberra Cup in 1984, we had Tricky One and All Humour in the race and were on our way with them in a two-horse float. Not long after we had left, my mother rang to warn us that she had seen 'Jacky' as we called this spirit. She said she had had a premonition that the float was going to break away from the car as we were travelling with the horses.

She had missed us by half an hour and did not want to frighten Susan with this message, but she rang me the next morning to see if we were all right. I asked her why she was worried and she recounted the warning. I had to sit down at that moment and tell her exactly what had happened to us the previous night. On the way to that meeting the float did come away from the towbar, and it was only the safety chains that prevented a nasty accident. I had then waited by the roadside with the horses while Vic went with a passing motorist who generously offered us the float he had at his farm.

We arrived at the races just in time to harness the two horses and go on the track. Vic won with Tricky One and I came second with All Humour (Miracle Mile winner Friendly Footman was third). It should have been a quinella well worth remembering. Instead, that successful trip to Canberra is noteworthy for another reason: the accurate premonition of my mother. From then on, when Mum claimed she had a premonition concerning Jacky, or we were alarmed by noises, we would not dismiss it lightly.

Glenn has seen Jacky quite a few times on the farm and Susan has seen him twice, but not as clearly. I have not seen him, but there have been times when I have heard unexplained noises around the house, or seen lights being switched on and off when no other person was about, and of course those episodes mentioned above. At the age of twelve, Glenn saw Jacky clearly, reflected in a mirror when he was washing his hands in the downstairs bathroom. He describes the apparition as Aboriginal, small but quite stocky in build, with what he said resembled a 'goatee' beard.

Another time when Glenn and Susan both saw Jacky, they were upstairs, about to take their showers. Susan bolted downstairs in fright. Glenn said he watched the ghostly figure walk into Susan's bedroom and he followed it in, and said to the figure that he was not afraid, but believed that he was looking after the horses and the farm. Jacky did not speak, but slowly disappeared after looking back at him for a few moments.

Before Glenn was married, he and his future wife Toni were watching a video in our lounge room when the apparition suddenly appeared near the curtains to one side of the room. Glenn told us he clearly saw Jacky, and when Toni turned to look at what had caught his attention, the figure disappeared. Toni later was not certain what she had seen, but had been terrified to see something going through the curtains.

When Susan was out riding around the farm one day she reported to me that she had seen that ghostly figure again. When I explained how Jacky was not a bad person and was only looking after the farm and horses, she was more able to accept it all. Of course, those who claim to have seen ghosts usually do find it a frightening experience.

On returning home one night after we had been out for dinner, Vic and I found a group of brood mares and foals running around the stable area. They had pushed the gate of their paddock open and were now being a danger to our racehorses.

The stallions, including the million-dollar horse Westburn Grant, were going wild and could have been badly injured, trying to jump the rails of their yards or kicking the walls of the brick stables. We called for Glenn to help and he came at a run and he said to us, 'Now

I know why'. There was no time for explanation until after rounding up all the horses and returning them to their paddock. Glenn then explained how the laundry door was continually banging, even though he had got out of bed and shut it securely several times.

At about 2am one morning when Glenn was about 23, the garage light came on and the wireless kept going on and off. Glen just turned them off and went back to bed each time. He discovered next morning that one of his good horses had got out of the paddock and had been galloping around the farm. Since then, we have an agreement that if any peculiar incident happens again, someone will go over to the stables and make sure all is well.

Some five years after these perplexing events, Vic and I had our friend Peter Ramster and his wife Doreen over for dinner. During the evening, our conversation turned to a subject which was of great interest to Peter: inexplicable phenomena. We related our experiences to Peter, who didn't seem at all phased by them but, to our great surprise, suggested he make a film of the events. Peter had produced various successful television films and documentaries, so we agreed, not thinking for one minute that we would be involved personally and have to re-enact the whole episode. Acting was not a talent with which Vic or I was endowed, but since the story was factual we went ahead with the film documentation. Peter made the film, and it was screened soon after, in a series of documentaries of the same genre, on a special program on one of our metropolitan television channels. Vic and I were given a video of the episode, which has since been shown overseas, and after sitting through it, we decided that we had best stick to training and racing horses.

Jacky has been quiet for quite some time now, but I am not too anxious to hear from him again either.

TWENTY

Pacer Puts the Bite on Me

A day I can laugh about now, but which was no laughing matter at the time, occurred during one of Vic's trips away, when I was working all the horses myself. Visiting me at the time was my friend Irene Angel, who was not experienced with horses. She was watching me pacework the stallion Tricky One, which I had in the gig, and another stallion, Duane True, which I was leading. Because we had a good covering of grass in the area around our track paddock, some of the broodmares were allowed to graze there, as they were unlikely to interfere with the horses being worked.

Around the stables Duane True was not a difficult horse to handle, but on this particular day he really started 'feeling his oats' when he became attracted to the mares. It was that time of the year, and he started acting like a stallion. He became quite contrary, reacting like stallions probably did when running with the herd hundreds of years before.

Perhaps I gave him a tug on the lead to get his mind off the mares and he resented it, as without warning he grabbed me from behind, sinking his teeth through my clothes and into my shoulder. There was this searing pain in my shoulder; he pulled back, and I was forced to let go of his lead. The horse immediately took off, galloping straight for the mares. I knew I was in big trouble.

Trying to forget about the pain in my shoulder, I was able to get Tricky One back to the stables and secure him. He had not reacted to the incident, not showing the same interest in the mares. Urgent action was required if we were going to separate Duane True from the mares. Without thinking, I rushed over to the motorcycle we kept for the boys to ride. The futility of this action then hit me; I had never ridden it before, and had no idea how to even start the thing.

One point was crystal clear. I could never expect to catch the stallion on foot. I shouted to Irene to run down towards the horses and make plenty of noise, hoping this distraction would keep them on the move. 'Just keep them running if you can,' I shouted to her, as my next course of action was to catch Susan's pony in a nearby pad-dock. Grabbing the nearest saddle, I found that it was moments like this that you seemed to have five thumbs on each hand. Knowing how serving just one mare could be harmful to our stud book, the thought intensified my actions.

As I was about to do my 'Buffalo Bill' into the saddle, I became acutely aware of yet another deformity about me right then. I couldn't get my foot into the stirrup, my foot seemed too large; either that or I had my boots on the wrong feet or the stirrups were too small. It was unbelievable: in my haste, I had picked the only saddle off the wall with elastic stirrup straps. After what seemed an age, I finally mounted, and galloped off in a rush down the paddock. It briefly passed through my mind what I would do if the stallion happened to turn on us both, now he was in such an aggressive mood, and with me playing 'spoil-sport' in wanting to deprive him of what nature may well have in-tended.

Duane True chased the mares down a lane and out into another large paddock, and all I could do was keep on chasing him. I rea-soned that if he was kept on the move he could only do one thing at a time. This drama seemed to go on for ages. Boy, was I glad to hear a vehicle somewhere in the vicinity of our stables. Two men had come out to Glen-Garry Lodge to talk horse business. Seeing me on the pony chasing the stallion, they were quick to size up the situation. It was only with their help that the three of us were able to finally round up the stallion and return him to the stables with the only damage done being my aching shoulder and wounded pride. After we had finished, Irene was full of praise, saying, 'Gee, Margaret it was just amazing how fast you saddled that horse.' My answer was 'Yeah, not bad' as I looked down to check on my ten thumbs and oversize feet; I went out and checked the stirrup leathers later.

Thanking the two men profusely for their timely arrival and as-sistance, I then went over to the house with Irene to survey how se-vere the bite had been. Somehow it had been almost forgotten in the heat of the fray, but now it was hurting like mad. There was no time for me to head off to a doctor to have stitches inserted, so Irene gen-tly rubbed antiseptic cream into the wound before adding plaster to the area so that I could return and finish working Tricky One. Duane True had had his exercise for the day—and I felt as if I had mine, too.

Duane True was a handy performer for the stable without ever really making the grade. Tricky One, so well behaved that day, continued to win races for us. In the two years from November 1984, he notched up a further 19 successes, with 11 of these at Harold Park. On one occasion we had three horses in one race, and claimed the trifecta with Vic winning with Young Welvan, me second driving True Delight, and Joe Ilsley and Tricky One, third. Vic later sent Tricky One to Joe when he considered the horse would race sounder if prepared on the beach.

It was also during the mid-eighties that my pacer, Grand Delight, won 17 races for me, with 11 of these at Harold Park. This gelding was by Grand Thor, and the second foal from our Oaks winner Cheryl's Delight. The year before she had produced the handy True Delight, the pacer that had given us our first big win as breeders when he won a $60,000 race. For some reason Vic did not rate Grand Delight highly, with his only drive on the gelding unplaced, but he was one of my most favoured pacers to train and drive. This horse gave me great pleasure and singularly the most success. I drove him in all of his 17 wins.

The first city quinella Vic and I fought out was in 1980 when he won with Grand Thor and I chased him home driving Ragtime Boy. This was the first husband and wife quinella at Harold Park, and possibly on any metropolitan track in the country. We drove quinellas in other races later on, usually with Vic coming first. One quinella that puts a smile on my face was when Vic not only elected to drive the former South Australian Robber John in preference to Speed Partner, but told its connections he expected to lead all the way. Robber John had drawn well off the front, and my horse was awkwardly drawn off the second line. Vic took his well-supported horse to the front and punters must have been all smiles a long way from home. After having little choice but to bring up the rear with Speed Partner, there came a bit of shuffling-up ahead, and I was able to get through along the rails and have my horse right on Vic's back.

Because of Vic's outstanding horsemanship, you never expected to see horses do things wrong for him in a race, so imagine my surprise in the last lap when Robber John began hanging away from the inside rail despite all Vic's efforts to keep the horse straight. When the leader was almost one horse off the fence, I cheekily pushed Speed

Partner into the gap and then through, going on to win by a half-length. Having once been given a hostile reception when beating my husband on a favourite, I brought this horse back not knowing what to expect from the crowd. This time I was given a hearty reception. Perhaps Harold Park punters had come to know how Vic and I were honest and both of us always tried to win. Robber John won just one race in Sydney, and ironically that was the night I drove the horse.

Speed Partner and members of the Frost family came to have a special affinity for each other. This followed Glenn's decision in early 1986 to give up his work with the council's parks and gardens and join us at home training and driving pacers. His first winner came at Bankstown on June 30th that year, and the horse was Speed Partner. Many of this pacer's 21 wins were with Vic in the sulky, but I drove him for several races, and our son Glenn drove his first winner with the horse so aptly named.

When Garry, our younger son, left high school, his immediate ambition was to become a trainer, and we were glad to welcome him into the business. This was just prior to Glenn's decision not to pursue his career in horticulture and also remain home with the horses, and become a driver.

Garry, on the other hand, stated that he wanted only to become a trainer, having little interest in driving in races. He did love animals, and enjoyed taking a horse out to graze on the long and green grass that grew outside of what we called the 'pick' paddocks, where horses in full work would be put out for several hours each day. Normally this grass outside the paddocks would be wasted. Garry for once demonstrated patience when prepared to stand with a horse for many minutes so that it could enjoy some green grass.

Whether Glenn's decision to work with the horses and his successful debut as a driver changed Garry's previous desire to train, I will never know. But before Garry's 18th birthday he upset me greatly when he decided to leave home, and moved to live in Moss Vale. It had always been my hope that the boys would live at home until they married. I would have gladly gone and begged him to reconsider, but both Vic and Glenn advised me to leave him be to sort himself out, as they were well aware our younger son had some growing up to do. Garry took on bricklaying, becoming an apprentice to a Moss Vale contractor who took an instant liking to him, encouraging him to learn the trade. But Garry was a restless soul, and it wasn't long before he again went looking for something else to do.

He wasn't the only one in my family proving to be restless. After some years of having a difference of opinion over the merits of living in the country to moving closer to a large city, my parents had finally separated. Dad remained in his country home while Mother moved in to Wollongong. She had never really come to grips in this large country trying to adapt to life well away from a city. I was saddened by the break, but both had made it clear that was their choice.

TWENTY-ONE

The Loss of Glenn's Thunder

It is the desire of all standardbred owners to possess and race a champion. To achieve this, some have bought progeny of stallions with reputation from abroad, rather than those of locally bred stallions, at yearling sales. It seems that successful locally bred pacers do not get the support from breeders that one would expect at these sales. Those who do use a local sire usually do so for the purpose of racing what they breed. If you look through any race-book at our major tracks you will find much evidence of some Australian sires that have excellent percentages when compared with many of the much-vaunted imports.

Vic's numerous visits to the US, where he was part of the racing scene, had never led him to believe that one had to turn one's back on a colonial-bred stallion to expect good progeny. For instance, when Vic and I, along with Ron and Margaret Swan, obtained the mare Dottie's Cape, for her first foal we thought nothing of breeding her to our horse Ringo. The result of this produced a colt we named El Trevino, which won more than $20,000 before Vic took it to the US as part of one of the teams he raced there, prior to selling. The following six matings for Dottie's Cape were to Prince Jeldi, Local Ayr, and the imports Kentucky, Tarport Low, Thor Hanover and Massie, in that order. Three of these four imports were considered top class sires, but the best foal this mare ever produced was sired by one of our own Australian-bred stallions.

When we introduced Grand Thor to his first mares between campaigns in 1980, Vic and I were more than happy to breed Dottie's Cape to Grand Thor. From these nuptials a colt was foaled the following season on October 23, the same day as our son Glenn was having his 16th birthday. Several years earlier, its three-quarter brother, Glen's Country, had also been foaled on Glenn's birthday.

Dottie's Cape had a rather difficult time foaling her latest offspring, and we actually had to give her assistance. Perhaps it was the handling we gave this colt while being born, and then helping him to take his first steps, that would see him develop the most affectionate nature. As a yearling, before being broken in, he had no fear of us at all. We could let him out of the paddock and allow him to feed on the lush grass that grew around the stables, knowing he would be no trouble. On occasion he would even come into the feed room behind me when I was making up the feed for the horses, where he would put his head over my shoulder wanting a pat, or playing on my sympathy to let him put his head into the oat bin. It wasn't difficult to find a suitable name for him. Being foaled on Glenn's birthday and by Grand Thor (the God of thunder), it was natural to name him Glenn's Thunder.

His three-quarter brother Glen's Country had been a most promising youngster, winning $20,622 in stake money before being turned out for a spell to give him every chance to develop. One day when out checking over the stock we found him limping, with a swollen leg. The injury had already become infected, and despite all efforts over the following days, the vet finally advised us to have the pacer put down. He had shown so much promise. But as good as Glen's Country could have been, this latest colt from Dottie's Cape would more than match him in every way. Some breeders spend a lifetime trying to produce a top horse. From limited opportunities in the breeding barn, we had bred several very useful metropolitan performers. Now we had come up with a colt that promised so much.

In keeping with our policy to race our own two-year-olds sparingly, the racing debut of Glenn's Thunder was delayed until March, then he won at his second start on April 16th at Penrith. He went on and won the Breeders Plate at Harold Park, returning to Penrith to win a Sire Stakes. The following season he won the prestigious R.C. Simpson Sprint at Harold Park and the Penrith Derby. On October 1st 1985, I got to drive Glenn's Thunder for the first and only time, winning with him at Harold Park. This was at a time when I was enjoying good success with Grand Delight, a pacer competitive enough to be in some classics. As good as I knew Grand Delight was, when driving Glenn's Thunder that night I found the difference in power and speed to be quite awesome.

A highlight of his four-year-old campaign was winning the Australasian Four-Year-Old Championship, now the Four & Five-Year-Old Championship. Vic was keen to give him a break from racing, but an invitation from the WA Trotting Association to contest their Group 1 four-year-old classic, the Golden Nugget, was most tempting. By the time we decided to take him and Grand Delight across to Perth, Glenn's Thunder had won 29 races—15 of these at Harold Park Paceway, and four down at Moonee Valley.

Vic and I flew down to Melbourne with the two pacers on a cargo plane on the Tuesday afternoon, where I was then to connect with a passenger plane to Perth the following morning, with the cargo plane taking the horses to the west scheduled to be not far behind. However, mechanical trouble prevented the cargo plane from leaving Melbourne that day after my flight had taken off, so Vic phoned the WATA office in Perth to explain the delay, hopeful that the horses would be leaving on Thursday morning. He arranged for a truck to take him and the two horses to a track where they could be given light work.

At this point, both horses seemed better off than me, as my luggage was back on the cargo plane stranded in Melbourne, leaving me with only the clothes on my back. A quick shopping spree was arranged for me in Perth to buy the things to last until my luggage arrived. But luck was still against the horses, with it being announced that the plane could not leave for Perth until Friday—the day of their heats for the Golden Nugget. Vic wanted to scratch the horses there and then, forget the race and go home. But with me already in Perth, he was persuaded to press ahead. Perth officials had also attracted Vanderport from Victoria, but it was Glenn's Thunder that publicity claimed was the champion four-year-old of the eastern states, and was the pre-race favourite.

If the unexpected delay in Melbourne was not bad enough to interfere with the preparation of two finely tuned horses, Vic became concerned when transporting them to the training track, when Glenn's Thunder, quite out of character, became upset and began lashing out and kicking the truck wall. He had never done this before. Now, travelling to and from the track for four days in a very large and unfamiliar truck had become a little too much for this young stallion that usually took everything in his stride.

Soon after arriving in Perth, Glenn's Thunder went off his feed and stopped eating his lucerne, which was most unusual for him. This did not prevent Vic from driving him to win his heat at Gloucester

Park easily; Grand Delight and me finishing fifth. Disaster struck the following day, when Glenn's Thunder pricked his hoof with a shoeing nail, which had been dropped on the floor of the complex where our horses were stabled. It was not a deep wound and was not considered serious, but Vic treated it carefully with an ointment as a precaution.

There were further heats the following Wednesday for those still hoping to qualify for the final, and Grand Delight produced his best to win. It was a very rewarding win for me, but it was a close finish. It looked as though I was going to lose with two furlongs to go; Grand Delight hung out, letting a horse up on the inside, presenting it with a good chance of beating me. My horse, however, fought back to score, and in winning that race we broke the two-minute barrier. Both our pacers had made it into the Golden Nugget. Vic and I became the first husband and wife to qualify two pacers for the final of a Perth classic, and I was the first woman to do so.

When campaigning horses away from home in environments strange to them, additional care and attention is taken for their well-being. Despite the early treatment Vic had given to the nail prick in the hoof of Glenn's Thunder, bacteria surprisingly became active in the area. The vet later explained that this was almost certainly due to the horse being stressed by the delay in Melbourne, leading to the suppression of its immune system, thus allowing the development of laminitis.

His problem had been added to because of possible dehydration during the plane trip and the fact that he had gone off his lucerne and would only eat grain. This leads to a phosphorous imbalance, leaving him more susceptible to the infection. Glenn's Thunder had more going against him than we realised. He became a very sick horse within a few days, and had to be scratched from the final. I was most reluctant to leave him to fulfill my obligation to drive Grand Delight that Friday night. Vic stayed with him until the time of the Golden Nugget, then came to see the race. I came fifth to Vanderport, driven by Anne Frawley. We then rushed back to the stables to be with our horse again.

Vic returned to Exeter, to carry on the business at home. For the next three weeks I slept in the back of a Kombi-van to be with Glenn's Thunder, occasionally falling asleep in the paddock alongside him. We made a shade that we could carry around, so that when he was able to move, which was not often, we were able to keep shade over him. It was so hot in Perth in the first days of January that he often had to be cooled off. I carried water to him for this purpose and for him to drink.

After several days, Charlie Stuart, the vet who attended him, operated on the nerve to his foot to deaden the pain, which must have been almost unbearable after the coronet band had broken away (the coronet band joins the foot to the leg of a horse). The vet had previously been unsuccessful when he attempted to freeze the nerve, hoping to avoid an operation. We were praying this would work, and had a glimmer of hope, even when the horse was so sick.

The vet, his wife and people around the vet's clinic were supportive to me. I had several meals at the vet's, I showered and ate breakfast in his clinic, and sometimes they would watch the horse while I slept. They would often come and keep me company in my vigil with Glenn's Thunder. The horse's struggle for recovery had endeared him to all those who came in contact with him. I was comforted by several get well cards for the horse, sent by wellwishers whom I never knew.

Ross Oliveri is a well-known, successful and respected trainer-driver in Western Australia. Ross and Jan loaned me blankets and some warmer clothes when the weather cooled. My wardrobe did not lend itself to the vagaries of Perth weather, because I had not made allowance for an extended stay. They would often pick me up and take me to their home for a well-cooked meal and give me the pleasure of their company and that of their small children.

Ray Holloway, one-time secretary of the sport in Adelaide before moving to Perth to take office there, was then the Racing Manager of Gloucester Park. In this period I became good friends with both Ray and his wife Golda. On one of those hot days Perth is well known for, Golda was sitting with me sharing the canvas covering Glenn's Thunder. We were talking about life in general, when suddenly, with no warning at all, the wind came up like a tornado, lifting Golda up in a fierce rush of wind and dust. She simply disappeared before my eyes in the cloud of dust. Being about five and a half stone in weight, dripping wet, the wind had picked her up like a piece of paper.

'Golda, where are you, where are you?' I called out in alarm:

A little voice with a quiver in it replied, 'Here I am'. It had come from the other side of the fence. It was incredible. I thought I had finally cracked, and found it difficult to comprehend how she had landed on the other side of a four-foot fence whether she had been blown over it, or had been driven through it by the wind. Yet, there she was on the grass on the other side. I ran over and helped her up, checking to see if she was hurt. She was a little shaken and sore, but not injured, thank goodness! As the wife of one of the most respected officials in Australian harness racing, I imagine that if that story had been told around Gloucester Park, both Ray and Golda would have been in for some teasing. The horse had withstood the mini tornado, and I have often wondered what poor Glenn's Thunder thought of the antics and shouts of these two silly women.

To entice me home, Vic entered Grand Delight in a race at Harold Park. I always drove this horse, and I felt he did not go so well for anyone else. He was a little cunning, and you had to get used to handling him, Vic drove the horse once, and even though he was a top horseman, Grand Delight galloped at the start for him. I always felt this was because Vic never liked Grand Delight, and the horse could feel it.

Grand Delight evened the score by beating Vic driving No Tie at Harold Park on 14th April 1981. Vic had led for most of the journey and I had been caught three back on the fence. I managed to push through and get a clear run in just enough time to beat Vic, and I didn't feel the least bit sorry for him, but did a little for No Tie's owner, Eric Gilleland. He knew that we both always drove to win, so he wasn't upset with me.

Glenn's Thunder had to be left in Perth. But because he was now able to stand, it gave us hope that he would survive this crisis. I was home for about two weeks when we received that fateful telephone call from Charlie Stewart saying that the pedal bone had protruded through the foot. There was no alternative but to put this magnificent four-year-old down. It was no easy task for Charlie, as he too had become attached to the horse and was well aware of the great fight he had so valiantly put up.

Glenn's Thunder had fought hard for 42 days after nearly dying twice in 24 hours in the first week. Horses normally can't stand much pain, and usually give in. But not this horse. He fought hard all the way. An interesting article in the Perth press quoted Charlie as saying, 'The grand horse deserved to live. It was so hard for me, having to be the one to end the life of such a great horse, but I had no alternative. If I hadn't, Glenn's Thunder would have died anyway, and in extreme pain.' Charlie Stewart went to the trouble of burying the horse beneath the trees on his property.

The death of Glenn's Thunder affected us greatly. It was about 12 months before we could even stand to look at a video of him racing or even talk about him without shedding a tear. He had the potential of becoming a champion and possibly a good sire of pacers. He had been treated carefully since we had broken him in as a yearling and had been raced sparingly, receiving all the love and care a horse can expect.

In the season of his passing he was voted New South Wales Harness Horse of the Year. Vic, Susan, Glenn and I went to the Hilton hotel in Sydney to be presented with the award. The actual trophy was a large framed picture taken after the horse had won the Menangle Cup, and I had perched myself on the side of the gig to save a walk back to the stables when the course photographer had snapped this picture.

That year we won five awards in all, presented by the Minister of Sport, Mr Michael Cleary. The other trophies were New South Wales Broodmare of the Year (Dottie's Cape); Vic and I were the Leading Owners; and Vic had again won both the Harold Park premierships for drivers and trainers. That award for Horse of the Year was precious to the family, as Glenn's Thunder had been a very special horse to us.

After the loss of Glenn's Thunder, Grand Delight went on to win more races at Harold Park for me, totalling 16 in all, and about $70,000 in prize money, not bad for an impish horse. He won nine races at Harold Park in one season and one at Gloucester Park, making it 16 metropolitan wins. This put him into second place in the award for the most wins at Harold Park in one season. He led for most of the season, but was just beaten by one or two wins at the finish. When his handicap made it difficult to win any more races at Harold Park, we sent him to Arthur Lawrence, a friend, to race in Brisbane.

Arthur had helped us build our stables in Dapto and came every day to help us with the horses, until he and his wife May, who was a Godmother to Susan, left to live in Brisbane. May was a lovely, quiet lady who suffered with a breathing problem and died several years ago. Arthur has never lost his interest in horses; he still owns a horse or two and for quite a while after Vic moved to Moobal he helped Vic with his horses.

This tragic loss was followed by another great loss for the family. Vic and I had gone to a fundraising auction at Canberra, necessitating an overnight stay. On returning to the farm we were met by an anxious-looking Glenn, who told us that Dad had suffered a heart attack and had been rushed to the hospital in Wollongong. Quickly grabbing a few essentials, I made all haste there to find my father in the intensive care ward.

For the next couple of days I stayed at the hospital, only leaving his side during the day to have a quick meal. The signs for a recovery seemed promising until on the fourth day he suffered a massive heart attack. Doctors told me he was then brain dead. I continued to sit there holding his hand, quite convinced there was still some feeling, a kind of bonding between us as I held his hand. Feeling that he was holding on for me, I told him that I loved him very much but it was all right for him to go, as I would be okay. It was only then, when I left the room for a few minutes to grab something to eat, that he finally gave up the struggle. George MacDonald Paterson died on the 11th May 1988.

There was so much I had inherited from my father that always made me believe our relationship was special. My sudden loss also made me think that I should have made even greater efforts to visit him more often in those four years he had been living alone. It is a regret I still nurse to this day. I made a promise to myself then not to ignore my mother, especially as she had then developed a serious loss of memory, a condition that would only worsen. After my father died, I suffered a lot of guilt for not giving him more of my time; the quick visits had always finished too soon for both of us. His face lit up when he opened his door to find me there, his love was so evident. Dad looked forward to my visits and we both enjoyed our time together, as brief as it was. I loved Dad and so wished to spend more time with him. My family have always meant a lot to me and I wanted to see them and be with them as often as I could. For, as much as my hectic lifestyle prevented my visiting family members on the coast, there was that pressure from home. This was an area of friction between Vic and me.

During my grief, I made a vow to myself that I would not let this situation develop with my mother. The direction my life has taken in these recent years has made it easier to give her much more of my time. As it has turned out, her circumstances now require more of my time.

Visiting the family took half a day at the very least when Dad was living in Dapto, Mum in Wollongong, Neena at Albion Park and Catherine near Warilla, which involved travelling about two to three hours to reach them all, and then I had to drive home, another hour away. Vic's family consisted of a sister, Pauline, and brother, Peter, and his mother and father, all living in the Dubbo area, so his visits to them were infrequent, although I encouraged him to visit them as often as possible. These visits were restricted to holiday periods when we could go with the children, as a family. So I was seeing more of my family than Vic was of his, and I felt that he was sometimes jealous of the close association I maintained with my family.

For our special family celebrations, Catherine and her family would travel to Exeter and she could be counted on to be the life of the party. She would always insist on helping with any last-minute preparations and clearing up during the night. Catherine was smitten by the Paterson's curse also; she had to be in there helping.

TWENTY-TWO

Tile business goes on the Slate

Garry's cousin Karen, my sister Catherine's eldest daughter, had earlier married Bruno Komel. They then operated a small business in Bowral, Highland Tile and Slate, a branch of his Illawarra Tile and Slate in Wollongong. Bruno kindly offered Garry a job working in the tile business. Not long after he began there, Bruno placed the business on the market. Thinking that we could help our unsettled son find his niche in life, Vic and I purchased the tile and slate operation for Garry in May 1988, hoping to establish him in a sound business.

A local boy was given a job as assistant in the tile shop; he presented himself well and gave the impression of being able to be trusted. He learned the work well and was able to be left in charge. Garry became less interested and was often absent, thus leaving the boy alone much of the time. This presented a temptation too great to resist and the boy began stealing from the shop, and went as far as cashing forged cheques. He had been allowed to do the bookwork, thus making his stealing a lot easier.

The problem came to my attention on notification of a huge overdraft, but not before a lot of money had been taken from the business and the shop left deep in debt.

Many hours were spent studying the accounts, and then I had to telephone every person for whom the cheques were supposedly written, to find those which had been forged. I also discovered that no cash was ever banked. We placed the situation into the hands of the police, but this was of little help with the overdraft. Only a small portion of the total figure was recovered. We could only prove that he had stolen the cheques, because he blamed Garry for the stolen cash. On the point of the cash, he had us, since it came down to his word against Garry's; it became a stand off and was unable to be proven.

Glenn was helping with the training of the horses and sharing the race driving with his father, and Vic had reduced his workload, a kind of semi-retirement. Therefore, the number of horses in work at Glen-Garry Lodge was less than we normally trained. It seems that with young Glenn not yet a proven horseman, owners were a little reluctant to leave their horses with him. To allow me to take a break from the horses to work at the tile shop, in the hope of getting the business back on its feet, Vic and Glenn took over all duties with the stable, and this gave Glenn the opportunity to race the horses I would have driven.

It was not easy working at the tile shop, trying to tidy up the mess the books were in, order the stock, organise tiling jobs, and serve the customers. Vic took on the task of driving our tile truck to Sydney once a week to collect the orders. With a great deal of earnest endeavour and some sleepless nights, I managed to turn things around, making the business a success. We added to our small staff a young man, Brett Daley, who was to become our son-in-law. When Susan was 19 she had begun going steady with Brett, a rather shy and reserved young man whom we respected and found extremely reliable.

Brett was doing only casual work at this time, so we gave him an apprenticeship as a tiler, hopefully to give him a trade. He eventually became a good tiler and did a lot of work for the shop. Unfortunately, we sold the business before he had finished his apprenticeship and the new owners didn't retain him. However, he had established a good reputation with some builders and secured ample tiling work. Later he joined the family business again, but this time he turned his skill to horse training with Glenn.

While we owned the shop, Garry and Glenn played indoor cricket at a complex a block away. Cricket was not my 'cup of tea'—I never really cared to watch the game let alone play it—but both Vic and I were roped in occasionally, to fill in for missing players. I can't claim to have excelled at the game; I didn't even know the rules, but we enjoyed some really great times on these nights, and I can at least claim to have given them a good laugh.

Eventually it was all too apparent that Garry just had no interest in the tile shop, and it was not my wish to continue as manager, so we sold it.

While I was working at the shop with Garry I managed to talk him into returning home. He began to work training horses for his brother Glenn. They had always been very close as brothers, playing sport and often fishing together, but an argument developed between them. This may have precipitated Garry's decision to leave home once more, to live with his girlfriend Lisa in Moss Vale, where he was welcomed into the family home. When Susan left home to live with Brett, I did not have the same concerns that Garry had given me when he moved out to live in Moss Vale, previously.

A blacksmith Vic called in to shoe one of the horses in 1988 was chatting away with him and happened to mention some blocks of land that were up for sale on Magnetic Island, out of Townsville. According to him, this was the only island around Queensland where one could purchase land that allowed you to develop your own 'island paradise'. Vic thought it sounded like a great investment, both money-wise and as a future retirement proposition. He flew up to the island (courtesy of the real estate company) to inspect these blocks. So impressed was he that he decided to purchase two of them, thinking he could make some capital gain and eventually retire there.

So enthusiastic was he to get moving on it, that he organised some friends to help Glenn with the horses, and Vic and I took three weeks off to get the project moving. We were joined in this project by our good friends Kevin and Ruby Wells, from the Sydney suburb of Mascot. Kevin was the manager of a cement company. We made use of the truck from the tile business, loaded it up with tiles and tools, and then headed north on the long journey to Townsville, crossing by ferry to Magnetic Island.

It had earlier been arranged for a Townsville builder to lay the concrete slab, then have a Queensland-built kit home sent to the island to be ready when we arrived. This would have given us the best part of three weeks to erect the kit home. We arrived on the ferry from Townsville to find that absolutely nothing had been done or delivered. That first week was wasted chasing up a builder, the tradesmen required, and getting the equipment we needed.

The four of us then worked like slaves for two weeks, laying the cement slab, then erecting the hardwood frame. The boys had managed to find a bricklayer and we became his labourers. Our 3pm Friday departure was fast drawing near, requiring us to work at a frantic pace. It was only after boarding the ferry that we were able to put up our feet and relax for the first time in more than a fortnight. This was Kevin's annual holiday, which says something about the man.

Vic and I returned to the island on several occasions to finish the home. It was well appointed and we were very happy with the final result of our combined efforts. At first we made good use of the local club, situated only a couple of blocks away, where we showered until our kitchen and bathroom were in service. The house was left unoccupied for long periods at a time and was always left open. The ferry was the only means of getting on and off the island, apart from a private boat, and this was some assurance that all would be well there.

After the ordeal and experience in building the first house on the island, we eventually screwed up the courage to build on the second lot around the corner. To prevent hold-ups this time, we took the kit home there ourselves. I always seemed to finish up the one to do the painting, and have never been good at this trade, always managing to get as much paint on myself as the walls.

We were still at Horse Shoe Bay working on the second house when Kevin phoned from Sydney to tell us that his elder son Jimmy had been crossing a road and was struck by a car, and was fighting for his life in hospital. A talented diesel mechanic and a keen sportsman, Jimmy had lived a robust life. Jimmy survived but, tragically, he is now a paraplegic, with brain damage, and confined to a wheelchair for the remainder of his life. Kevin and Ruby were devastated. But both they and their other two children, Debbie and Robert, have remained steadfastly devoted to his care. Many changes had to be made around their home to accommodate for Jimmy's handicap. They have purchased everything necessary to make Jimmy's life as pleasant as possible, from building a spa to adding a crane at the edge of the swimming pool, as an aid for Jim's therapy.

Our dream of making our fortune and retiring to Magnetic Island never eventuated. In fact, we later sold both homes for about the price they had cost us to build, real value for the new owners considering the amount of labour that had gone into them.

TWENTY-THREE

The Joys of Westburn Grant

Millions of dollars are spent at yearling sales each year, with buyers hoping to buy a champion or at least a horse capable of winning races, but the best pacer we ever had would be the result of a free service!

Much the same can be said for Glenn's Thunder and Grand Delight. They were the offspring of Grand Thor, a stallion we trained and had served six mares with during a spell from his racing program. Three of the best horses we ever owned were born on our property and cost only the veterinary fees for their birth to obtain! Glenn's Thunder would definitely have gone on to win more cup races had he lived, and Grand Delight won about $70,000, thus indicating that we don't always have to pay millions for top horses. Chance does play a big part in the breeding game; as it has been said, each horse is a four-legged lottery ticket!

Some years earlier, New Zealand's Barney and Colleen Breen had given us Jan's Daughter to train. Barney had selected Vic because of his reputation as a straight-shooter. It was a happy association with the Breens, who later sent us their mare Westburn Vue, a good race mare that won some nice races at Bankstown, Bulli, Penrith and Menangle. She actually broke a pedal bone during the running of the 1980 Bankstown Cup, still managing to finish fourth to Gammalite.

The competition to attract good quality mares to any sire is keen, even fierce. After Queensland businessman/breeder Kevin Seymour imported Land Grant, he offered numerous free services to breeders who owned proven or well-bred mares that would enable this son of Meadow Skipper every chance to succeed. Among those to accept this offer were Barney and Colleen Breen. The mare they sent to this stallion was Westburn Vue, a daughter of the fine broodmare sire Lumber Dream. She herself had taken a record of 1:58 before breaking down.

The result of that service was Westburn Grant.

We always gave young horses three or four preparation programs as yearlings, with a little spell in between. The preparations consisted of being taught to tie up and lead, to be mouthed, to accept the hopples and harness, learn to pace with long reins, then, later, accept the gig and driver and pace on the track. We could usually tell by the end of these preparations whether a horse showed any promise. When they have had sufficient work to be pushed for a furlong or two, they will usually demonstrate their speed capability. It is not often that a yearling does not show what potential it has at this stage, and then produces it later. It can happen, however.

Right from a foal this one had been gentle and easy to manage when broken-in by Glenn. He was born with no white marks on his body. But as a foal out in the paddock, he had been soaked by rain, then scalded by a hot sun. This left little scabs all over his back and led to us calling him 'Spot' around the stable.

The colt took to pacing readily and was blessed with no bad habits. One morning when I was working another horse at the same time Glenn was on the track with Westburn Grant, he called to me: "This is the one!" Even then he was convinced this colt would make into a fine pacer.

Glenn drove Westburn Grant three times as a two-year-old, winning all three starts, including a classic race, the Globe Derby Mile at Harold Park, in February 1989. Westburn Grant had shown that he had well above average ability with these races, and was to be prepared for a big campaign next season.

Glenn had only been driving for three years, thus his lack of racing experience gave cause for Barney and Colleen to feel that Vic would be much more experienced in handling the budding star in his forthcoming career. Glenn was sidelined at this time, and unable to drive for about three months after sustaining a broken wrist following a motorcycle accident.

I felt sorry for Glenn, but realised that Vic, being one of the best trainer-drivers anywhere in the country, would be the one to develop the colt's racing career. This was a fact I had to contend with throughout the whole of my racing career. Vic had decided to 'retire' a short time earlier, preferring to become a part-time performer. He had planned to help Glenn get established as a trainer-driver by himself. But it was Westburn Grant's outstanding ability that actually enticed Vic back into full-time driving again.

During his season as a three-year-old, Spot gave us a nasty surprise when we discovered that he had developed sore feet and could suffer much pain with them. Vic took him to Camden University and was told by the head veterinarian there in no uncertain terms, to 'Get another meal ticket, or move to the beach.'

To be told: 'If you continue to work the horse on hard tracks, you will not have a horse to race, because his feet just will not stand up to it' was grim news indeed, for the four of us. We discussed the problem at length and decided that we would not give up that easily. Spot's ability was all too apparent, so we were prepared to take any steps necessary to give him every chance to develop.

Spot had to be trained on a beach somewhere, but this was no easy hurdle to overcome. Our complex at Exeter was at least an hour's drive from Seven Mile Beach, the nearest one, which was near the little town of Berry on the South Coast. This beach is used by Kevin, Terry, and Chris Robinson from Berry, a top harness and thoroughbred racing family. Kevin, the father, was a top pacing trainer and driver for many years, but diverted to the thoroughbred sport several years ago, leaving the pacing side to the boys.

Vic travelled there every second day to fast-work the horse, and used special boots that covered the whole hoof for jogging on our own track. This would have been almost impossible to do if we had still had the number of horses in training that we had before Vic decided to ease down. Opportunities arose when I was able to go to the beach with Vic. This gave me a chance to exercise while he worked the horse. On completion of Spot's fast work, I would unharness him and ride him into the salt water as further treatment for his feet. This gave Vic some time out for his exercise.

On the days when we wanted to time Spot, to estimate how his preparation was coming along, I would sit on the side of the gig while Vic drove slowly along the beach watching a little device attached to one of the gig wheels, which measured out his required distances. When the mile, half mile, two or three furlong marks, were reached, I would jump off and make marks in the sand, clearly enough for Vic to see as he was passing them during Spot's workout. Invariably, Vic continued his measuring up to the two mile mark, which required me having to run the two miles back to the starting point. I often wondered whether his training program included me as well as Spot. Either way, it kept me trim.

As a three-year-old, Spot raced 13 times for 11 wins, including the New South Wales and Victoria Derbies, and it was then that he made his first plane trip. This was to race in the New Zealand Derby and the John Brandon Series. We took him to Prebbleton, a little town near Christchurch, where Barney and Colleen Breen lived.

Westburn Grant travelled on a cargo plane, secured in a wooden container, which had similar partitions to that of a horse float, but much narrower. This prevented the horse from moving around too much while the plane was in flight.

Vic and I had some experience in airfreighting horses, when we travelled with them to the United States to race and sell there. Therefore, this being Spot's first trip in an aircraft, and with our previous experience with airfreighting, we were expecting some nervousness, but Spot, to our pleasant surprise, took it in his stride—accepted it in his usual calm manner, and acted like a seasoned traveller. Air transport can be extremely frightening for horses, due to the rapid ascending and descending. For safety reasons, occasionally a horse has to be put down if it becomes too restive.

Many horses are sedated for the flights, but we were very fortunate, never having the need arise where Spot required anything to sedate him. He stayed calm and relaxed the whole trip, even dozing off at times. Vic always travelled alongside him, and I whenever possible, in the cargo hold on every flight he made, and to watch this beautiful horse in transit filled me with an intensely warm feeling and a real sense of pride in this unusual animal. If it is possible to love an animal as much as a human, I loved Spot.

Westburn Grant was so impressive in his campaign in New Zealand that he was named the New Zealand Three-Year-Old of the Year, a great achievement for a visiting horse. He won the New Zealand Derby, and the heat and final of the John Brandon Triple Crown Series in effortless style, and thousands of New Zealand hearts into the bargain. Of course, the fact that Colleen and Barney Breen, the breeders and half owners of Westburn Grant were local, made it a popular win for many in the district, as the Breens were highly respected enthusiasts. Vic and I stayed with Colleen and Barney for about three weeks and Spot was well housed in one of Barney's stables. The short stay proved to be a well-earned holiday for the three of us, though it was not so leisurely for Spot.

There was a private track nearby where Vic was able to take the colt for some light jogging work. In order to minimise the risk to Spotty's feet, I would walk the track, taking on the job of picking up any stones or obstacles from its surface. Barney was often asked later, by the owner of the track, 'When is that beaut "stone picker-upper" coming back?' This was a job I always seemed to do automatically, whenever and wherever we worked the horse, even on the beaches.

Spot was named the New South Wales Harness Horse of the Year as a three-year-old, after a remarkable program of racing. He was defeated twice only, winning 11 out of 13 starts, and two placings. One of his defeats was when he raced at Bankstown in the Australian Derby, a month after flying back from New Zealand. As well as appearing a little tired, he had to endure a very hard run when pressed by Rockleigh Victory, one of the late Vinnie Knight's best horses. Spot took out third place. Vinnie Knight was a well-known Victorian trainer-driver, and tough opposition; he gave no quarter and asked for none.

Rockleigh Victory had defeated Westburn Grant once before, placing him second, contesting the Victorian Harness Racing Cup. Westburn Grant had his moment, during the running of the New South Wales Derby, when again these two horses were pitched together. Westburn Grant drew number two barrier, Rockleigh Victory drew the barrier directly behind Spot. From the outset, Vic took our horse straight to the front and Rockleigh Victory came up quickly to challenge for the lead, heading into the first turn. The pace was on, and during the last two laps both horses were running close to 29 second quarters, but with 600 metres to go Vic gave Westburn Grant his head. It was home time for them both; the field was left trailing some 20 metres behind. He broke the three-year-old track record that night.

The bright spot of 1990 was Glenn's marriage to Toni Urquart, a school friend. They made their vows in Saint Aiden's Church at Exeter on the 8th April 1990. Toni, who was so shy and quiet, had once written in a school magazine, as part of the class's set project, that her ambition in life was to go out with the 'Frost Boys'. It was not so important at first which one, as she admired both, but she was relentlessly teased about the article by schoolmates.

Toni actually went out with Garry a few times and then married the other 'Frost'—Glenn. Toni is extremely pretty and made a beautiful bride, Glenn looked handsome in his grey suit, as did Garry, who was his groomsman. Thankfully we have a video of the wedding, which has Garry in it.

Toni is one who is happy at home with her family, not needing the bright lights. On the other hand, Glenn is one who enjoys life and action, possessing a real adventerous streak in his make-up. Her mother Colleen and father Ken live in Exeter and are her mainstay and constant babysitters, especially now that I am no longer living close by. I used to drop in to their home for a cup of tea, but now only see them on occasional visits home, if they are there. Toni worked since leaving school at White's Store in Moss Vale, where she was a valued employee. She gave this up to support Glenn in his stables, at first having to learn to trust horses before she could learn to handle them.

As a three-year-old, Westburn Grant became known as 'The Prince of the Paceway', and a recognised champion throughout Australia and even was known to some in the US. A computer simulated series of races was carried out by an American journalist named Bob Wolff, using information on 64 of the world's best pacers, which included our horse. On the completion of the computerised series, Spotty was rated (even if narrowly) the second best pacer in the world. Even though this was a hypothetical exercise, and none of these races ever took place, it did no harm to Westburn Grant's reputation. This was reported in the New South Wales Harness Racing Gazette, July 1992.

Fans began to gather at the race venues whenever Westburn Grant was appearing, and clubs were always very keen to add him to their program, in an effort to be assured of a good following and turnover for that meeting.

Because Westburn Grant was so popular, and did not have a trace of meanness in his nature, I began the practice of taking him over to the fence that separated the public from the horses. This allowed the people waiting there to see him, and gave them the chance to pat him and take photos, if they wished.

Spot was a truly remarkable horse. Even immediately after winning a championship race, and not yet cooled off, he would stand quietly and lower his head gently down, to allow children to reach out and pat him. On most occasions when Vic brought him back to the stalls after a race, he would tell him to 'Stay!'; untied, he just stood there, like a big dog being told to sit. There were several people taking off his gear one night, when one of them dropped the cart, a shaft on either side of Spot, onto the asphalt, with a resounding bang! Most other horses would have bolted, but ours never moved. In all my years of travelling to race meetings, I haven't ever witnessed this phenomenon from any other horse, before or since.

At some country meetings there was no separating fence between the horses and the crowds. There were times, in such situations, when I was able to take Westburn Grant off to the side for a quick graze, if the grass was green and lush, and children would come over out of the crowd to touch him. Some wanted their photo taken with Spot, and we lifted them up onto his back, at times, for that special picture, to the delight of the parents as well as the children.

As inconceivable as this may seem, keeping in mind that he was a stallion, and stallions are usually not noted for their gentle temperament, he displayed exceptional care with his movements when children were around. He would even lift and hold a leg up if a child came too close, to prevent his treading on their feet, or bumping them. The horse seemed to know what was required of him in those circumstances and responded accordingly.

It became almost customary for me to allow the public to have close contact with him, wherever we went. He became known as 'The People's Horse', and he seemed to enjoy the attention people gave to him. Spot was such a treasure to us, and because of the great admiration that the racegoers had for him, we felt we could share him. The response of the people was overwhelming, and I believe that this was a factor that gave this horse a fighting edge, enabling him to bring forth his greatest efforts of strength and endurance in times of desperation. Westburn Grant never let us down.

Vic and I went shopping in Myer in Melbourne one morning. As I handed my credit card to the assistant to pay for my purchases, the girl, after reading the name, looked up in surprise and said, 'Oh you're those people from Sydney whose horse is racing tonight.' We were just as surprised as she, at the interest that people had taken in Westburn Grant.

Most of the races he won as a three-year-old were classics, and carried big prize money. Consequently, he became a millionaire pacer at the tender age of three. By the time Westburn Grant was a four-year-old he had added numerous Grand Circuit races to his list of wins. The Miracle Mile is the most prestigious race one could wish a horse to win; even being selected for it is a privilege. It requires a strong horse with brilliant speed and endurance to take on this event. The race is over a mile and is restricted to six horses, and only the best horses racing in that year are invited to enter. Spot was invited to enter this race three times in consecutive years, and won the first two.

There is always very keen competition among the trainer-drivers throughout Australia and New Zealand, for an invitation to enter the Miracle Mile. The task of selecting the field carries with it a great responsibility for officials from Harold Park, to keep close observation of all eligible horses racing in every state, to ensure that the best six are invited to compete.

When the Miracle Mile was run on the 24th November 1989 at Harold Park, I was in London, on business for the tile shop we had bought for Garry, and a reporter from Harold Park contacted me in the hotel where I was staying and allowed me to listen to the race over the telephone.

It was a wonderful and thrilling experience, standing there with a phone in my hand, so far away from where it was all happening, waiting for the great race to commence. I am sure the reporter was confident that Spot would win and wanted to hear my screams of delight and get my reaction to the win, first hand. I was very impressed by this most generous gesture offered me, and I can't satisfactorily describe what a joy it was to hear the broadcast, as the race was in progress.

To hear the result there and then was so much better than being told later. The reporter was by no means disappointed by my reaction to Westburn Grant's victory that night. It was morning where I was, and should anyone have been passing the door of my room at that precise moment when Spotty passed the winning post at Harold Park, I have no doubt that I would have had a visit from the boys of Scotland Yard, in no time flat. Vic was even brought to the phone quickly for me to congratulate him, before the presentations.

Westburn Grant had taken all before him, his talent was well known throughout Australia. His popularity in the pacing circles had made him a big drawcard anywhere he appeared and, as a result, racing club secretaries worked very hard to attract him to their states for the big races. The Western Australian Trotting Association persisted in their efforts to persuade Vic to nominate the horse for the Golden Nugget, the very race for which we had taken Glenn's Thunder to Perth. Alan Parker from Gloucester Park, Perth, would have to get first prize for his efforts in 1989. Vic had told him after Glenn's Thunder's death there that he would never return to Perth with a horse, for any race. As Spot was regarded as the best pacer racing, Alan was desperate to get him to race in the Golden Nugget that year, but was reluctant to ring Vic to ask. It took a great deal of courage to make *that phone call* and Alan was surprised and pleased when Vic told him he would give it some consideration, after talking it over with the other owners.

The large prizemoney on offer was too much to dismiss lightly and after long discussions with Barney and Colleen Breen, we decided it was worth taking the risk. The decision, based on the fact that it would be a very remote possibility for history to repeat itself.

Alan was under great pressure while waiting for Vic's decision, before he could make the necessary arrangements, but to add salt to the wound the local newspaper ran a headline saying, 'Frost No to Perth'. He knew that the writer of the article could not have had first-hand information, and now he just had to sweat on Vic's decision.

Alan was told next time he rang that we would make the trip, but we wanted to race in the Max Treuer Memorial at Bankstown on the Monday night, 4th December, and could only fly out on the Wednesday. This caused a major problem for Perth as the airlines were only flying once a week from Melbourne at that time, due to the airline strike, and that flight was on Monday, which made Wednesday impossible, under the circumstances. Most people would have accepted the fact that it was just not possible to fly the horse to Perth, and accept defeat, but Alan went to unbelievable lengths, and actually managed to get Ansett to put on a special cargo flight on the Wednesday for one horse!

Of course it took many phone calls and meetings. He had to make a special trip into the city, to pay the huge fee in advance, directly into the airline's bank account. He said that a Melbourne Cup galloper had wanted this special flight, but according to Alan, Spot was more important than any 'trumped up galloper'. He derived great delight from being able to phone the local paper with his news, 'Frost Yes to Perth'.

'Being able to have Westburn Grant in Perth was worth every cent and every bit of effort,' he said afterwards. Because Spot won both the heat and final of the race, the club received some excellent publicity from the great horse. The fact that our luck had changed for the better and that all had gone smoothly, gave Alan Parker and Ray Holloway great satisfaction, for they had been almost as worried as Vic and me, having the fear that disaster could strike again. They were so relieved and elated by our success. We certainly were thankful and delighted, not just because Spot had won the Max Treuer race before leaving for Perth, and then the Golden Nugget in Perth, but also by the fact that all was well with Westburn Grant.

Given the tragic episode with Glenn's Thunder four years before, we were a little anxious and cautious. On this occasion, however, all went well. In the running of the race, Spot set the fastest half-mile ever run in Perth, by pacing his last half-mile in 56 seconds. Not even the great Village Kid, the local idol, had set such a fast half, and it showed the Western Australians just how fast the New South Wales pacer was, forewarning them of the threat he was to their Grand Circuit races.

Westburn Grant was almost unbeatable when he was allowed to lead in his races. In this final he drew barrier one, the best draw possible, to enable him to take charge of the race from the outset. He led easily and held off all challenges, winning by eight metres, from Whitby Timer and registering a fast mile rate of 1:58:8 for the 2500 metres. My mother was partially responsible for Vic drawing this desirable barrier number. Being British, she had always taken great delight in teasing Glenn, who was a keen follower of the Australian cricket team. When the English team won in Australia, Mum enjoyed phoning Glenn just to hear his excuses. This year the draw was done by having twelve people stand and hold up posters, each with funny sayings on them. Vic, being well aware of the cricket rivalry between Glenn and his Grandmother, chose the poster on which was printed the words, 'Beat the Poms in cricket'. The poster was turned around, and there to our great surprise and delight was printed the beautiful number ONE. Vic could have hugged his mother-in-law.

After the Golden Nugget, on the 15th December, we stayed in

Perth for the Benson and Hedges Cup the following week. The final was to be held on the 5th January 1990. This was Westburn Grant's first clash with the local idol Village Kid and it made headlines. The first heat was expected to be a real battle between these two champions. The local fans were sure that the horse that had ruled harness racing's classics in WA would be the victor. We never doubted the ability of our horse and he didn't disappoint us in the first heat. What was expected to be a major battle, the 'Clash of the Titans', became an easy victory for him, much to the sorrow of the Kid's connections.

The final was, once again, expected to be a real thriller, and a fierce contest between the two great horses; no other horse was even considered a threat. Vic jumped Spot to the lead ahead of the Kid and felt very happy to have his danger directly behind him, on the fence. He could keep the Kid in a pocket there, by dictating the speed of the race, and ensuring a horse was kept in the 'death seat' on the outside of Village Kid.

Vic had only the last furlong to go and he felt he had a horse full of running (plenty in reserve), as Spot was well on the bit. Vic thought that all he had to do was keep the Kid in and release his grip when a horse made a run from the back of the field. He was incredulous when the horse let go of the bit and almost pulled up; Spot had never quit in a race in the whole of his racing career. He was almost unbeatable when allowed to dictate his own terms in front as he had been allowed to do this night. When he dropped out of the race, he pushed the Kid back with him, thus spoiling his chances of winning also, and robbing the crowd of the expected battle between the two champions. An outsider, Tarport Sox, at 33/1 in the betting, came from the rear and won the race.

The crowd was silent and neither the people nor Vic and I could take it in. Some said our horse had choked down, as horses sometimes do when they pull and are restrained. Vic knew this was not the case, Spot never pulled hard, but only held firmly onto the bit. Vic had to front up to a stewards' inquiry, which is usual in such dramatic situations. However, at the time Vic had no possible explanation for what could have happened to cause Spot to stop.

Vic said later that he had heard of an incident taking place at Randwick thoroughbred races three weeks before when the use of a laser gun had been cited. This instrument, apparently, is aimed at the head of a horse from some remote distance. When the trigger is pulled, it causes a high pitched screech that only the animal can hear, causing it to slow down and even stop. Vic felt that this or something similar could have been used on Spot that night. The horse had been totally untroubled during the whole of this campaign and had been working brilliantly.

This could have been used by someone who had put Spot 'in the bag' with a bookie and obviously stood to win a lot of money if the horse could be stopped. We will never know what really occurred, we only know that something extraordinary happened to our horse that night in Perth. Nothing like that ever happened again. If Westburn Grant was beaten, there was always a reasonable explanation for his loss. More often than not, it was due to the pain caused by his foot problem.

When the horse had cooled off after that race there was evidence that he had a sore back, which required constant attention in the following weeks. On the way back east we stopped off in Adelaide, where the horse won the South Australian Cup, before having our colours lowered at Moonee Valley in the Victoria Cup. The Inter Dominion (Westburn Grant's first) that season was in Adelaide, with our young stallion receiving constant treatment throughout the series for his back, which was not serious, but his recovery was slow and he performed below his best. The Westburn Grant that took to the track for that series was handicapped by more than his opposition. Spot won a heat and was placed second in his two others, before finishing fifth in the Grand Final to the outsider Thorate. There was never any other occasion in the whole of Spot's racing career, where he raced less than his best.

Westburn Grant made amends for his defeat by Tarport Sox, and was described as 'awesome' when he won the Benson and Hedges Cup the following January, 1991, and again in January 1992.

On the occasions these two great horses, Village Kid and Westburn Grant, were matched against each other, the racegoing public and the media were never disappointed by the spectacle. The wonderful pair were described as the 'mighty prize-fighters', and most of their races were just that: a thoroughly good fight.

Westburn Grant was named the Australian Harness Horse of the Year three times, New South Wales Harness Horse of the Year four times, and the Grand Circuit Champion, after these convincing wins, and scooped almost all of the votes for the awards.

Spot was again the Grand Circuit Champion in 1991 when, as a five-year-old, he backed up to win the Miracle Mile once more. He won the Australian Pacing Championship and made another trip back to Perth to win the Benson and Hedges Cup on 4th January 1991.

Once again we were met at the airport by Alan Parker. Vic, I and our prized possession were given the same wonderful hospitality from the WA Trotting Association that we had come to know and appreciate. We were always most careful as to where Spotty was stabled, and were again able to use the facilities of the Fremantle stables. Vic wasn't as concerned about *our* accommodation, but we were more than satisfied with the well-appointed and comfortable motel nearby.

At this time, races were still being conducted at the Fremantle raceway, and the committee members were in their offices at the track each weekday. They were always so obliging if we needed anything, and often one of them would come over to the stables, just to ensure that everything was running smoothly. We travelled from Fremantle to the Gloucester Park track in Perth where The Western Australia Cup was held. It was then sponsored by Benson and Hedges.

During this campaign, Westburn Grant was to encounter a challenge by Sinbad Bay, driven by Vinnie Knight, for the Cup that year. Sinbad Bay had beaten Spot in their first heat clash. Vic's strategy was hopefully to give his horse a not-too-hard run, because of his strenuous campaign, but as it happened, Spot was also balked by Vinnie's whip on the home turn. On the strength of this, Sinbad Bay was touted to win the final. Both horses contested separate heats that New Year's Eve. Vinnie Knight had let Sinbad Bay roll, winning his heat of 2100 metres in the mile rate of 1:55:7. Spot ran his heat in an even faster time, half an hour later, forcing his critics to be less vocal. In the final, Vic led and cruised to the front. When Knight made a run around the field with Sinbad Bay, Vic upped the tempo so that they ran their last mile in 1:54:96 at the end of 2500 metres. Alan Parker later commented to me that he felt sorry for Sinbad Bay. Vic only let Spot go at the top of the straight, when Kellie Kersley (driving Icarion for Ross Oliveri) ran into the back of his cart, flattening a tyre. Spot set a race record of 1:57:8 for the 2500 metres, only beaten in 1998 by Our Sir Vancelot.

It was after this race that tragedy struck for the second time in Perth. Vic was working Spot in preparation for his next race, the Foundation Cup, to be held in South Australia the following week. The previous night, I had learned by telephone that my sister, Catherine, then 54, had cancer, and that the disease was too widespread for any hope of recovery. Sleep did not come easily that night, so Vic insisted that I sleep in the following morning, while he went off to fast-work Spot, having to do without my usual help.

Westburn Grant was only working at about half-pace, when Vic heard a 'crack' like a gunshot. Spot lunged sideways and almost fell. Vic pulled him up and got out to see what had happened, only to find that Spot could not put his hind leg on the ground. It was the sound of a breaking bone in the stallion's hind leg.

The sudden ringing of the telephone startled me awake and, as I reached out to pick it up, I was overcome with a feeling of dread. The premonition I felt was proven correct, but did not concern Catherine. Vic was almost in tears as he broke the devastating news to me over the phone, regarding the horse's crippling injury.

Vic managed to get all the gear off Westburn Grant by the time I arrived. A number of helpers quickly appeared, enabling us to almost lift the large horse onto the float. We rushed him to the Murdoch University, where we were told to ask for a veterinarian, John Yovich.

We had it in our minds by now that the only option for the animal was to have him put down, which was usual for a broken leg. Our episode with Glenn's Thunder came back to haunt us on the journey. The trip to the university took about 20 minutes and I could almost feel the agony that Spot must have been going through.

On arrival, we were met by a young veterinarian. His youthful appearance didn't inspire us with great confidence. Thinking the young man was a student, Vic said 'I have come to see a Mr John Yovich.'

'Right,' the young man answered, 'you're speaking with him.' Our first impression was soon dispelled. His confidence and expertise exceeded our expectations by far, as we watched his examination of the horse.

X-rays of the horse's back leg revealed a fracture of the pastern bone, just above the foot. We waited anxiously for the fateful verdict, expecting the worst. To our absolute amazement and joy, John Yovich made the statement, 'I can save him, no doubt about it.' We immediately assumed he meant for stud purposes only and considering what we thought was in store for Spot, we were overjoyed at this. He went on to explain quite definitely, not only could he save our horse's life; Westburn Grant might go on to race again. We were stunned.

Not knowing the brilliance of that man at that stage, we did not believe it possible and told him that if he saved Spot's life we would be eternally grateful; *if* he could get Spot back to the races, that would be a big bonus. We did not think for one minute that our horse would ever race again.

It took both Vic and me quite a while to be convinced that the horse could really get back to racing, and achieve that peak racing form he was in before his injury. Eventually we accepted the man's word and agreed to leave Spot with him for the operation to be performed.

John operated on the leg and we stayed in Perth, keeping Spot company each day, until we were confident that he would pull through. We left Spot at the university and flew home.

Approximately three months after his operation, when the horse had recovered enough to travel, Vic flew to Perth to bring him home. As he entered Spot's stall, Vic almost had a fit when the horse, being so pleased to see 'the boss', double barrelled the brick wall at the back of his stall. Vic was seen to change through fifteen shades of white in as many seconds.

On his return to Exeter, Garry was the one who could give Spotty the most time and walked him quietly for exercise. We could not allow him to gallop in a paddock, so he had to be taken for walks every day. Garry loved animals, especially this horse, and it was thanks to him that our pacer got all the exercise he required. Garry spoiled the horse by picking some of the special grasses that were normally out of reach of the horses, in their pick paddocks, and giving him these each day. Old Spotty relished the attention and was recovering steadily.

That year of 1991 was a year of trepidation, as we watched Westburn Grant's steady but dramatic recovery. This was also the year that Vic was given a special party for family and friends to celebrate his 50th birthday, and it was good that my sister Catherine was able to attend. It was the last time we were all together. As usual, she presented her happy face, told her jokes and gave every indication of how much she was enjoying herself, but the ravages of her illness could not be disguised.

His first start back to racing was in the flying mile at Newcastle, where he sat outside of Thorate for the whole trip and won by three and a half metres in the race record time of 1:55:6, smashing the track record and taking half a second off the time he had set in winning that race the previous year.

We travelled with Westburn Grant to Tasmania to contest the Australian Pacing Championship, when he was a six-year-old. Tasmania was the host state for the championship event that year. Some old friends, Trudy and Bruce Beaudinette, owned a hotel in Derby. They once had a pacer called Beleen. We had become friends when Bruce had brought Beleen to us to race in New South Wales, and stayed with us at Dapto, years before.

Vic developed a successful combination with Beleen, winning numerous races at Harold Park. Bruce had taught the horse to drink beer from the bar and to eat Lifesavers, and the horse apparently was sharp and keen to learn. Beleen had to 'dry out' at our place, I am afraid, because no-one had time to take him to the local hotel, but I am sure he would have been made welcome there, if we had.

Bruce told us about a suitable beach at Bridport, a 50-minute drive to the north-east of Launceston, whose track (Mowbray) is identical to that at Brisbane's Albion Park. We accepted his advice and he gave us his father-in-law's address. Arrangements were made for Vic and me to meet Bill Hall and his wife June, who were taking care of our accommodation requirements.

Bill and June confided in us later that it was our down-to-earth and helpful attitude that gave them the courage to offer two 'noteable people' the opportunity to stay with them. They had been expecting two stuffy, posh and conceited people who would prefer to stay in a flash motel rather than stay with them in their 'little home', and were surprised to find that we were just ordinary folk.

Our stay with the Halls was most pleasant and we enjoyed the time spent in their company immensely. This was the beginning of a lasting friendship. In fact, after my smash, they rang and offered me the chance to come for a holiday and stay with them again, and it is my wish to be able to take their invitation quite soon.

Working a horse on a beach is very different from track-work, the main difference being the times that the horse can be worked. On the track a horse can be worked at any time during the day, but on the beach the times are governed by the tides. It has to be low tide to be able to work on the wet sand and not have waves rolling over the horse's legs, which meant there was a need to determine at what times the tide would be low.

As a result, working on the beach could be at anytime during the day and often we had to leave home at 5am or earlier to get to the beach and gear up Spot in time to finish his work before the tide changed.

At Bridport beach one morning, we arrived at about 6am, geared up the stallion and walked up the steep hill to the beach, only to find that the tide had brought in an enormous amount of stones. They were all over the sand and it was impossible to find two miles of clear sand anywhere on the beach. The only thing we could do was to take off his gear, put him back onto the float and take him to another beach an hour away and hope we would be able to work him there.

This time we were fortunate, the tide was still low enough to work our horse. We walked the beach before we geared up Spot and found it good enough to give him the work necessary for his big race. This beach was not as good as the Bridport beach, but solid enough and not covered with stones, which presented the greatest threat to the horse's weakness, his hooves.

Several days before that Australian Championship, Vic had clocked Westburn Grant to have paced a mile in 1:50, faster than any standardbred had ever been timed in Australia. Of course, pacing in a straight line does eliminate the stress and strain of racing around bends. But whichever way you looked at it, this time was quite sensational.

On the day of the race, Franco Ice and Westburn Grant jostled for favouritism when betting opened. I was later told by one of the many guests from the mainland, being entertained in the committee room, how a usually well-informed gentleman had entered the room and mentioned that he had it on reliable authority that Westburn Grant had easily bettered the Australian record when trialling on the sand several days earlier. At the mention of this, more than a half-dozen people quietly left the room and then made a beeline for the book-makers, which in turn generated further support for those still trying to decide. Westburn Grant was sent out a pronounced favourite and was untroubled to win with a mile rate of 1:57:3. He had been making a habit of creating new track records.

On the night before the final of the Championship race, we attended the Albert Hall in Launceston, where we were presented with the award for the Australian Harness Horse of the Year for 1991 by the Premier of Tasmania, Mr Michael Field. This was the third time that Westburn Grant was named the New South Wales and the Australian Harness Horse of the Year and also the Grand Circuit Champion in the one year.

As if to live up to the prestigious award, Spot won the Pacing Championship with ease, beating a top field. He won a lot of Tasmanian hearts as well with his courageous effort and his great comeback to the racetrack after his breakdown in Perth less than 14 months before. This trip to the Apple Isle was followed by a placing to Christopher Vance in the Miracle Mile at Harold Park, then a second to Franco Ice in the Treuer Memorial at Bankstown. It was announced that Franco Ice would be going to Perth for the rich Western Australian Pacing Cup. The decision to take Spot to Perth had to be agreed to by Colleen and Barney, along with Vic and myself. The Breens were were keen to enter the horse in this race, and in spite of some misgivings, Vic appeared to have, the decision to take Westburn Grant to the west again was made.

Before the trip west, we took Spotty to Queensland for the Pacing Championship, and stayed at Hastings Point with our friends, Doug and Pat McMillan. Doug was an owner-driver himself and was the son of the former well-known driver, Sutton McMillan. Their training complex was situated very close to a beach, which was most suitable for Spot's preparation. They made us extremely welcome on the many occasions we raced in Brisbane. Sadly, Doug has since passed away after a short illness.

The Championship was held on 19th October 1991, and Spot was narrowly beaten by Franco Ice in world-record time. One minute 55 seconds for 2100 metres. Westburn Grant had several great battles with Franco Ice, whose career would be tragically cut short by a serious leg injury.

TWENTY-FOUR

A Christmas We Will Never Forget

* ' The death of people whom we love brings sorrow and pain,
But if our loved ones know the Lord, our sorrow becomes their gain'.

Vic and I would be away in Perth with Westburn Grant for the running of the Benson & Hedges Cup (now known as the WA Cup), taking us away for Christmas that year. So we had our family Christmas dinner on the Wednesday of that week. This wasn't the only time that we weren't able to be home with the family for Christmas because of a trip to Perth.

Our younger son brought his girlfriend Lisa out for our family get-together. Lisa is the younger daughter of Dianne Lewis. The evening was a happy and most enjoyable occasion. On the day before we were to leave for our flight to Melbourne, on the first leg of the trip to Perth, we called Garry, inviting him to come out and see us, and to receive his Christmas presents.

We asked him if he wished to return home, but he said that he was happy living with Lisa and that they were soon to become engaged. We made it clear to him that our home was always there for him and that we loved him very much, and I am so glad that we did. We said our goodbyes, and stated that we would be home in about a month.

Early the next morning we drove to Sydney and flew from there to Melbourne, where we had to wait overnight for the next leg of the flight to Perth. That night, during the stopover, I felt a compulsion to ring Garry. I picked up the phone, considered a minute, then replaced the receiver. We had only just left him. I thought I would wait until we were settled in Perth before ringing him again.

This was to be the one decision that I will regret having made for the rest of my days.

We arrived in Perth with Westburn Grant. There is such a lot of work getting the horse off the plane safely and onto the float, with all his gear, the gig and our luggage as well. This is why we didn't become alarmed when Ray Holloway, now retired and serving on the association committee, said to Alan Parker: 'The police were supposed to be here, but they haven't arrived yet.' He then told us to ring home. We didn't understand the significance of his comment about the police.

We had already been nonplussed by the strange reception from Alan Parker. He would be there to meet us at the airport and to take our horse to his pre-arranged stable, and us to our accommodation. He always made every effort to ensure that our stay in Perth went well. Vic was amazed that Alan this time could not shake his hand when they met.

This time was different, his meeting was subdued, even had a faint coldness about it. He seemed reluctant to talk. Alan left us quickly to load the horse and belongings onto the float. He put our bags, containing our clothes and money, into the car he had hired for us, and while I was on the telephone, Alan just drove away without a word. The importance of his action wasn't realised until later.

Using our mobile phone, I tried to ring Glenn at Exeter, but the line was continually engaged. I began to worry a little, thinking that something may have been wrong on the farm or with the horses. After many more attempts, and finding the phone was still busy, we really became anxious.

Vic and I exchanged ideas as to what the problem may have been, but drew no conclusion. Vic had to go over and check that all the gear had been picked up. No-one present, who had been informed of the dreadful circumstances, enlightened us. It must have been an awful time for them, knowing, but not being able to tell us.

After what seemed to be an eternity, I finally got through to my daughter-in-law, Toni, Glenn's wife. When I said 'Hello' she just said, 'Oh no, oh no,' over and over.

'Toni; What is it? What is it?' but she could only keep repeating the same words.

'Toni, is it Glenn?'

'No'

'Is it Nicki?' (Their daughter.) Again, the only word she would utter was 'No'. I was absolutely terrified by now as I knew something bad had happened and could not determine what!

'Toni, tell me, tell me. Is it Susan, or the children?' for some reason I could only think it had something to do with someone who lived on the farm.

'GARRY'S DEAD,' she uttered finally.

It was as painful for Toni to pass on this tragic news to me, as it was for me to hear it.

Blindly, I threw the mobile phone away from me, which hit against the side of a truck and broke.

Screaming, 'Garry's dead, Garry's dead,' I just ran in a blind panic, aimlessly around the tarmac of the cargo receiving area of the airport.

Not until much later did I even consider the horrible way in which Vic was to be given the news that our son had been killed. I don't believe there is any easy way to be told that your much-loved, strong, agile and handsome 24-year-old son is dead. I *do* know how devastating it was for me, to be informed bluntly by telephone, as I was. What I *don't* know is how shocking it must have been for Vic, being informed as he was.

Uncontrollably, I continued running around the tarmac until a man who knew me grabbed me and forced me to stop. I was hysterical by this time, and it must have been no easy task for him to calm me down.

Vic heard me scream that our son was dead and ran, shocked, to pick up the mobile phone. He was hoping that Toni would still be on the other end to talk to, and find out what I was saying. The phone had broken almost in two when it had hit the truck and was out of action. Vic was devastated, in a state of shock, and was desperate to find out what had happened.

Who helped Vic at first, I don't know, but we were led into an office at the airport by Ray Holloway and given a telephone to ring Glenn again. The staff made us tea and coffee, but to this day neither Vic nor I can remember drinking it. We then learned the whole story. The shocking way the accident had happened, causing Garry's death, and how my daughter Susan had found her brother lying dead beside the water tank below his bedroom window.

Neither Vic nor I was in any fit state to make the necessary arrangements for our immediate flight home.

Ansett Airlines, being made aware of our circumstances, had made available, free of charge, two business-class seats on the first available flight out of Perth that day. Being Christmas Eve, this must have been no easy task, and we will always be grateful to the generous gesture of that top airline. We were driven directly to the passenger terminal and escorted aboard the aircraft. We had no money and no luggage.

The friendliness and generosity of the West Australians that we had met was typified by the actions of Ray Holloway that night. Ray gave us $100 for our use on the trip. During the flight, the kindly flight attendants made every effort to comfort us and make the flight bearable. Nevertheless, the trip seemed to take forever. When we landed at Sydney airport, I felt numb and my legs did not seem to belong to me, almost unwilling to move, so I had to be helped off the plane. Still in a confused state, I then walked unsteadily through the terminal, where we were met by our good friend Kevin Wells. He drove us first to the mortuary at Bowral, where our son's body was held. He gave us his support by coming in with us to identify Garry; an experience I would wish to forget, but cannot. I see the vision of Garry lying there before me, as I leaned over to stoke his lovely curly hair, as clearly today as I did then.

From Bowral, Kevin then drove us home to Exeter, where the family was waiting, along with our local church minister, and Janet and Ron Greason. Janet and Ron had helped the family through the day and helped Glenn paint the tank to save us from seeing the blood that covered it. They stayed on and slept the night at our home.

Glenn, as best he could, gave Vic and I the dreadful details of the last 24 hours.

Evidently, after Garry had said that he would not be coming home until we returned, he had changed his mind and rode his bicycle out to the farm at about 10.30pm.

Vic and I had prevented him from driving the car, because he had been driving while drinking a little too much. We had promised to give it to him as his own when he stopped drinking. Inadvertently, Garry was left without a key to our house, because it was still on the ring with the car keys.

On arriving home and not having his house key, he proceeded to enter by his bedroom window. I discovered now that this was the way both Glenn and Garry gained access to their rooms after being out late at night. The bedroom was situated at the end of the house over the garage, and the window was above a cement water tank. The boys would climb onto the tank and pull themselves up into the bedroom window.

This window was very rarely locked. On this one occasion, Vic had locked the window because we were going to be away for a month. This was after having heard the local constable of police say how there had been a few recent robberies in the area, and those going away should make sure all doors and windows were locked.

As was Garry's usual practice, he climbed onto the tank to make his entry and found the window locked. Apparently, while trying to open the window in the dark, the glass broke, cutting his right arm at the elbow. The glass severed a major blood vessel. He then apparently fell from the tank to the ground, where he may have been unconscious, and as a result of the cut, bled to death. The doctor said that from the evidence he would have died quickly; to know this was such a relief to both Vic and I. It was unbearable to think of Garry lying bleeding, in the freezing cold, all through the night.

Arrangements had to be made for the funeral to be held on the following Saturday to enable our trotting friends to attend.

The day of the funeral arrived. It was raining.

The service took place as arranged at the Exeter Anglican Church, and was attended by some 600 or so relatives and friends. Local policemen volunteered their services to control the traffic, which was unusually heavy in our little village, on that day.

Garry was buried in the cemetery, in the grounds of the Sutton Forest Anglican Church.

Westburn Grant was still in Perth, being trained and cared for by Colin Brown, a trainer that we had not previously known. John Yovich, the veterinarian, had arranged this for us.

There was still another heat to be contested for the Benson and Hedges Cup, before the funeral was to take place. Glenn volunteered to go to Perth and drive our horse in that heat, despite the way he was feeling and the effect that people, giving their condolences, would have on him. He returned to Exeter the following day.

Westburn Grant failed to take out a place in this qualifying heat. However, this did not prevent the horse's inclusion in the field for the Cup. Due to Westburn Grant's exceptional ability, he was deemed eligible for entry in spite of his failure in the heat. The Final of the Benson and Hedges Cup race was to be held the week after Garry's funeral was scheduled.

Still I wonder whether it would have made a difference to Garry's life if, on that night, in Melbourne, I had not hesitated to make that phone call. On reflection, after many 'what ifs' and 'if onlys', the unalterable fact remains that our son is gone, leaving a great void in our hearts. Life goes on, as it must, but the trauma of his loss has left its mark on each member of the family. The impact on his sister Susan's life, particularly, is still evident after much counselling. Glenn gave the impression that he was coping a little better, but we found out later that he had not coped as well as he had appeared to.

Being only a week since Garry's funeral, neither Vic nor I had any intention of returning to Perth for that race. Our decision was reversed by the persistent encouragement and wonderful support of our friends, who seemed to leave us alone only long enough to sleep. Not willing to risk separation from our family again, we agreed to go back to finish the series only when our daughter Susan agreed to come with us and bring her daughter Monique. Glenn had to stay at Exeter because he had horses in training, so could not come with us.

We arrived and were met at the airport by a very subdued, but relieved, Alan Parker, and were taken to collect our horse. We thanked Colin, the trainer we had left our horse with, for his very generous help. On collecting Spot, we found that he had fretted for us. He had never been in anyone else's care since he had been born, and had not too easily accepted the separation.

When Vic worked him later that day, his comment was that it was a waste of time coming back for the race. Spot had always been trained on the beach, but Colin, with whom we had left him, had quite a big team of horses in work, so could not afford the time to travel to the beach to work him there. Therefore, Spot had become sore in his feet, and he didn't work very well that first time, when Vic hoppled him. Vic's comment to Alan was, 'I don't know if we will be there Friday night. I will ring you if I have to scratch him.'

With only six days to go before the race, the pressure was on Vic to try to soothe Spot's painful feet and to improve his condition. It seemed an impossible task in the time we had left, but nevertheless we applied ourselves intently to Spotty's training. With his workouts on the beach, and walking in the salt water, we were able to reduce the severity of his inflamed hooves. When Vic and I arrived at Gloucester Park with our horse, Alan Parker was the first to ask how Spot was, and Vic replied, 'I don't know if he can win, but if we get an easy quarter, he will let them know they have been in a race.'

At Gloucester Park Paceway we were swamped with people offering us their condolences and best wishes for the race.

The race will never be forgotten by all who attended that night; January 3rd 1992 was a very dramatic night in the sport of harness racing.

TWENTY-FIVE

Spot Defies the Odds

* 'We may not know what the future holds,
but we can trust the one who holds the future'

Westburn Grant and Franco Ice had been dominating the big important races that season, but our horse had been the victor most times. The night of the Benson and Hedges Cup, it was mainly predicted that Franco Ice would win, because of the way our horse had performed in his heat, aggravated by the fact that Vic would be driving in the race and feeling the extreme pressures of the past few days. Franco Ice it seemed had the rich Grand Final at his mercy.

Franco Ice started a short-priced favourite. Spot's price had been set by the bookmakers at 10/1, the first and only time he had ever been at double-figure odds and one of the few times he was not favourite.

He had not fared well in the draw, starting out wide in barrier nine. When the field was dispatched, Vic did the unexpected from his bad barrier draw; he went away fast and Spot dashed to the lead. Driving to instructions, Brian Gath settled Franco Ice at the rear of the field. Not wishing to see Westburn Grant dictating the pace out in front, the Victorian reinsman swept around the field, to have Franco Ice up on the outside of our horse with two laps to go.

The favourite was noted for his stamina and Brian upped the tempo by allowing his horse to increase the pressure on Spot. The roar from the crowd was quite deafening, as these outstanding horses turned on a two-horse war in the last lap. As the two champions went stride-for-stride and head-and-head together, the noise became louder and louder.

Even though there were local horses and drivers in the race, the only names I heard called were 'Spot' and 'Frosty'. The shouts of 'Come on Spot' and 'Come on Frosty' were enough to bring tears to the eyes of the hardest heart.

When Westburn Grant went over the finishing line first, I doubt if

I have ever heard a more sustained roar of support from any harness racing crowd. The crowd seemed to be greatly moved by the paradox of our triumph in tragedy.

Vic, Susan and I were very emotional at the presentation of the trophy, and our responses to the speeches were short and subdued. But we can never forget the warm manner in which Perth people supported the win by our champion that night. Almost 12 months to the week from when he suffered the fracture to his hind leg that almost ended his racing career, and a little less than a week since we had buried our younger son, the people of Perth had risen to the occasion almost as one.

The spectacle of Westburn Grant and Franco Ice racing together drew so much attention that a video was made for posterity, called 'The Summer of Frost and Ice.' I cannot view this video, even now, without breaking up. There, before me, in full colour and action is the race that Westburn Grant won against Franco Ice, the week after Garry's death. The roar of the crowd, giving us their full support, is clearly audible on it.

Vic and I both firmly believed that old Spot had, in some way, sensed the sadness and the intense emotion of the moment, and had reached into the very depths of his being to draw out all the power he had within him, to win that race for us. I believe he was lifted by the great roar from the crowd that night, and carried by the support that they gave him for his monumental effort. I know that Vic and I certainly were. I could feel the empathy of the crowd as they shouted their encouragement to Vic and to Spotty. It was beyond me to express the intensity of my feelings during those moments, just as it was for me to control the huge lump in my throat and the tears from my eyes.

While we were in Perth for this race, Glenn rang to tell us about a rare act of sportsmanship by the Mittagong RSL second grade cricket team, during the game played between them and Glenn's team at Exeter oval.

Our local paper carried the story, which we were given a copy of when we returned home> In it the editor congratulated the Mittagong team on 'their actions'. He said, 'It is second to none I have ever witnessed during my sporting career.' He wrote the full story of the events and said it was a touching story, which began with the death of

180

the local cricket and soccer star Garry Frost.

We had given Garry for Christmas, amongst other presents, some cricket shoes and a cricket bat that he had longed for, a special type of bat and one that he hoped would enable him to score 100 runs in the next week's competition. He had boasted that he would do this the very first time he used this bat. He was never given the opportunity to make his predictions come true!

Glenn and his cricketing mate Andrew Smith, knew of Garry's yearning desire. They went to Garry's grave side and there pledged to their brother and friend that they would score the century with Garry's new bat in the next match, the following Saturday.

The match was on their home ground of Exeter and it was because of their pledge to fulfill Garry's wish that they forced themselves to play, when it was still a very sad time for them both, especially Glenn.

When it was time for the home team to bat, they became anxious to reach their goal of 100 runs, and were urged on by their team mates. The opposite team, at this stage, did not know of this burning ambition of the two players. Andrew, unfortunately, never managed to make too many runs that day, although he was usually a good batsman. Glenn quite often made high scores and this day he was batting so carefully and trying with all his skill and strength.

Luck seemed to be against him. He was on 96 runs when the skies opened up and down came a torrential flood of rain! The opposite team called the match off. The Exeter team knew what this would do to Glenn and Andrew, and went over to the other team and told them what was in progress.

In pouring rain, they said 'Come on Frosty, get yourself back out here, we are going back on.'

Glenn and Andrew were elated with the offer to finish the game, and rushed back onto the field, with their team mates. In seconds, they were all drenched, but no-one noticed it now; they all had the ardent desire for Garry's wish to become true. Glenn went back to the crease and faced the bowler once again, with hope and dedication. He scored the next four runs needed and the other players rushed to him with hugs of congratulations and support.

It was a very emotional time for Glenn and the two teams, and a lot of the players went to Garry's grave, to tell him that it had been done. It is a custom for Glenn and some of the team to go the grave each Christmas Eve, with beers, and have a drink there with their best mate.

It was absolutely stunning to be told of this wonderful act of sportsmanship; it has made me cry to write and read this story, but with it comes a warm glow to my heart that makes it worth the sadness and pain.

Garry's death has touched the lives of so many people, the publicity of it and the magnanimous support of family, friends and the trotting people has brought into clear focus the great importance of family to many. I have had letters from people sharing with me their change of values and their life's direction, and know of some who now take more time with their loved ones and place less value on material things.

My friend, John wrote a poem that which carries a great deal of meaning for us. I would like to share it with you:

The Hundred Runs

The sky was clouding over and there was still some game to play,

One hundred runs off Garry's bat was the order of the day.

Glenn was standing at the crease, his score was near the ton.

I'll get those runs I promised, Garry, watch this *next* shot son.

The rain came down in torrents, the teams walked off the field.

There was bitter disappointment, for one hundred was not the yield.

The other team was made aware of the promise that Glenn had made.

'Get back out there Frosty!' they all said, and ply that trusty blade.

The teams went out again, all eager to continue play,

A grand display of sportsmanship was witnessed on that day.

Glenn clipped the next ball off to leg, he took another two,

His score was slowly creeping up, but he was still short a few.

In the pouring rain the game went on, the lads were soaking wet,

The bowler ripped a wild one, to Glenn, who's bat was set.

Howzat! The bowler shouted, as the ball glanced off Glenn's pad,

The umpire stood a moment, then ruled; Not out! My lad.

A mighty hook to silly mid, brought up the final run,

Glenn's promised hundred, off Garry's bat, was well and truly won.

The teams came off all wringing wet, knowing the effort that they gave

They went to celebrate the final score, standing by Garry's grave.

Vic and I were managing our lives and our grief with some difficulty that summer, but were given some solace by the challenge Westburn Grant faced in the gruelling Inter Dominion Championship hosted by Moonee Valley. This was only a month or so after the Benson and Hedges Cup. On the way home, we stopped over in Adelaide, where Spot won their biggest race, the South Australian Cup.

If Westburn Grant was to do well in the four races within a fortnight of the Inter Dominion series, the horse had to be trained on a beach. In desperation, Vic phoned our Melbourne friends, Ken and Cynthia Norton, with the challenge of finding a suitable beach, a stable and a place for us to stay. Melbourne is a fine city, built around Port Phillip Bay, but is not noted for having a suitable beach which allows for a horse to be worked there. I know Ken accepted this request with a feeling of helplessness, as it seemed that we were asking for the impossible.

Ken told us how it all fell into place, after driving up and down the coast with Cynthia looking at various beaches, he finally selected a little-known place called Venus Bay. As it turned out, this was ideal for what we wanted. It had a good stretch of firm sand and not too many stones. The big bonus was that nearby were toilets with an outside tap, ideal for us to wash our horse after his work. Ken's search for suitable accommodation for us and our horse nearby had also born fruit. The stables, only a few minutes from town, were just what we wanted, with a walkout yard, and another important feature, a place for Spot to wander for a green pick. The couple who owned it were most helpful and gave us a very warm welcome.

The house we secured for the fortnight was situated on the side of a hill that provided a commanding and most beautiful view of a lake. I love being near water, and enjoyed it to the full. It took little urging for me to make the time and allow myself the luxury of being able to sit outside, look out over the glorious panoramic view and experience the feeling of calmness and peace that it gave. There was no telephone in the house and we were too far out of transmission range for our mobile phone to work, so we were not bothered by the press, as would have been the case at most Inter Dominion Carnivals. We both found the town pleasant and friendly, and we often ate out at the local hotel. We knew the beach would help the horse, and those two quiet weeks gave us precious time to recuperate.

It has always amazed us that people think that owning and training a champion is just a matter of taking him to the races and winning. They only see the glory and joy of it. Only those who work in the industry can know the tremendous amount of stress and hardship that goes with keeping a horse at its peak and then having it produce its best in every race.

Westburn Grant was almost always expected to win, not just to produce a good run. It was a load in itself to ensure that his training maintained his feet in as pain-free a condition as possible, let alone always having to keep him in top form.

Vic and I were dedicated to the training of all our horses, but it was impossibile to *guarantee* Westburn Grant's winning. His physical condition, the position he drew at the barrier, the calibre of his opposition, the absence of hindrance on the track, and many other factors such as his feeding and accommodation came into play. Even though we knew we had done absolutely everything we could to produce Spot at his best, we suffered a lot with the stress involved.

Having a champion horse carries with it a responsibility for maintaining the integrity of the owners, the trainers and the drivers. A champion today can be a 'has been' tomorrow, but it is how the champion is remembered, both by the public and the press, that determines how that responsibility was met. Westburn Grant was a grand horse and a champion and has made his unique mark in pacing history. Granted, the joy and excitement and the monetary gain derived from Westburn Grant's racing made the strain and effort worthwhile, but it certainly was not all 'beer and skittles', and we have the scars as the proof.

A catholic priest, Father Brian Glasheen, blessed our racing colours a few days before the final of the Inter Dominion. This was something we never had done before. We had come to know Father Glasheen because he was from an old trotting family and was a regular at Melbourne meetings and often travelled to the Inter Dominions. Therefore, when he offered to bless the colours we gladly accepted, and maybe this brought us luck! We learned later, from Max Agnew, that Brian had once been seen to bless the colours of another horse that then ran nearer last than first. When Max mentioned how the blessing had not worked, Brian had replied: 'Don't you know the difference between a blessing and the last rites?'

The undisturbed atmosphere surrounding Westburn Grant's training prior to the big race, paid off; winning the biggest race on the racing calendar in Australasia. This even is often referred to as the 'Melbourne Cup' of harness racing! What an experience! Spot had won! We had won!

Vic had driven in six of these prestigious Grand Finals and had never been close to winning. This time it was different; he was driving Westburn Grant.

A huge crowd had gathered to watch the strappers, Kevin Wells, Ken Norton and Steve Bottoms, take the gear off Spot. As the unharnessing was taking place, someone in the crowd started off a 'three cheers' salute, with a tumultuous result, followed by a very vocal 'For he's a jolly good fellow'. Once again words fail to describe my rollercoaster emotional state.

A small girl came out of the crowd with a special gift, a bunch of carrots for her hero!

The celebrations went on into the early hours of the morning, at a quickly arranged meeting for friends who were in Melbourne for the race. Beer or champagne, I can't remember which, was drunk from the large Cup for a few hours that night. Neither Vic nor I have ever been drinkers, but he enjoyed quite a few that night, and so did I! Vic was invited to appear on a televised sporting program the following morning, but it would seem that the makeup department had their hands full. Despite their efforts, his appearance brought forth comments on the extent and intensity of the celebrations. To be truthful, I didn't think he would make the interview!

Just before leaving for home, we called in to see Ken and Cynthia to thank them for their most valuable contribution to our success. Cynthia had decorated the entire sitting area of their home with ribbons in black and white, our racing colours, and she had a spare set of colours on a dressmaking model, standing in a corner. Vic and I was delighted and very impressed by Cynthia's most thoughtful gesture and demonstration of the Norton family's support. This was the rare occasion we didn't stay with them. Normally most of our racing in Victoria involved a weekend only, therefore Spot was already prepared when we arrived, and a beach was not necessary.

Harold Park management invited us to parade Westburn Grant on the track a few weeks later. The evidence of Westburn Grant's popularity was made patently clear by the large crowd of spectators that presented that night to witness Spot's parade. They had made a special enclosure, near the betting ring and the stable area, for the public to come and see the horse, and to have their photographs taken with him.

Kodak, Fuji and Agfa had a bonanza; there were many reels of film exposed that night. Many people came to take advantage of the opportunity to take a photo of Westburn Grant or have a photo taken with him. Many children were included in those photographs.

Spot was his usual elegant and gentle self, showing that poise and control that had endeared him to us at the outset. He stood quietly, allowing anyone who wished to stroke him, and never once showing any sign of irritability.

The Harold Park Trotting Club had retained the services of a security guard to keep him under surveillance, for which we were most appreciative. Even though the risk was there, I found it difficult to understand why anyone would want to hurt Westburn Grant. Vic and I had to leave the area continually, because Glenn was driving three of our other horses that night and these needed our constant attention also. Our loyal friend, Kevin Wells, Spot's strapper for his entire career, was with him every moment.

Spot was led onto the track following two attractive young ladies holding a banner between them, with the writing 'Welcome Home Champ!' blazed across it. Underneath were the words 'Westburn Grant', then 'Spot', as well as five black stars bordering the print. The banner was carried the length of the straight, as Spotty was driven quietly by Vic from behind, displaying his Inter Dominion rug draped across his back.

Glenn drove two winners (a double) this night. Reporters mistakenly thought that this was the first double he had won, but Glenn had won two doubles at Harold Park previously, when he had driven Spot as a two-year-old. The horse had won, and had been a winning leg in each of the doubles. Glenn said he felt as if the horse had influenced his good fortune that night as well.

When Australia was making its bid for the Olympic Games, Vic and Westburn Grant were named ambassadors for our country. Vic says he is Australian through and through and we were both proud that they were given this honour. A special set of colours were struck and presented to Vic and he wore them with great pride in the remaining races of Spot's career. Vic felt that he and Westburn Grant were given their chance to play a part in the hard bid to hold the games in this, our beautiful country.

Those colours (the five coloured rings on a white background) were worn in several classic races and were carried to victory quite a few times. One of these races was Spot's farewell race at his home track, Harold Park, where he was sent out sentimental favourite.

Westburn Grant did not let the race crowd down; he won his last start in New South Wales and farewelled the crowd with a display of sheer Westburn Grant, with the style and panache that he had displayed as a two-year-old, and that was his hallmark throughout his competitive life.

Many horses are required to compete until they cannot match the opposition any longer, and usually their last races are in much lower grades. Not so with Spot. His very last race was the Brisbane

Inter Dominion at Albion Park Paceway in 1993. This was the third time he qualified for the final of this most prestigious race. He finished sixth in this final, but bowed out a champion.

It was ironic that it was not the broken pastern for which he had his operation that finished his career, but he was plagued with front leg problems for the last year or so. Vic puts it simply, by saying that his front fetlock joints had finally worn out. Arthritis had taken over these joints in a very chronic way and were causing so much pain to Spot that he just could not do his best, no matter how much he tried. As Vic said, 'His heart was willing, but his legs weren't able.' I think that this is exactly the case.

Vic would say that, even though his body hurt, Spot would keep on going, and he just could not allow the big-hearted horse to keep doing this any more. This stallion would have gone on trying, we felt certain that was the character of the great horse. But the love and respect we had for Westburn Grant prevented us from subjecting him any further to the rigours of training and racing. He earned the right to retire from racing with grace and dignity, befitting the calibre of horse he was. Barney and Colleen also felt this way; they had always wanted the best for their horse.

The large crowd urged him on in each heat, and he rewarded them with a heat win, sitting in the 'death seat' (the hardest place to win from) to do so, and a second and third in the other heats.

An air of sadness prevailed as we took the harness off our champion, but we were so thankful that Spot had retired without coming off lame after the race. The fact that he was to retire without further injury eased a little the sadness that went with the knowledge that Westburn Grant would never race again.

Many of his admirers came to touch and stroke him for the last time and there were a few tears shed that night. There were those who thought that Spot could race again the next year, but we left them without doubt that his racing days were over. He was to be retired to stud in Victoria. This was a job, we thought, that old Spot would really enjoy and take on with the style so characteristic of him.

Vic and I were invited to stay at the Pelican Beach Resort at Coffs Harbour, with Spot as a special guest, and on the way home from Brisbane we booked the horse into this lavish resort. He actually marched up with us to the reception desk and stood by watching

Vic and I sign the register. Of course it was a publicity stunt for them, and reporters took photographs of Spot at the desk.

He had to be moved to the showground and sleep in a stable there, while we had the benefit of a warm bed and a hot breakfast the following morning.

His career tally was 67 starts for 38 wins, 11 seconds, 7 thirds and 4 fourths, so he actually finished in the first four placings 60 times. Some 22 of his wins were paced in under two minutes, and he won 10 Grand Circuit races and 14 group one races.

Vic was asked to give a brief description of a champion, and he summed it up by saying, 'It takes speed, stamina, courage, the ability to sprint twice in a race and a good head.' Spot had all of these qualities, but his courage was the most outstanding quality, and it was this horse that gave Vic and me the courage we needed to carry on, at the worst time in our lives, and to be able to go back to Perth after Garry's funeral.

Hopefully we will be able to breed another horse with at least some of Spot's ability, but it would be nothing short of a miracle to own another Westburn Grant. Nevertheless, we intend to keep trying, such is the way of the racing fraternity, and perhaps one of our mares may surprise us.

After he left the stud in Victoria, Spot was home at Exeter for a few months, running in the paddocks with the geldings. Of course, he left the other horses in the paddock with him in no doubt as to who was 'boss', and it was good to see him in good health and running free in the paddocks he loved. He has well and truly left his mark in harness racing. In my mind, Vic Frost and Westburn Grant, together, say it all. They are both firmly part of Australia's harness racing history now.

TWENTY-SIX

My Search for Answers

'The tests of life are not to break you, but to make you'

Garry's death had devastated our immediate family. On our return from Perth, following the Benson and Hedges Cup the week after Garry's funeral, setting about our normal routine was no easy task.

Westburn Grant was given a well-earned spell for a few weeks. During his rest period, we had numerous other horses to work. We worked hard and functioned at home as best we could, but our lifestyle was anything but normal. Vic had semi-retired and was now carefully selecting the horses he would train and race.

Vic and I had won enough money from our share in Westburn Grant at this time to clear the debt on our homes and build other structures necessary on the farm. Spot had been a godsend!

Glenn lived on our farm with his wife Toni and their baby daughter Nicole, in a house we had built a couple of minutes walk from our own. Glenn was doing most of the driving and training from our stables now and Vic and I helped him with his horses, as well as working our own.

Susan and Brett were not yet married, but were living with their 18-month-old daughter Monique on the farm also, but at a distance of approximately half a kilometre away, in a home we built for them. Their home was built close to the stud complex and close to the road that ran past the front of the property, because it was Susan's intention to be responsible for any of our future breeding programs.

The situation allowed Vic and me to see the family members most days. I think it was the attention that we were able to give to the two little girls, Monique and Nicole, that eased us through that dreadful time after Garry's death.

Parents who have lost a child of any age know that intense feeling of pain and grief that follows. I felt numb; many things that I did were done almost automatically. I seemed to have lost the ability to feel. I had dulled awareness as well as suppressed emotions. I had experiences of driving through our town, and not even remembering

190

passing through it. In a sense I was on 'automatic pilot'.

Just one month after Garry's death, Vic's mother died of cancer.

My sister, Catherine, whom we expected to die because of terminal cancer, was admitted to a hospital in Berry, near Nowra. I visited her regularly, just to sit and talk with her. Despite the excruciating pain she suffered, toward the end, she showed remarkable strength and endurance; no-one can remember Catherine ever complaining. When asked how she was going, she would always say, 'I'm fine', nothing more. Seeing her in pain and watching the cancer take its toll on her body, made it very difficult to sit there without breaking down. I managed to control myself until I stepped outside her door, on my way to the car.

Catherine died on Good Friday in April 1992. I was still so affected by Garry's recent death that I could not feel the full impact of her death, even though I loved this gentle sister of mine. Neena, and Catherine's family, seemed to be much more affected by Catherine's passing than I was. The guilt for what I imagined to be an inappropriate grief response, that I felt for Catherine at the time, caught up with me later, but I was advised that this was because I was still grieving for Garry and could not respond any more than I had.

Nevertheless, the guilt I experienced for the loss of Catherine, and the guilt I experienced after Garry's death, stayed with me for a long time. It was made more intense because I had taken the car from Garry, due to what I believed was a drinking problem that needed curbing, somehow expecting this action to make him consider the error of his ways. I believed that this had contributed in some way to his death.

Vic and I were not coping very well. I certainly wasn't. I would burst into tears anywhere and at any time, be it my local supermarket, with company or by myself, if for the slightest reason, something or someone reminded me of Garry.

A friend took us to meet an 86-year-old lady, Bant Iliff, who lived in Bowral. She has been helping families cope with the loss of a loved one for 26 years. Expecting a frail old lady, we were surprised to meet a sprightly, very alert octogenarian who still had the air of a school teacher about her, which she had been in her youth. Bant ran a spiritualist group at her house, where people met once a week, to listen to tapes and for discussions. Vic and I both were invited to attend. Bant never accepted any money for the time she gave to helping people who were in need of comfort, or for imparting her belief in life after death for their loved ones.

Bant taught us that we do not die, we merely shed our cumbersome body, and our spirit passes on to a much more beautiful place than this planet. We are always met by a loved one, who has gone before, to help us grasp the fact that we have 'died'. This phenomenon, apparently, is hard to believe, by the one newly passed over. At this stage, the person is still in close contact with Earth and can still see those they have left behind, being aware of their homes and all their earthly possessions, just as things were before they died.

During these discussion groups, Bant explained that the recently departed were distressed to see the suffering of their loved ones on Earth, without being able to help. This is because those on Earth cannot see or hear those in the spirit form. Souls now in the spiritual realm want so much to ease the pain of those left grieving, but it is not possible, so they have to allow the grief being suffered to take its course. All they can do is to pass on their love and strength.

That there is life after death was what we were so desperate to learn and understand. This lady passed onto us as much as we could absorb, certainly enough to calm us and to have us feel that our son was in a beautiful place. Vic came to these meetings for about a year, but stopped when he felt he had learned enough, but I continued to go for another year or so.

This group also believed in reincarnation, that is, we return through more than one life cycle on earth. They say that, before each life, we choose what lessons we need to learn during that life, to assist us in our spirit's evolution. If we have given out hurt, distress or injuries to others in our last life, we may choose to live the next life where we are required to learn to handle these hurts or distresses ourselves. If we have been very poor we may choose a rich, abundant life. We choose the country we live in, our parents, titles, in fact every aspect of our lives to enable us to learn new lessons from each life. Everything that happens to us in our lives, happens for a reason, and we are expected to learn from the experience. The spiritualists state that it is always a matter of choice and not compulsory.

No matter what we might do, nothing will prevent the things from happening to us, that are set for us to experience. If we choose a life as

Great triumphs are born out of great troubles.

physically or mentally disadvantaged, a long life or short life, no-one can in any way stop this happening. This helped to explain a lot in our case, as so many things could have been done, seemingly, to prevent Garry's death. Many people have had feelings of guilt since, because they did not do what they had felt they ought to have done, at the time.

For instance, his girlfriend Lisa had gone out to visit a friend, without Garry; he had not wanted to go with her. On what seemed an impulse, Garry left the house and rode off on his bicycle, not telling Rod and Diane, Lisa's parents, where he was going. Rod wanted to take Diane with him and drive around looking for Garry, especially at our place. They knew we were away, so they resisted this, because they thought that Garry would not have ridden his bicycle all the way out to the farm (about 12 kilometres) to an empty house at that time of night.

If we had not locked the window, if I had not taken the car from him, if he had gone to Glenn's or Susan's house, even for a key, if he had slept in the unlocked caravan parked near the house, *if, if, if, if,* so many *IFs*. People told me afterwards that they had the opportunity to do something at the time, which they later felt could have prevented the accident, but didn't for some reason.

At this time I honestly didn't know what to believe about reincarnation and who chooses our lives, us or God; I was still searching for the answers. It was so important once, to think that I would come back again and again and be with the people I love, in different ways each time. Probably because I thought then that there could be no place anywhere as good to live as Earth. I have since learned that there is another place. I believe in the existence of heaven, that place where I will be in the presence of the Lord. Now, it is of no importance to me as to whether I have many lives or not.

All my life I have believed in God and Jesus, but I thought that heaven was like a cloud, and we floated around in this in some way. I was terrified of dying and thought that when we were dead, we were 'finished', but now I am not so afraid of dying. My expectation is that I will be reunited with Garry and my other loved ones, who have gone before me.

Glenn is the most caring and devoted son and, with his wife, Toni, has been so supportive in these last few years, but I can't stop missing Garry. Just to hear his laugh once more—I can dream, can't I?

Susan and Brett have been a tower of strength to me in these times, also, and I will always be grateful to them all. I hope that I will be there for them in times of need, as they were for me.

Vic and I always felt that Garry knew he was only going to have a short life. He lived life to the full, fitting as much into it as he could, travelling on fishing trips and other adventures with Glenn or his mates. He was engaged before, but he broke off the engagement before the wedding could take place. His last girlfriend was Lisa.

He would say to me often, when I asked him to stop drinking or to take care of himself, 'Mum, I am here for a good time, not a long time.' Looking back, it now seems that he was certain of an early death.

This would frighten me, and I would reply, 'Garry, I want you here for a long time, as well as you having a good time.' He said once to a friend, who had a little girl, that he would never have a child of his own, as he would not be here long enough. I believe that is why he broke off the engagements and lived as he did.

The Spiritualist Church at Bowral was the one that I had been attending during that early period after Garry's death, and I was greatly influenced by the teachings. In September 1993, I arranged an overseas holiday, to Britain.

During a visit to my Aunt Rina in Scotland, I talked her into going to the spiritual church at Kilmarnock, which is not too far from Glasgow. I liked the service there and I booked in to see a clairvoyant who gave readings, and only accepted a donation for the church as his fee.

Aunt Rina agreed to go with me, and I was stunned by the messages that I received from this man. He told me that he had the spirit of a young man with him, and this young man loved me very much. The man went on to describe to me many details of my son's death. He described the short ride to our home, a circular driveway (which there is to the garage), the fall involved, the attempt to break into the window, an argument Garry had had with his girlfriend and other details of that night.

This argument had not been known to me at that time, but later it was confirmed, as more of a misunderstanding than an argument.

Garry sent his love to his sister, whom he wanted to surround with flowers, and to comfort her and his brother.

Glenn and Garry had fallen out about a month before the accident, and we were so glad that their differences had been resolved the day Garry came out for his Christmas presents, before we left for Perth.

'Garry' said that he understood now many of the things that we had tried to teach him, and it would have been much better for him, had he taken notice. He said that, at first, he had not been too happy to be there, but now he was happy, and the only thing that made him sad was that we were so sad. He said that we had to go on with our lives, especially his sister, who was still not handling it all that well, and put the accident behind us.

This man had not been given my full name, he only knew me as Margaret, and I guess he may have been able to tell I was from Australia by my accent, but he could not possibly have known me, or my background. If this had been in Australia, I would have been more sceptical, because he could have gleaned some of his information from the newspapers. A Sunday paper in Australia had reported the accident on the front page, giving the impression that we had locked Garry out of the house. It would have been an easy task, at home, for this man to get many details of our lives. But here I was in Scotland, far from home, and away from any chance that anyone could know my circumstances in any detail.

This gave his revelation to me a more than reasonable authenticity, I had to admit, and it did give me some consolation to know that Garry was somewhere at peace.

Life in 1994 seemed to be always in a state of flux, swinging from an emotional high to an emotional low and back. The only stabilising influence that year was the preparation for Susan's wedding. Susan and Brett were married on 25th February 1994, at Saint Aiden's church at Sutton Forest. Monique, who was four by then, was a flower girl, along with Glenn's three-year-old daughter, Nicole. Susan was a beautiful bride and looked exquisite, and Brett cut a handsome figure on their wedding day, and the little flower girls were just gorgeous. My niece Lisa Broadley was one of the bridesmaids. She and Garry were close friends, and his absence from the family gathering affected her, as it did all of us. It was particularly hard for Susan that day, because Garry's grave was in the church grounds. The church is also next door to Brett's parents.

Susan chose a carriage drawn by two white ponies to take her and Brett, both to the wedding and to the reception at Moss Vale. As we followed them along the road to Moss Vale, it was wonderful to see cars pulling up and people getting out to take photographs. Susan, Brett and the carriage presented such a pretty sight, resulting in some delightful photographs.

If the loss of Garry had been a most traumatic blow to me, then it was surely the same for Vic. He seemed to change a lot in this period. I put this down at the time largely to the loss of our boy. But it seems there were other things then on Vic's mind as well.

I came back to the farm one day a little earlier than usual and found a young lass at the stables whom I had seen at Harold Park speaking with Glenn. I had naturally assumed that here was another member of the fairer sex who had found Glenn to be 'interesting'. If the girl, whose name was Gail, had initially displayed fondness for our son, this had taken a surprising change. She had come to see Vic.

Three months after Susan's wedding, and about two and a half years after Garry's death, Vic asked me for a separation for a few months, 'to sort himself out'. No amount of pleading could change his mind, so I booked a trip to Canada and Scotland, intending to stay away for four months, giving him the time he thought he needed.

When the arranged date for the trip to Canada arrived, Vic drove me to the airport. It was my intention to stay for a month with a lady who had been asking me to visit her since our meeting on a coach tour of Europe, several years before. I thought I would be able to stay away for the four months, but after a few days of this lady's company, I found I could not remain with her for long. In other circumstances, I could have enjoyed a lazy, relaxing holiday, but the mental turmoil I was going through was almost like an extended grief. Garry's death was still painful, and now I felt that, by this separation, I was going to lose the others that I held dear to me.

Being in a very stressed state, I would walk for miles and miles around the streets of Dundas, to tire myself enough to enable me to sleep a little at night. The excessive walking blistered my feet. I would often go to a nearby coffee lounge at night, to drink coffee and read books on positive thinking, while Hertha (the lady I was visiting) watched war movies on television; the very last thing I wanted to do. I had to keep busy, but Hertha didn't show any enthusiasm to travel or

Never give up or give in!

do the 'tourist thing', so it was not helpful, either for me or for Hertha, to have me stay with her any longer. I am sure that she must have been driven to distraction by my restless energy.

After leaving Dundas, I hired a car and drove to Ontario to visit my Aunt Betty, whom I had not seen for many years. She lived near a lake, which I was able to walk right around each day. Being near the water gave me some sense of peace. I stayed with my aunt for about four days. She was very pleasant to me and made my stay as happy as she could. I returned to Hertha's place for another couple of days, then flew out to Scotland, to my Aunt Rina's home in Ayr.

This aunt is my late father's sister, a most caring and gentle lady, whom I love very much. Aunt Rina is a petite lady in her seventies, and has been widowed for some 20 years or so. She has a soft round face; her wavy, grey hair is kept short and she still has a twinkle in her eyes. The stay with her helped me immensely, and I was able to calm down quite a bit. Aunt Rina is a Christian lady and so was my other aunt, her sister Jeanette, who lived close by, and they both did as much as they could to make me feel better.

My Aunt Jeanette asked me whether I wanted Vic to come back to me, and if I did, she would pray for this. I was not sure how to answer her question. Having given this very question hours of consideration on my trip, I had come to the realisation that somewhere along the way of us both working long hours to keep the stable a success, we had lost the real meaning of communication. I was now more like a friend to him than a wife. It was in such circumstances that Vic probably became impressed to have a woman not much more than half his wife's age, interested in him. So we prayed together for the right solution to the problem.

Aunt Jeanette died not longer after I arrived home.

While in Scotland, on this visit, I had another reading, from a different medium. This time I was given messages from my son, confirming his happiness and his love for us. He was full of advice for me, for my life now, with warnings of certain things to avoid. He was happy that Susan was at last beginning to accept his death and not grieving for him so much.

After a month, I returned to Australia and was met at the airport by Glenn and little Nicky, who put her arms around me and did not want to let me go. The feeling that this gave me was so comforting.

Glenn had horses racing at Bankstown that night and had to go to the races directly from the airport, so after a 24-hour flight, I had a long night ahead of me before I was actually home.

After finally getting to bed, I did not surface the next day until about mid-afternoon and, on waking, had to check the clocks; I just could not believe I had slept so long.

It seemed to me that, because Vic was the better trainer and driver, and could do all necessary farm activities, it would be better for all if Vic stayed and I moved out. As all the children lived on the property at Glen-Garry Lodge, in my agonised state I could not envisage my being able to see them so often. I thought I was going to lose them, if I had to leave the farm.

Any loss of contact with my children and grandchildren was a situation that I could not bear to think about. I had lost one son and could not stand the thought of losing any other children, no matter how it came about. Toni and Glenn by this time had a son, Andrew, and Susan was pregnant at the time, giving birth to a son, Hayden, a few months later. Both families now are blessed with one daughter and one son each. The two girls have always been great pals, but the boys needed a little more time to become good mates.

After a few days of discussion with the family and Vic, it was finally decided that it would be best if I stayed on the farm and helped Glenn with his training, and Vic would leave. I guess it was mainly because I was the one more willing to help Glenn with his overall work. Vic wanted to train his own couple of horses and to drive just a few of Glenn's, for fast-work. It was not because Vic was lazy, but he had set his mind on less participation, and had no desire to start training and racing too many horses again. He was living in our caravan with Gail, his present partner, at Berry, a little village south of Wollongong and an hour away from Exeter. They were training horses on a nearby beach, and decided to stay there.

Vic was forced to change his decision on an early retirement when he moved to Moobal, near Twead Heads in northern New South Wales, where he purchased a property on which to live and train his team. He races mainly in Brisbane now. We are still friends, and often consult each other on matters of mutual concern.

The family was so thoughtful and helpful to me in those following few weeks. The telephone would ring and Glenn would say, 'Mum,

ABOVE: After numerous quinella's with Vic, from the late 1980's Glenn and I finished one-two in various races. This was one in which I won with Liberated and Glenn was on Our Revenge (No 6). We are seen returning to scale together.

BELOW: Glenn's Thunder is paraded for the photographers after winning the Cranbourne Cup and being presented with his garland of flowers. This wonderful pacer would have gone a long way in the sport but for his untimely death.

ABOVE: Westburn Grant overcomes a broken leg to return to Perth and win the WA Pacing Cup. Seen here at left after the presentation is the veterinary surgeon who saved his life, Dr John Yovich. That's our friend and strapper Kevin Wells holding the horse, and the breeder and part owner of Spot, the late Barney Breen.

LEFT: While most of Westburn Grant's work was at the beach, here he is with Vic doing fast work especially for the photographers. Once the horse was recognised by racegoers and officials as a champion, we did our best to cooperate in the build-up to the major events.

ABOVE: Westburn Grant at the beach. Note how the horse just stands there perfectly still as it awaits on Vic to change from his clothes into bathers so he can then take Spot into the water having finished their fast work.

BELOW: Our great pacer captures the most prestigious pacing event outside of North America, winning the 1992 Inter Dominion Championship at Melbourne's Moonee Valley. After three hard runs in a week, it was those few days at the beach which helped him bounce back in the final.

One of the ploys the photographers adopted with Westburn Grant was to ask Vic to drive the horse slowly along the beach and have me running beside them. I guess this type of exercise was more helpful to me than it was the horse.

The last race for Westburn Grant. This was the Inter Dominion in Brisbane. Note the colours Vic is wearing are the official Olympic Games colours following Vic and the horse being made official ambassadors as part of the bid to gain Sydney the 2000 Olympics.

WESTBURN GRANT p, 1:55.6h

Brown Horse 1985

LAND GRANT (USA)- WESTBURN VUE (NZ)

Date	Track	Place	Driver	Rate	Distance	Stakes	Race Winner)
07-07-88	Penrith	1	G. Frost	2:08.3	2020m	$1,050	2YO of $1500 Stake
22-07-88	Harold Pk	1	G. Frost	2:03.5	1960m	$3,491	2YO
29-07-88	Harold Pk	1	G. Frost	2:03.9	1960m	$3,648	2YO
02-12-88	Harold Pk	1	V. Frost	2:03.7	1960m	$3,492	3YO
30-12-88	Harold Pk	1	G. Frost	2:02.8	1960m	$3,491	3YO
14-01-89	Moonee Valley	2	V. Frost	2:04.0	1940m	$3,634	VHRC Cup (Rockleigh Victory 1ST)
20-01-89	Harold Pk	1	V. Frost	2:02.1	2350m	$9,975	Harold Pk Guineas
28-01-89	Moonee Valley	1	V. Frost	2:00.4	2380m	$6,720	Victoria Derby Heat
04-02-89	Moonee Valley	1	V. Frost	2:00.8	2380m	$50,800	Victoria Derby Final (G1)
10-02-89	Harold Pk	1	G. Frost	2:01.0	1609m	$16,625	Globe Derby Mile
17-02-89	Harold Pk	1	V. Frost	2:01.3	2350m	$5,000	NSW Derby Heat
24-02-89	Harold Pk	1	V. Frost	1:59.0	2350m	$66,500	NSW Derby Final (G1)
15-03-89	Addington	1	V. Frost	2:03.3	2600m	$39,000	John Brandon 3YO Championship
18-03-89	Addington	1	V. Frost	1:59.2	2000m	$39,000	John Brandon Flying Stakes
25-03-89	Addington	1	V. Frost	2:01.7	2600m	$97,500	NZ Derby(G1)
29-04-89	Bankstown	3	V. Frost	2:02.3	2540m	$9,450	Australian Derby (G1) (Rockleigh Victory)
11-11-89	Canberra	1	V. Frost	1:56.8	1609m	$6,400	Canberra Mile
24-11-89	Harold Pk	1	V. Frost	1:57.9	1609m	$122,500	Miracle Mile (G1)
04-12-89	Bankstown	1	V. Frost	2:02.6	2540m	$68,125	Treuer Memorial (G1)
08-12-89	Gloucester Pk	1	V. Frost	1:59.1	2100m	$7,000	Gold Nugget Heat
15-12-89	Gloucester Pk	1	V. Frost	1:58.8	2500m	$76,000	Gold Nugget Final (G1)
22-12-89	Gloucester Pk	1	V. Frost	1:57.9	2100m	$14,000	B & H Cup Heat
31-12-89	Gloucester Pk	1	V. Frost	1:58.3	2100m	$14,000	B & H Cup Heat
05-01-90	Gloucester Pk	9	V. Frost	2:01.4	2500m	$1,000	B & H Cup Final (G1) (Tarport Sox)
13-01-90	Globe Derby	1	V. Frost	2:00.5	2645m	$57,200	S.A. Cup(G1)
27-01-90	Moonee Valley	4	V. Frost	1:58.9	2380m	$11,560	Victoria Cup (G1) (Sovereign Cloud)
10-02-90	Globe Derby	2	V. Frost	1:59.3	1800m	$4,850	Inter Dominion Heat (Jane Ellen)
14-02-90	Globe Derby	2	V. Frost	1:58.6	2230m	$4,850	Inter Dominion Heat (Gaelic Skipper)
17-02-90	Globe Derby	3	V. Frost	2:02.5	2645m	$2,350	Inter Dominion Heat (Kylie's Hero)
24-02-90	Globe Derby	5	V. Frost	2:00.0	2645m	$8,000	Inter Dominion Final (G1) (Thorate)
24-08-90	Harold Pk	3	V. Frost	2:02.9	2350m	$800	Open Pace (Love To Spare)
14-09-90	Harold Pk	1	V. Frost	2:04.4	2350m	$6,400	Open Pace
28-09-90	Harold Pk	3	V. Frost	1:59.6	1609m	$800	Open Pace (Love To Spare)
06-10-90	Newcastle	1	V. Frost	1:56.1	1609m	$12,400	Newcastle Mile
12-10-90	Harold Pk	1	V. Frost	1:56.5	1609m	$6,400	Open Pace
20-10-90	Albion Pk	1	V. Frost	1:57.4	1609m	$55,900	Queensland Championship (G1)
03-11-90	Moonee Valley	1	V. Frost	1:57.0	1940m	$63,000	Legends
09-11-90	Harold Pk	1	V. Frost	2:00.5	2700m	$64,000	Italian Cup
16-11-90	Harold Pk	7	V. Frost	1:59.3	2350m	$1,500	Australian Pacing Champ. (G1) Almeta Boy)
30-11-90	Harold Pk	1	V. Frost	1:55.6	1609m	$180,000	Miracle Mile (G1)
10-12-90	Bankstown	2	V. Frost	2:01.0	2540m	$18,200	Treuer Memorial (G1) (Thorate)
26-12-90	Gloucester Pk	2	V. Frost	1:58.3	2100m	$3,800	B & H Cup Heat (Sinbad Bay)
31-12-90	Gloucester Pk	1	V. Frost	1:56.7	2100m	$14,000	B & H Cup Heat
04-01-91	Gloucester Pk	1	V. Frost	1:57.8	2500m	$179,900	B & H Cup Final (G1)
12-10-91	Newcastle	1	V. Frost	1:55.6	1609m	$14,000	Newcastle Mile
19-10-91	Albion Pk	2	V. Frost	1:55.0	2100m	$17,200	Queensland Champ. (G1) (Franco Ice)
02-11-91	Moonee Valley	5	V. Frost	1:55.8	1940m	$280	Legends (Almeta Boy)
11-11-91	Launceston	1	V. Frost	1:57.3	2100m	$69,375	Australian Pacing Championship (G1)
29-11-91	Harold Pk	3	V. Frost	1:57.2	1609m	$21,250	Miracle Mile (G1) (Christopher Vance)
07-12-91	Bankstown	2	V. Frost	1:59.2	2540m	$19,600	Treuer Memorial (G1) (Franco Ice)
27-12-91	Gloucester Pk	6	G. Frost	2:00.5	2500m	$0	B & H Cup Heat (Zakara)
03-01-92	Gloucester Pk	1	V. Frost	1:58.1	2500m	$182,523	B & H Cup Final (G1)
11-01-92	Globe Derby	1	V. Frost	2:00.7	2645m	$43,840	S.A. Cup (G1)
08-02-92	Moonee Valley	5	V. Frost	1:59.4	2380m	$3,700	Victoria Cup (G1) (Franco Ice)
22-02-92	Moonee Valley	2	V. Frost	1:59.1	2380m	$3,343	Inter Dominion Heat (Level Advice)
26-02-92	Moonee Valley	4	V. Frost	1:57.8	1940m	$1,115	Inter Dominion Heat (Level Advice)
29-02-92	Moonee Valley	3	V. Frost	1:59.2	2840m	$2,229	Inter Dominion Heat (Christopher Vance)
07-03-92	Moonee Valley	1	V. Frost	1:59.4	2840m	$252,000	Inter Dominion Final (G1)
24-10-92	Newcastle	2	V. Frost	1:57.2	1609m	$3,000	Newcastle Mile (Joshua Tree)
14-11-92	Bankstown	2	V. Frost	2:01.0	2540m	$19,000	Australian Pacing Champ. (G1) (Franco Tiger)
27-11-92	Harold Pk	4	V. Frost	1:56.7	1609m	$10,000	Miracle Mile (G1) (Franco Tiger)
27-02-93	Moonee Valley	4	V. Frost	1:56.7	2380m	$9,000	Victoria Cup (G1) (Master Musician)
19-03-93	Harold Pk	1	V. Frost	1:57.3	1609m	$13,000	Golden Mile
17-04-93	Albion Pk	3	V. Frost	1:56.9	2100m	$2,250	Inter Dominion Heat (Blossom Lady)
21-04-93	Albion Pk	1	V. Frost	1:57.5	1609m	$14,500	Inter Dominion Heat
24-04-93	Albion Pk	2	V. Frost	1:58.0	2600m	$4,500	Inter Dominion Heat (Master Musician)
01-05-93	Albion Pk	6	V. Frost	1:57.8	2600m	$4,000	Inter Dominion Final (G1) (Jack Morris)

CAREER SUMMARY
67 Starts 38 Wins 11 Seconds 7 Thirds $2,374,016 Stakes
27 starts in Group One races for 14 wins and 6 placings
In 60 out of 67 starts finished in the first four horses

ABOVE: The survivors of the Paterson family who had migrated from England to Australia. We had come together at the Botanical Gardens, with my Mother second from right, with her son Eddie, and daughters Neena and myself.

BELOW: Glenn and his wife Toni and their two children Nicki and Andrew during a break at the stables for a cuppa. Glen-Garry Lodge has a stabling complex for 28 horses. Note the machine in the loft in the background for making chaff.

My friend John and I pictured at my home at Exeter, shortly before making my decision to leave the farm and purchase a small home at Oak Flats close to a beautiful lake. All my life I have felt at peace when spending time by water.

Sunrise from my backyard overlooking the lake at Oak Flats. At last I feel at peace with my life and my search for answers. My family often visit me here, while Vic and I have remained good friends

The most precious thing I have in this world – my family. At back is my son-in-law Brett and his wife Susan, with Glenn and his wife Toni. My grandchildren from the left are Nicki and Monique, along with Hayden and Andrew.

tea is on the table.' I had to go over and eat. I guess they knew I would not bother if I had to prepare something for myself at home. I appreciated this attention very much, but after a few days, feeling that I could manage, I protested that it was too much for them.

They took no notice at all of my protests. The phone would ring and 'Tea is on the table Mum, get yourself over here before it gets cold,' was the statement I heard when I picked it up. If I had not finally refused their offer, and commenced getting myself back into a routine again, I think this could have become a habit.

In the mornings, Susan would come up for breakfast, bringing the two little ones, to keep me company and, I suspected, with an ulterior motive; checking to make certain I was eating. I had lost weight and didn't have much to spare as it was, and they had worried about me. It was most comforting the way Glenn, Susan and their respective little families demonstrated their concern for me. They kept a close eye on me until they were satisfied that I was able to operate with some normality again and get on with my life with a show of confidence.

Once again, I became 'hooked on horses and racing', and devoted a big part of my day to their training.

Once a week I encouraged the two girls, Monique and Nicole, to come to my house and sleep over. They loved to sleep in my bed, and I enjoyed having them with me, but they were restless sleepers, and wriggled and thrashed me with their arms and legs during the night.

We nestled into bed, one on each side of me, and they took it in turns to pick the stories for me to read. I had quite a lot of children's books, but the book that was most frequently chosen was one containing my 'Jesus' stories, as they called them. It became mandatory for me to sit with an arm around each one of them, and make a bell sound when it was time to turn a page, which they did in turns.

When Andrew became old enough to sleep the night, he sometimes joined us, but two of them had to sleep in the spare bed in an adjoining room. Hayden joined us later, when he too was old enough.

The girls loved to have a baking night and I taught them how to bake pastry. Monique loved to make one filled with apple, as long as I peeled and cooked the apples, but Nicky always made one with jam. The results of their efforts were enjoyed in the stables, or at home the next day. They are both now able to make a good pastry.

Except for measuring the ingredients into the bowls, I encouraged them to do most things themselves. They sieved the flour, mixed the ingredients, rolled out the pastry and spread it with the fillings. Andrew loved to help out by scraping the bowls, after the icing had been put onto the cakes I baked for the stables. He took his task seriously, but managed to apply as much to his face and his clothes as he removed from the bowls!

After helping Glenn for about nine months, he said to me one day that he was going away for a couple of days, and that he had put me down as driver of his horse, Golden Peace, racing at Fairfield on Tuesday, 27th September 1994.

'Glenn!—I can't do that, I haven't even had a drive at a gymkhana yet, I haven't driven for years, I can't drive in a race before I get the feel of it again!' I gasped, in exasperation. It was Sunday afternoon, and too late to go to a gymkhana now to refresh my skills.

Glenn's nonchalant reply was, 'Mum, you will be right, it's all set now; you are down to drive him on Tuesday.'

So that was that. I was given little choice but to drive Golden Peace. The casual attitude of solving a problem is typical of Glenn. As it turned out, I drove Golden Peace and won. This was my first race drive after an absence of about six years. The win was an added bonus.

The thrill of the race and the feel of the horse before me, responding to my signals once again, started the adrenaline flowing. I experienced that irresistible need to race again and was made aware that horses still held an important place in my life. I knew very quickly that there would be no resistance from me when the next offer to drive was made.

The congratulations and the welcome that I received that day were a balm to my bruised heart, and I knew that I was back. Once more I was in the environment that I loved: *harness racing.*

By this time, Glenn had a large team of pacers in work and often had two in the same race at Harold Park. It didn't take much persuasion for me to take the drive on one of these, each time it occurred. Soon, I was driving there most race nights, and enjoying them all.

The long drives home after the races were not as easy to endure. We would sometimes stop at a Chinese restaurant for a meal on the way home, because we didn't always have time to eat at the track. Often we would not have eaten since lunchtime. The stopover would make it a much later night, but no-one complained.

In the area of self-improvement, I had done a lot of work on myself, with tapes, books and lectures. Also with techniques for releasing anger, positive thinking, loving oneself and letting go of one's ego and other aspects of life that are a hindrance to one's peace of mind. I attended many seminars on these subjects and bought a lot of the tapes and books on sale on the night, which I found very helpful. I learned a lot from these. I firmly believed that 'when the student is ready the teacher will appear', and at this stage of my life, I was looking around for the teacher.

Later, I re-read 'The Power of Positive Thinking', a book written by a minister, Norman Vincent Peale. Even though I had read it six years before, the book now held much more meaning for me. I had an insatiable need to read his books, and would buy any publication of his that I could get my hands on; they almost became bible-like for me. I found them to be so inspirational, and they filled me with hope and a great feeling of peace. I would go to secondhand book stores and buy any books of his that I could find, giving them to people that I knew who were having difficulties in their lives. His words have changed quite a few lives, as well as my own, for the better.

Once, I only wanted to read books about the New Age, then self-improvement, graduating to Norman Vincent Peale, but now I was being introduced to the Bible and *its* teachings.

Affirmations became a big part of my approach to a day, and this made a difference in my thinking and my attitude to life. I had been a person who had to please people, drive a good race and always try to do the right thing, where possible. It mattered greatly, for me, to have people agreeing with my actions.

This new thinking gave me a completely different outlook on things, particularly with race driving. When I went onto the track now, I would say to myself, 'all is well with my soul', something my friend John had urged me to do. Of course, I still assessed the field, and then decided the best race strategy for the horse I was driving. Some horses perform better if they lead, some if they have a sit behind another, some if they sit outside the leader, and others work better from the rear. The horse's performance depends heavily on whether it is a tough horse (a horse with endurance and stamina) or a sprinter (a horse with speed). One has to assess each horse's particular ability, then try to place it in a position, during a race, best suited to maximise this ability.

Now, however, it was not so important for me to seek the approval of others. I gave of my best and that was all that mattered to me.

The irony of this was that I seemed to be driving better and was finishing in a place most times, and winning some races as well. There was no pressure to please others now, I was actually enjoying myself instead.

Before my separation from Vic, I had met John while attending his clinic for treatment. I had gone home to Vic after the first appointment, and said that I had met the most caring and dedicated man I have ever met, apart from him.

John is a Christian man and we used to talk about our opinions of faith (mostly mine; he is a great and caring listener) during my visits. After my separation from Vic, I started to lean on John for strength in these matters. We eventually began going out together and now he is a very big part of my life.

There have been many times throughout my racing career that gave me great excitement and pleasure. But there were a lot more times that you would call ordinary. On 18th October 1994, I was given an opportunity for the former sort of time. It gave me great satisfaction, in this sport that I loved, to add to harness racing history once again—this time it was a first for harness racing in the world.

Liberated won for me at Harold Park, and my son Glenn came second with his horse, Our Revenge, making this the first time in the sport that a mother and son had ever driven a metropolitan quinella. Vic and I had several times achieved the honour of driving husband-and-wife quinellas. The first time was on 25th January 1980 and now, 14 years later, I had achieved a quinella with my son. This is one record in my career that I am very happy to have achieved.

The following week Glenn won a race with Our Revenge and I came second, driving Liberated—another mother-and-son quinella. Mother and son taking out the quinella two weeks running, first one way and reversing the order the next, is certainly unique. There would

*Kind hearts are the garden, kind thoughts are the roots.
Kind words are the blossom, kind deeds are the fruits.*

not be many mothers and sons driving together anywhere; it is a very unusual occurrence. The hugs from my son were as pleasing to me as the cheers from the crowd.

Each week I continued to drive in races and to work in the stables every day. Glenn had forged ahead in the Harold Park premiership and I was eager to help him as much as possible. If he could win the premiership, this would be his first time. We were both keen for him to achieve this goal, as his father had done on five different occasions.

My biggest fault then, if I can call it that, was my being a workaholic. There was a compulsion to do anything that I saw needed doing, and because things had to be done right, I was driving myself too hard.

My mother, as I have said, had these flashes of insight which she would relate to me. She said to me continually, 'Margaret, you have got to slow down'. After continuing to ignore her warnings, she said to me one day, 'Margaret, if you don't slow down, you are going to be stopped.'

I was trying to slow down, but, as I had done in all my life before, I could not rest when there was a job to be done.

TWENTY-SEVEN

Hanging Up My Colours

** 'Asking God for miracles is no
substitute for not using God-given means'*

The last race I would ever drive in took place at Harold Park Paceway on 16th June 1995. The previous week I had driven the pacer Just Baz in a race where Glenn was behind the stablemate Westburn Fella. This time, when both horses were drawn to clash again, Glenn had elected to drive Just Baz off the second row, and I would be behind Westburn Fella on the extreme outside gate off the front.

There was a reason why Glenn changed the drivers over for this event. Just Baz would race in any other position without pulling, except when caught leading the outside division. The previous week that is exactly where I found myself trapped with him. In this position, outside the leader, he would pull hard, wanting to take the lead, and was very difficult to restrain. This would push the leader to set too fast a speed for this stage of the race, as well as tiring the horse that was pulling.

No matter how hard I tried, I could not prevent my horse from pulling and increasing the race speed. In hindsight, it would have been better if Glenn had surrendered the lead with Westburn Fella. If a stable has two horses in one race, you have to be careful that your tactics are not misconstrued by punters (and stewards) when a horse surrenders the lead to a stablemate. Stewards also are usually good 'readers' of a race. It is their duty not only to keep racing fair, but to ensure that racing be seen by the public to be fair. Handing over the lead to a stablemate can be fraught with risks of suspicion. Mindful of this, drivers don't always make the best decisions suitable for their horse.

The next week, both horses were again drawn to compete together. Just Baz had caused Westburn Fella to lose the previous week's race by his pulling, so to lessen the chance of this happening again this week, the decision was made for me to drive Westburn Fella and

Glenn to drive Just Baz.

Due to my memory loss, I am unable to give an actual blow-by-blow account of this race, therefore the description has been derived from several sources: from the observations of eye witnesses and the re-running of the video film of the race, and the feelings conveyed are those that I remember from previous experiences. My last recollection of this episode was calling for 'room'.

On this night, I had earlier watched Glenn win two races from his three drives. I had not had a successful night with my previous two drives, being unable to secure good positions in either race. I finished only fourth and fifth, and had suffered interference when driving Gold Fury in his event. Hoping for a better result in the last race of the night, we went on to the track, wishing each other luck, as we always did. On that cold, wet Friday night, we were oblivious as to how much luck we were going to need.

The number six gate from behind the mobile starting barrier at Harold Park (which I had drawn), is out wide on the front line, a position that is almost impossible to lead from, unless your horse is a brilliant beginner, and providing those drawn inside you don't wish to engage in a cut-throat early battle for the lead. Glenn had drawn the back line, so he would undoubtedly be at the rear of the field on settling down.

The steward called us to the start, 'Get them up to the gate, drivers,' and the mobile moved off. We jogged into our positions on the gate and were working up speed when the starter signalled the driver of the mobile to 'go', with the two arms of the machine folding in as the vehicle cleared the field. I pushed forward immediately to gain my best position. Others inside of me had the same idea, and I was trapped out in the 'death seat', outside the leader. Westburn Fella was not fast enough to take the lead away from the horse inside of me. I did what was usual in this position; I took hold of my horse to ease the speed of the outside line, hoping to encourage something from the rear to go forward and give me cover. Such tactics can often lead to a driver from the rear coming out to take advantage of the slower pace and whip around the field. A wet track is also usually inviting for someone to come from the rear and make an early move. But for some reason my strategy failed this night, and I was parked outside the leader for the race.

One lap from home the bell sounded. This is to ensure that all drivers know it is now just one circuit of the track to the finish. The sound of the bell is a signal that sees the tempo of the race increase dramatically, as those up front do not want to get caught napping by a horse in full flight from the rear. The driver who had been good enough during the race to have worked his way into the favoured position of one-out and one-back, was Glenn. As he waited for the right moment to make his run, Just Baz's hot breath was blowing down the back of my jacket.

Westburn Fella was a good horse, but did not have the stamina to race outside the leader, breaking the breeze for an entire race. A hard run such as this is usually enough to take the edge off any late sprint, and he was feeling the pressure. One does not give up in these conditions, as you try to hold your horse together, nursing it for as long as possible. Knowing that Glenn was the one right behind me, it would have been my hope that, if and when my horse reached the depths of its staying ability, it would not hamper Glenn by tiring too soon, and force him back with me.

Just Baz by now had a horse moving up three wide past him as the field raced down the back straight. Glenn could not make his run until the horse on the outside gave ground.

The pacer out three wide kept grinding away, and around the last bend was up into a position outside of me, and began veering in under pressure, hampering my position. Danger signals would have been going off in my mind, requiring me to call out for room, expecting the driver to pull off and give me clearance.

Other drivers had started moves from the rear of the field now, and bunched and gathered speed, each struggling for his best position. The horse did not pull off, the gap was closing, and I was being pushed onto the horse inside of me, giving me nowhere to go. Frantically, I tried to draw the driver's attention to the critical position I was in. I know the feeling of pain involved in hitting the hard track— and broken bones!

I was calling for room and urging the young driver on my outside to pull off, but at this point of the race, when every driver's concentration is centred on winning, my pleas went unheeded.

Up until this occasion, the need for me to call to other drivers for room was extremely rare, but I would have been aware of the real and

Do not be afraid, only believe. Mark 5;36

present danger in the closeness of his sulky's wheel, and continued my frantic plea for room. Under the frantic pressure of racing up the home straight, his sulky wheel was ever so close to my horse's legs. With most of the field right behind me, this was a situation one could feel real fear. My fear was not only for my safety, but knowing my son was right on my back. If I went down, he would probably go right over the top of me.

My worst fears were realised. The interference that happened so suddenly, caused my horse to break stride, stumble and fall, sending Westburn Fella crashing onto the track, flicking my gig into the air and catapulting me face-first into the gravel. On videos of this incident, I landed just in front of my fallen horse, resulting in one of the worst falls to have taken place in the long history of Harold Park.

The accident could have been a lot worse, had it not been for Glenn's quick assessment of the situation, and his rapid response, pulling his horse back and away from me.

Three horses came down in the smash, but the other two reinsmen were not badly hurt and were able to walk away. I was not so fortunate.

Immediately after the fall, I was totally unaware of anything, and the events that followed were related to me much later. Westburn Fella was lying on the track on his side, head toward the winning post, his legs and hopples were tangled in the legs of another horse on its side, head in the same direction. Both horses were lying stunned by their fall. My gig was demolished.

Face down and still, with my arms outstretched, I was lying on the track, just inches away from Westburn Fella's head, until he was moved about two feet further away by the men present. Our strapper Kevin Wells had been one of the first to reach the scene, and with my horse lying so close to me, he positioned himself on Westburn Fella's head to restrain it from any sudden movement.

The race went to its completion, only a short distance from the crash scene. Glenn immediately turned around and jogged back to the fallen horses, and gave his horse to a willing hand. I'm told there seemed to be a delay in the arrival of the ambulance.

In the meantime, Kevin Wells was still lying on Westburn Fella's head, restraining any sudden movement, and Neil Day, a driver, was lying on the other fallen horse's head, restraining it also.

Because the seriousness of my injuries could not be ascertained from the position I was in, no-one was able to move me away from the precarious spot, so close to the tangled horses, until the ambulance arrived.

Westburn Fella was lying quietly, until the other horse tangled with him began to struggle. The horse had been quiet, and only commenced struggling when somebody began to unharness it while it was lying on the track, despite the protesting shouts of 'Hold on! Hold on!'

The horse sprang to its feet, less than two metres from where I lay. Glenn was standing over me, and as the horse came up, Glenn leapt across that narrow gap, and with both hands on the frightened horse's neck, literally pushed it off balance and away from where I lay.

The ambulance had arrived by this time, and the officers had begun their examination of me. A great relief was felt by those standing around me when an officer turned me onto my back and they saw the air bubbles in the blood from my nose, as I breathed.

'She's alive, she's alive,' my son Glenn whispered.

The heavy fall onto the track caused multiple injuries. My head injuries were the most obvious. I was taken, unconscious, to Royal Prince Alfred Hospital, and was critical for most of the night. John accompanied me in the ambulance. Glenn, Vic (who had been racing that night), John Dumesny, the racing manager from Harold Park, and Keith, a friend who works where we stable our horses on race nights, drove to the hospital, and stayed until they were told that I would live.

There have always been race falls in harness racing. Usually the drivers get up and walk away. Some people that night stayed late at the track, some went to the office, and others remained in the stabling area, all hoping to get some encouraging news about my condition.

Some friends told me, months later, that they had been driving in their cars on the night of the smash when they heard a voice on the radio station 2KY, urging people to pray for Margaret Frost who had been injured badly at Harold Park Paceway during a race that night. I am very grateful to the man, Rod Fuller, for this, as I now know the power of prayer and am sure that they were a big help in my recovery.

Cast all your anxieties on Him because He cares for you.   *Peter 5:7*

Both my nieces, Jennifer and Lisa, Neena's daughters, who live in Sydney were at the hospital every day. They often allowed John to go for a coffee or meal, as he hardly left me at weekends and travelled from Wollongong after his clinic finished each night.

Not all the injuries were known at this point, and it ended up taking several months to discover the full effect of the smash. At first the main concern was for my skull, then the eyes, as my right eye had been damaged so badly that I was unable to open it at all. My face was badly swollen, my lower lip and chin were cut, and some front teeth were broken, and there were other cuts and bruises around my eyes.

For several days, I was floating in and out of consciousness, I am told, and did not know much of what was going on or who had been to visit me. I had much pain in my chest and electrocardiographs were performed. These proved negative.

Scans were taken of the brain the night of the accident, and the doctor told the family I had suffered damage to this area, but it was not sure to what extent. The diagnosis, at first, was that I had a fractured skull, because it was thought that cerebrospinal fluid was leaking from inside the skull out through my nose, but after further assessment, fractures were not confirmed.

For the first 24 hours, the hospital was inundated with calls, from wellwishers across the country, to such a degree that the incoming calls were jamming the switchboard and interfering with the hospital's function. The hospital staff's request that people refrain from calling the hospital was broadcast over the racing radio station 2KY. A private phone was installed by my bedside, and my visitors took the calls.

Great difficulty was experienced in remembering who my visitors were, even though they may have been family or friends of long standing. John would inform me who my visitors were, and later reminded me of them.

My friends and the harness racing fraternity responded in their usual extremely generous way, with flowers, cards and phone calls to wish me well. My room gave the appearance of a well-stocked florist shop, almost packed to capacity. Even in my dazed state, during those first days in hospital, I was made aware of the open-hearted generosity of the harness racing fraternity, emphasised by those members who came to visit me.

My visitors informed me that, in the early days of my time in Prince Alfred, I was rambling on about driving again the following week, and getting out of hospital by the end of the week, to finish my preparations for a charity auction that I had started, to assist Susan in her efforts to raise money for Ronald McDonald House. She was an entrant in a Charity Queen competition that was going to be held at a ball to raise funds for this favourite charity of mine. We had also planned an auction in conjunction with this, to be held at Sutton Forest Hotel, and I had a lot of organising left to do. Of course I was not going to be there, and Janet Greason took over the rest of the work, helping to make the auction a big success. Susan went on to win the Charity Queen title, thanks to Janet and our supporters.

After ten days, I was transferred to the Lawrence Hargrave Rehabilitation Hospital at Thirroul, where I was well taken care of. My memory was still impaired, and I was in need of further therapy; even now I still have problems in this area.

Still suffering much pain, I was finding it almost impossible to fall asleep at night without the aid of an injection. Sometimes I was almost begging for one. I have never been one for taking medicines, preferring to put up with pain, rather than give in to taking drugs. The next few years changed my mind on this score, for I needed some rather strong medications to be able to cope.

The pain was not subsiding just with rest and therapy, and the doctor in charge sent me for further tests, for chest pain, right shoulder pain and facial pain. I was still having pain with chewing and was unable to open my mouth easily since the accident.

One test revealed that my gall bladder was functioning poorly (about 16% of normal). A Wollongong specialist ordered an X-ray of my jaw, which revealed that it was broken in two places, one on each side. The fractures were left to repair by themselves; since they were not displaced fractures, any interference with them now could complicate and impair their healing.

They sent me to Shellharbour Hospital, to have the gall bladder removed on my birthday, and I returned to the Thirroul rehabilitation centre for another couple of weeks.

The pain did not recede, much to my dismay, and I was still having severe pain in both shoulders, arms and back. I had to sleep with my arms resting on pillows, and on my back. This was never my preferred position, for I had always slept on my side. I am still looking forward to the time when I will be able to sleep the way I would like, without any pain.

Treatment gave little improvement, and I had to resort to using pillows under my legs or knees, which relieved the pain enough to allow me to sleep. I am so lucky to have John to treat me quite regularly, thus reducing the overall pain markedly. Without him, I know I would be suffering a great deal more.

My right eye was causing a lot of concern and I was still not able to open it. There was nothing they could do at Lawrence Hargrave Hospital; I was only advised to wait patiently for some sign that it would eventually open by itself. I was still having difficulty in remembering who my visitors were, and had to be reminded often of many things.

The Lawrence Hargrave Rehabilitation Hospital discharged me after about six weeks, and I returned home to Exeter. I had difficulty doing any work at home, particularly any chore that required me to lift my arms above my head, as in hanging washing on the line.

Toni and Susan helped where they could, until I learned to throw the clothes over the line with one hand, then peg them, while I held the clothes down by the bottom, with the other. John was a tower of strength in my difficulties, and at weekends, he did most of the ironing and household chores.

For all the years I lived at Exeter, our family doctor was Richard Kwong, who sometimes used acupuncture in his practice. I was still suffering so much pain, that I consulted him. He used this procedure on my right eye, which then began to open, a little at a time. After some months, my eyelid had almost fully opened, but my eye muscles, giving upward movement to the eyeball, and my vision, have not recovered.

The impaired eye function remaining is thought to be due to the residual brain damage. I can't see things to my right or below me, when I am looking straight ahead. For me to have reasonably normal vision, now, I need complicated bifocal lenses in my spectacles, but these were not made available for almost 12 months after my accident.

For a year, I had been attending an eye specialist in Sydney, but he had been more concerned with what could be done to correct the damage to my eyes. It was my local optometrist, Tim Mckinnon, who suggested the spectacles that made such an unbelievable difference. I no longer had to walk with my head in the air to prevent double vision. Tim's expertise had performed for me what was nothing short of a miracle.

My restricted vision is a big problem in a busy thoroughfare, as people can rush in front of me, not realising my problem. I once tripped a lady over, who stepped in front of me. She became quite angry with me, and this made me become anxious in a crowd. When John is with me I tend to make him walk on my right side. If he isn't, then I walk next to the wall or buildings, wherever I can, so that no-one can cut across me.

The severe pain was still prominent in my shoulders, so Dr Kwong sent me to the Bowral clinic, where I had scans done on the right shoulder first; these revealed a rotator cuff tear that required surgery. I had to go to the Mater Misericordia Hospital at Crows Nest, Sydney, for the operation, and I expected to be out of pain after this was performed. Not so! I was bitterly disappointed!

For several months after the operation, the pain was almost unbearable. I always prided myself on being tough, but this was far worse than the broken collarbones and other injuries that I had suffered previously. I had to take the strongest painkillers I could obtain, and rub liniments into the area every few hours. John put hot-water bottles on the shoulder, which soothed the pain, but we found out that this was not the best procedure to follow. The heat of the hot-water bottle caused the whole area of the chest and shoulder to hemorrhage, which caused a lot more pain and discomfort. We then resorted to ice packs, which John replaced every few hours to give a much better result.

It was necessary to have physiotherapy for about six months—always a very painful treatment—to recover the use of my shoulder. I learned exercises to assist with this, to do on the carpet, and bought myself weights, which I used to pull my arm back and sideways.

Gradually I regained my strength, by having to lift the weights, but at first I could not even lift my arm without a weight. I persevered with the exercises, in spite of the discomfort and pain, in my determination to become well.

To multiply your joy; count your blessings

My vision got me into trouble a fortnight after the operation on my right shoulder; when a young girl bumped me as she hurried by, I cried out with the pain, causing the girl to feel very badly about it. This would normally have been nothing, but the jar on the arm, so soon after the operation, was about the worst thing that could have happened. I have since learned to hold my head at the right angle to see better, even with my new specs, and to continually turn my head directly to the right, and to look down. It is amazing how pain can teach you new habits.

Before I learned to do this, I caused myself to suffer a very bad cut to the lower part of my left leg. I had gone for a walk around the farm, which I did often, and was looking around at the animals and birds, and I did not look down to step over a log. I misjudged my step across the log, failing to see a branch protruding, and struck a sharp part with the back of my leg, which cut into my jeans, making a jagged hole on the lower part of my left calf.

Susan bathed and bandaged it for me, and told me to go to the doctor for a check-up, but I could not see the cut too clearly and thought that it would heal. For once I should have followed my daughter's advice; it was a very deep tear and it really should have been stitched.

When John saw it a few days later, he let fly with some of his choicest language; he was frustrated (to say the least) with me for not getting medical treatment. He said I had taken a big risk of getting an ulcerated leg. After several weeks of bathing and dressing, it eventually healed, leaving a nasty scar. I am more careful where and how I walk now, and when I go downstairs I make sure to look down as I walk. Even so, it is impossible to look down all the time and I have suffered two other very bad cuts to my legs, which have left scars.

The other shoulder was still as painful, so I was sent for another scan, which showed that the left shoulder had a rotator cuff tear, but a bigger tear than the one sustained by my right shoulder. I had to face another operation, knowing that the shoulder would never be fully usable if I did not have it. I was dreading having to go through this ordeal again, but had faith in the specialist, Dr Caldwell, who gave me much credit for my efforts. He asked me to write a diary on my exercises, which I did, for any interested patients. He was amazed that I was prepared to go through another rotor cuff operation. He says that most people think one is enough to bear, which I certainly agreed with, but I felt I had no option in my case.

The second operation was performed at the same hospital, and this time I knew what I was in for. Ice packs, painkillers and the Chinese liniment that I had found the only help after the first operation. Another six months of physiotherapy and exercises followed.

In all of these hospital stays, my mother and sister were so good, visiting me regularly and accompanying me on the train on my visits to the Sydney specialists. My nieces, Jennifer and Lisa, visited me in hospital and Lisa drove me home each time from the Mater Hospital.

It is quite a struggle making myself fit and reducing the weight I gained. I was unable to do much walking for the first year or so, but then I started walking every day, three miles or so around the trotting track, picking up any stones as I went.

Jogging was one exercise I tried, but running gives my hips pain, which is caused by the damage to the spine, and the pain can become so severe that I can't sleep. I have to be content with walking and, since moving to Oak Flats, swimming in the pool, which is heated in winter. I did hope to play tennis again one day, but this will most likely be out of the question.

My friends say they think I look better, just the way I am, and I shouldn't worry so much, just thank God that I am alive and well.

John was able to confer with the doctors at the hospital and also with Dr Kwong from Moss Vale later, and they spoke with him often. He had access to most of the scans and X-ray reports taken, and knew of the injuries that I had received. We both know that it is nothing short of a miracle that I am not confined to a wheelchair, or indeed, that I do not have more serious injuries. This has led me to continue my search for answers.

Lasting joy comes when you put Christ first.

TWENTY-EIGHT

My Final Acceptance

*'We lose the joy of living in the present
when we worry about the future'*

My life had become fearful and depressing since my tragedies. I had turned to affirmations and positive thinking, and was reading as many books as I could on this subject. I attended several seminars, and I heard some of the leading lecturers on these subjects. I bought many of their tapes, which I played frequently, and even when driving I would have a tape running.

Feel The Fear And Do It Anyway was a book I read when my marriage ended; the affirmations in this book were a great benefit to me. I would say these affirmations over and over while walking, working, and any time I felt afraid of the future, and I can truly say they worked very well. I would go from feeling fearful to feeling much calmer, while saying them, and I began to eat better and feel more confident.

Each day would begin with meditation, and would end with an evening meditation at bedtime, helped along by a specific cassette for that purpose. They had the desired effect of allowing me to face the day better and permitting me to sleep at night.

Even with these changes that were taking place in my life, I was attending Bant Iliff's group and the spiritual church at Bowral, and I looked forward to the meetings. I still had a deep and intense need to hear something of Garry, which, occasionally, the groups were able to satisfy for a time.

My life has been directed in many coincidental ways since my accident. Not long after my smash, a girl who was serving me in a coffee shop, where Diane and I often met for lunch, told me about Capernwray Bible College, which is only five minutes' drive outside of Moss Vale.

This Bible college had been there for a long time, but I had not been aware of its existence before this. I began to attend lectures there each week and became enthusiastic to learn more. The college and the lecturers there were a great source of knowledge and encouragement, and became a very important part of my life, until I moved to Oak Flats in June 1998.

Students come to the college from all over the world, with quite a few from Canada. The age of a student doesn't seem to be a barrier for attending; men and women of all ages come there, including families. They have such strong faith in Jesus Christ and the Bible that I have since asked myself why I have ever doubted.

Five or six students came out to the farm one afternoon each week, where we enjoyed fellowship and a meal together. I made pancakes and other goodies during the week to have on hand for them when they arrived; what they thought about the treats was evident by the lack of leftovers. Suffice to say that, after the visitors had gone, my dog Robbo would sit, looking up with his big brown eyes fixed on me, waiting for the leftovers. Needless to say he was very disappointed many times.

As I looked down on him one time, I was provoked by his expression, to think, 'How fortunate it is that animals can't speak.' Because Robbo frequented the stables, I don't think I would have cared for the colourful way he could have expressed the way he felt.

While I prepared dinner, the students were able to amuse themselves by looking at the horses and any activities being carried out on the farm at the time. They could swim in the pool near the house, weather permitting, or play tennis, if they wished.

For dinner, I always tried to prepare something special because, apart from my liking to cook, I also enjoyed their company, and wanted to give them a meal that was a little different from the college menu. I made sure they had a cake or two to take back to the college. They were always most grateful and showed their appreciation, but I was thankful to them for the fellowship and inspiration that they gave me in return.

On their return to the college each night, it gave me great pleasure to go back with them and join in with the evening lecture. Sometimes I would go to a Thursday night's lecture as well, and once stayed at the college for a week's 'taste and see'. This is a very inexpensive way of sampling living in at the college, if one is interested in taking a term or two there. I had thought of spending some time at the college, as a means of giving me direction in reading and studying the Bible, because I felt as if I was not learning quickly enough.

Let us consider how we may spur one another on toward love and good deeds.   Hebrews 10:24

The week I attended, they had an Irish lecturer there by the name of Ray Andrews, whom I had heard before, who is now the head of the Australian branch of Abiding Life Ministries. He was so inspiring. I gained some wonderful insights from his lectures, into some of the vexing questions that hindered my progress in achieving some understanding of the Bible's teachings.

When John came into my life, we began to attend church and to pray together. We attended Saint Aiden's, the little Church of England Church at Exeter, at first. Then, more frequently, the Wollongong Uniting Church, the 'Church on the Mall'. The minister of this church, the Reverend Gordon Bradbury, is a most enthusiastic and inspiring minister. He has given me much encouragement; his gentle and caring approach has banished many doubts that I had been harbouring.

John says that the spiritualist teachings to which I had been exposed put me on the bottom rung of a ladder, and that I am now moving up a rung at a time. I know that each of these areas of my learning has made a contribution in some way to my developing faith. Opening my spiritual eyes to the need of faith and the assurance it brings has enabled me to cope a little easier with the stresses surrounding me.

The teachers of self-improvement and positive thinking tell us that we can do it by ourselves; we only have to love ourselves, think positively, banish our negative feelings, forgive everyone including ourselves and all will be well for us. This does work—it did for me—but it did not give me what I was lacking or looking for in my life: an enduring sense of peace.

Ray Andrews' seminar, held during the week I had spent at Capernwray, had been on these same principles, as embraced by the teachers of self-awareness, but doing the exercises with God's help and taking Self out of the equation. What a revelation! I only have to ask! It is amazing, I only have to ask, and His love and help are immediately there for me.

John had always been trying to tell me that we can't do it alone, we have to do it with God's help, and now Ray Andrews, a man who has lectured all over the world, was telling me the same thing.

When I finally received enough answers to my most pressing questions, and turned to God for comfort, I began to understand what had been present all the time. God's all-surrounding, *unconditional love* for *me*!

For about three years now, I have actually been doing it with God's help, and anyone who knows me, who hasn't seen me for a while, is amazed at the difference in my appearance. They say that they have never seen me looking so happy and relaxed. One would think that this should have been the case when I had everything: three beautiful children, a loving husband, wealth, fame, a farm, and horses, when there seemed to be nothing more I could have wanted.

After losing my son, then my husband, then nearly my own life; left with pain, scars, double vision and a loss of so much sight; having lost the ability to play competition tennis, which I enjoyed so much, as well as my horse training and driving career totally gone, I probably should look anything else but happy and relaxed.

God has a plan for my life, I believe, and I accept this now. I am aware of the need for me to let go of my worries, doubts and plans for each day and let Him do the work in my life. I guess what I am trying to say is, to use a phrase I have heard before, Let go and let God! I accept that everything that happens in my life is used by God, to strengthen and to encourage me to rely more and more on Him.

There is an element of toughness built into us by God, I believe (the resilience of the human spirit), which I needed and found in my most desperate of times, an inner power to withstand difficulties in times of helplessness. I have learned not to give up or give in. A renewed faith has increased my tenacity and taken this former belief to a new dimension. With Him nothing is impossible.

An enormous struggle had been taking place within me, between the Spiritualist concept of life after death for everyone, and the biblical teaching which states that Jesus Christ is central to my acceptance before God in eternity. Most churches teach that Jesus Christ, because He first loved me, died on the cross, giving His life for me, personally; paying the price for me, personally; making me, personally, presentable before God. That is, if I accept that fact by faith, out of gratitude for the price He paid for me, personally; I then receive the Spirit of Jesus Christ into my life, giving me an inner strength and a sense of purpose, as well as an assurance for eternal life.

Grappling with these two concepts caused me much heartache, but I had to resolve the dilemma once and for all. The arguments for life after death were very convincing and there are many publica-

The best way to handle a problem is to hand it over to God.

tions to be read on the subject. The thought of my son burning in hell was unbearable, and weighed heavily in favour of life after death. As I continued to be mentally and emotionally pulled this way and that, I came across the verses Luke 23:42–43 in the Bible, which told about the thief on the cross, accepting Jesus as the Son of God at the last minute before his death, and being saved. I don't know whether Garry was a believer or whether he called out during those last moments of his life, but he could have. I do know however, that either way I am now at peace, being assured that Garry is in God's care. While I am alive on this Earth I have a free will—free to come and go and make any choice I so wish, relatively speaking—but when I die, I am in God's court.

Initially, it was much more comforting for me, before I became a Christian, to believe as the Spiritualists do, that we all go to another world, to the level achieved by our evolution during our lives on Earth, than to believe that we go to Heaven only if we accept Jesus, and go to hell if we don't. Their philosophy certainly made Garry's loss more acceptable.

I have done much searching to find an answer that satisfies me. I can't prove, and it is not my aim to prove to anyone that my belief is correct, or that my faith is the only one. I just know that I have Jesus in my life now, and I am assured of an eternity with Him, and I do not need or want any other faith.

Since my change of heart, I believe I have been shown some amazing examples of the power of God at work in today's world. I have had my prayers answered in the most convincing ways. I have been encouraging my family to believe and have faith in Jesus also, and I suspect, by the feedback, none too subtly.

A most remarkable episode occurred one day, after I had perpetrated a rather foolish and thoughtless act. On the morning in question, against advice, I was helping at the stables, and I drove two horses, then I was going over to the house to start my housework, when I saw my dog Robbo scratching. I started running the water into the laundry tub, in which Robbo was to be bathed, then ran over to the incinerator, situated in a small paddock behind my house, which was filled with the scrap papers, and set a match to them. There was no wind, and even though it was very dry, I thought it would be safe.

Some Capernwray College students were coming for a barbecue the next day, so I was in a hurry to make some preparations. I commenced scrubbing Robbo; this was not his favourite game and, being a rather large dog, I always had to struggle with him. Perhaps wrestle with him may have been a better description of the procedure, if given by an observer.

We were making so much noise that I did not hear the crackling until I had lifted him out of the tub to dry him off. The noise then was frightening.

Letting go of Robbo, I rushed outside to see flames leaping all over the paddock. I screamed for Glenn, only to see him, Brett my son-in-law, Ian the blacksmith and Toni, running around frantically, with hoses.

'Mum what a stupid thing to do!' Glenn shouted.

Then a minute later, 'Mum, call the fire brigade, it's out of control!'

Ringing the Bush Fire Brigade straight away, I was assured a fire-truck would be manned and dispatched immediately. I ran back at once, to help douse the flames, when Glenn yelled again to me.

'Mum, ring them back. We have it under control.'

By the time I rang the Brigade back to cancel the alarm, the truck had already left for the farm, even though the man tried to stop it. The fire-truck arrived a minute later, followed by another five men in their own cars. The fire was examined and any hot spot was hosed down to make sure it was safe, leaving no possible chance of the fire rekindling.

The next morning Glenn said to me, 'Mum, I hope that when you said your prayers last night, you thanked God for putting out the fire. It was completely out of control and the long grass was well alight. We had no chance of stopping it ourselves. It just suddenly became controllable.'

It was so good that Glenn had given credit to God for the phenomenon and I certainly gave Him thanks myself.

Another prayer that I believe was answered for me, was for my Scottish cousin's daughter and son-in-law, who had lost a five-year-old son in the Dunblane shooting. A man had shot children at random at the school and their son was one of them. I rang my cousin at the time and even went to visit her and the family, when I was in Scotland after the shooting, but her daughter had shut herself off from

For God so loved the world that he gave his one and only son, that whoever believes in Him, shall not perish, but have eternal life. John 3:16.

family, friends and everyone and would not see me.

Giving consolation is not an easy thing at any time and all I could do was listen as my cousin talked her way through her grief. Where I could, I encouraged her to lean on God for comfort and not turn away from Him, as so many people do in times such as these. She was finding it so hard to come to grips with the reason, why? Which is always the perplexing and unanswerable question in these circumstances: there never seems to be a reason.

My effort of keeping in touch and continually praying for them all was rewarded one day when I phoned, and was told that her daughter was pregnant. She had another younger son, about three years old, and the daughter said to her mother that if she had another son, she would hate God, as the baby could never replace the son that they had lost.

She was blessed with twin girls!

It seemed like a miracle to me and I thanked God for this, and hope that all will be well for that family, and that the two beautiful babies will ease their sadness.

Never, in my wildest dreams, could I have realised just how much I was going to need the amazing power of prayer in our little family's life.

KYB a know-your-bible course for women, which I had been introduced to when I was at a low ebb, was another of the 'coincidental' happenings in my life. I attend these weekly KYB groups as often as I can, to study the Bible and share our answers to the questions arising from the lessons. I have been helped greatly by the studies and the encouragement of the other women.

The words of the Bible are not easy to understand, I admit, but with the help of this group, John and the Church, it is becoming a more acceptable book to me. This book is something I am continuing to learn from and know that the learning will be ongoing, but I have a firm belief that the teachings of the Bible are instrumental in my salvation. Not just my spiritual salvation, but my physical and mental salvation, and my quest for peace. That peace of mind that 'passeth all understanding'.

No longer do I feel that life will be perfect when I get the better partner, the better house, the better job, when I have more money, importance and on and on. These things take a much lower order in my list of priorities. I now take the time to 'smell the roses'.

The peace that I feel as I look out my back door across the lake, seeing it in its various moods, with its multitude of wildlife, assures me that my God is with me. What a privilege it is to have a stirring in my heart that I have never experienced before. To have my 'spiritual eyes' opened to reveal to me the glory of His creation. Begging the question as to why? Why did it take so long?

God's timing is perfect, even in death.

TWENTY-NINE

One Last Attempt at Driving

'Success consists of getting up just one
more time than you've fallen down'

About three years after my accident, and directly against my
doctor's and John's advice, I succumbed to the need to be
involved with horses once again. I can never understand anyone who does not love horses or is frightened of them. They are a
most gracious animal and I could not control my desire to work with
them again. I did tell Glenn that I only wanted to drive pacework, but
once I had my bottom on the seat and the reins in my hands, I felt the
adrenaline rise again and could not resist the occasional fast drive.
Pacing is a form of driving we don't consider dangerous; the horses
are not pushed to maximum speed.

One morning I commenced paceworking a horse without checking the gear very thoroughly, trusting the strapper to complete the
work. After the first lap I noticed, in the horse's shadow on the ground,
that a rein was caught up; it had been put under the breastplate. This
is not dangerous, and I was going to ignore the problem and continue
working the horse, but Glenn called out as he went past on his horse,
informing me of the harnessing error. It was then that I decided to
stop and make the alteration. I eased the horse off to the side of the
track, out of the way of the other drivers.

My horse had been responding well while pacing, and I expected
him to stand easy, as most of our horses did, while I made the adjust-
ment. But when I got out of the gig and walked up to undo the offending rein, he became fractious and refused to stand, so I placed him in
front of the barbed wire fence at the side of the track. This proved to
be no deterrent; he managed to pull away from the fence and continued to prance and fidget. The horse's tossing head and my impaired
eyesight made it very difficult for me to replace the rein on the bit.
With much pulling and being pulled, I managed eventually to complete the task. This time, unfortunately, a buckle failed to engage its
keeper.

Since my race accident, it is necessary for me to wear glasses constantly. I have one pair which correct my double vision only, and another pair which are bifocals. These give me close-up vision as well as correcting my double vision. On this day I was wearing the glasses for the correction of my double vision only. Vision without spectacles is a nuisance; I can manage for short periods, but it is not a pleasant experience. It is a bit of a joke among the family, particularly with the grandchildren; they call my eyes 'funny eyes'.

Scrambling back into the gig that morning, I started down the track, but had only gone a furlong or so when the rein came through the saddle and ended up in my lap. If the horse had not been so nervous previously, when I had stopped, and was out of the gig, I would have kept him going until he eventually grew tired. But, because of his agitation, I thought the best thing to do was to turn him in small circles with the other rein, and hope to slow him down enough for me to jump out of the gig and pull him up. This was a practice which had been used successfully on previous occasions.

My plan did not work this time. I pulled him to the right, toward the inside of the track, where there were little hilly tufts of grass. A wheel jolted over one of these and I was tipped out of the gig onto the grass. The speed at which I was travelling was not sufficient to give anything else but a light fall, but because of my spine and severe shoulder damage, I was hurting badly and could not get up; walking was out of the question.

Brett was the first to arrive with his horse, at the spot where I was lying, telling me to wait while he went to bring the car for me. I had no choice but to wait! Glenn came for me, helped me into the car and took me back to the house. He made a few comments, some of which I would prefer to forget. He said, 'Mum you shouldn't have been hurt so much with that fall, I would have rolled as I fell and wouldn't have been hurt at all.'

He also said, 'What a stupid thing to do, how could you have done such a silly thing?' referring to the way I had adjusted the rein. I realised only then that he was not aware of the extent of the damage that had been done to my eyes, and that my bifocals were essential for me to see clearly. It took a lot of explaining and some time before he could grasp the extent of my difficulty.

Then Glenn fired me! He realised only too clearly then the danger of my driving and the risk to the remainder of my life. I did not

We're stronger when we stand together.

want to be in a wheelchair for the rest of it and decided right then and there, finally, to call it quits.

Never again to take up the reins of another horse! It was a most difficult conclusion to draw. The pain in my shoulders and hips, which once again became my constant companion, underlined very clearly that a definite decision had to be made, leaving me with no option as to what that decision had to be.

To help take my mind off matters for awhile, John and I travelled to Victoria for a holiday in December 1997. We stayed one night at Terang, and the next day we were driving through Glenormiston when I suddenly realised what the sign meant to me. 'John,' I said excitedly. 'This is where Westburn Grant is standing at stud. I've got to see him. I really must see him'.

Glenormiston College is a major agricultural complex that some eight years earlier had taken its horse breeding course a step further by standing stallions commercially so that students could gain practical experience. The first stallion they stood was the imported American pacer Black Gamecock.

Not an enthusiastic lover of horses, John rather reluctantly agreed to visit the college with me. We arrived to find that the students and studmaster were away on holidays, even though this was still the stud season. I was later to discover that the studmaster was seriously ill with cancer. This had caused a limit to be placed on the number of mares the college would accept that season for the several stallions there.

Surprised at this, I found a lady there who told me there were five stallions on the property. She pointed us in the general direction when told of my association with Westburn Grant. When nearing the area where the stallions were, I began calling, 'Spot, Spot', not really expecting any response, as it had been almost four years since I had seen him. When some fifty metres away, one stallion began to whinny, as if in answer to my call.

I went through this fence and it was Spot. I put my arms around his neck and gave him a hug, while he put his head down onto my back, just as he would with me some years earlier. It felt so good seeing him again.

THIRTY

A Sad Departure

'People who care, are people who share'

W hen the possibility of me having to leave the farm first became evident following advice that any further deterioration of my eyesight would prevent me driving a car, I was devastated. I expected to continue living at Glen-Garry Lodge and always being there for my family whenever they needed me. I just loved the place. The thought of leaving the farm after all this time was untenable. After a great emotional struggle, common sense prevailed, for I knew, deep down, that my options were very limited.

Reluctantly, I came to the conclusion that, if I had to leave my family; the country's peace and quiet; the joy of being able to sleep without fear, with the curtains open at night, and be able to see the moon and stars shine through my bedroom window, I could be consoled by a home near water. My being near the sea or an expanse of water has always given me a sense of peace and calmness also. Neena was very much aware of how I felt about the possibility of having to leave Exeter. We had spoken together at length on the subject, and I had given her a description of the type of home that I would accept as a reasonable substitute for Exeter. That is, if such a home existed, and then of course at an affordable price.

One morning I received a telephone call from an excited Neena; informing me that while out walking her dogs, she came across a house just like I had suggested. She went into some details about how it had just come onto the market, and how it needed some renovation. The garden had so much obstructing the view of the nearby lake, but with a little clearing this problem would be solved. My sister informed the agent how I was most interested, and put down the deposit. I actually bought the home by telephone, site unseen.

The following day I went down to see the acquisition for myself and loved every bit of it. The home needed painting and larger windows in the kitchen and dining room, so as to take advantage of the view across the lake. In both our opinions, these changes would give it a 'million dollar' view.

Glenn and Brett came down with all the necessary tools to cut away all the offending trees and bushes, and pulled down the offending sheds that were blocking out the view. What a difference those changes made! To be able to sit and work at my computer, eat my meals and look out across the lake from the back section of the house, is just so delightful.

My moving to this area proved to be a blessing for both Neena and myself, as we are good friends and able to support each other so much. Barry having advanced Alzheimers disease and Neena having to take care of him with such devotion, demonstrating the patience of a saint, a description she will only too readily deny. John and I enjoy their company and join them sometimes for tea, at weekends, at either their place or mine. As John listens 'with his heart', and is so patient, he is a good companion to Barry for those few hours. Being around the same age, he is able to relate to many of the memories that Barry still has. It is also good for Neena to have someone with whom she can talk, and share her views, who will respond and carry on a conversation, which Barry is now incapable of doing. It is so sad to see a man who was once clever and competent struggling to put a sentence together. He is almost blind now, not a fault of his eyes, as they are medically declared sound, but I understand it is due to the effect of the disease. It prevents the brain from interpreting what the eyes see. He is unable to do many things for himself and is very dependent on Neena's assistance.

Barry and I have always related well to each other, and still do, even with his limitations. I am able to joke with him about his difficulty and compare it with the results of my injury, which was the cause of my reduced vision, and we agree that we will be healed together either with medicine or by the grace of God. I tell Barry that I pray for us both each day, and leave the outcome in God's hands.

Even though my move to Oak Flats has taken me from Exeter and away from the close proximity of my children and grandchildren, there is a big plus: I am able to visit my mother more often.

After the loss of Catherine, Mum, a great-grandmother now, became a substitute grandmother to Catherine's eight grandchildren. She could be relied on to babysit at any time for the three families. Catherine's daughter Karen, who lived at Berry with her husband

Bruno, often took Mum down to spend the weekend with them. She loved the children and was always willing to stay. Any activities that required the presence of a grandmother were ones that Mum readily undertook for any of the girls.

One of the teachers at Berry school, which Karen's girls, Candice, Amy and Rachel and son Scott attend, was discussing the effects of World War II in England, giving rise for them to mention that we had survived one of the worst hit areas of England. The school then asked Mum to give a talk about her experience. Mum accepted after a little struggle. She has always been of the opinion that she is not very clever. Because of her broad Scottish accent, she was a bit shy to talk even in front of little children, for fear of them not understanding her.

To Mum's joy the class were enchanted by her talk and bombarded her with questions, to which she responded with delight. The teacher enjoyed listening too, and thanked Mum profusely for her effort. Occasionally, in spite of her memory loss, Mum will recall the talk and tell me about it. She was given a sense of pride and a boost of confidence by her experience. To cap it all off, a young student in class 5B, Hayley Gray, wrote a letter to Mum on a large page, containing notes that she had diligently taken down from Mum's talk. It had been well written in running writing, by the little girl, and then sent to Mum, in case she 'might like to keep it'. Mum was very impressed by the gesture evidenced by someone so young. The letter is still in her possession, but the significance of it is lost on her now.

Mum has dementia and she lives in a little unit in Diment Towers, in Wollongong. In the last couple of years, her loss of memory has become more evident. Her short-term memory is almost non-existent, and yet I can still converse with her about things in the moment and of days long ago. I make every effort to take her out for lunch frequently, or John and I take her out to dinner at night, whenever we can. Mum has an excellent dress sense and always presents beautifully, but before I call by to pick her up, I have to ring to remind her that I am coming, directing her to write the message immediately onto a white board on the wall near her telephone.

Her door key presented her with a major problem. It was always missing at the most inopportune times. I managed to solve this problem, for a time anyway, by obtaining a key chain that retracted into a container about the size of a small shoe polish tin. Remembering her

People who care, are people who share.

room number was a problem for her also, so I had her room and floor number engraved on the front of the container. After this innovation, on my next visit with her, as I entered the building and was walking down the hall to the door of her unit, I saw Mum walking toward me from the other end. She was just coming down from lunch, but there, clutched in her hand, was the key.

As I left her that day, after saying my usual farewell with a kiss and a cuddle, I turned and walked away, but before I reached the exit, I looked back and saw her standing at her door, watching me leave. In that instant my attention was drawn to her smallness, paleness and fragility. I realised then how important my mother is to me. I turned away quickly, hiding the tears that blurred my vision.

Recently I decided to get her a new hearing aid to replace the one that had been lost for months. I felt that she was missing out so much, with her limited hearing. She now was to wear one in each ear, replacing the single one she wore for years. Her dramatic memory loss does not allow her to accept new things readily, and having to wear two aids has presented her with a major dilemma. One hearing aid has already been lost, despite my frantic search. I have not been able to solve the problem of her carefully removing the remaining aid and putting it in a safe place, where neither the staff at the 'Towers' nor I can find it.

The staff and I have tried to encourage Mum to leave the surviving aid in her ear until the night nurse comes on duty. But in spite of the sign I printed and stuck on the wall in clear view, she hasn't as yet left it in her ear this long. There must be a solution but, as yet, I have not found one. This has created a great deal of difficulty; apart from the hearing aid needing to be removed and cleaned each night, the situation gives rise to the concern that Mum, even as forgetful as she is, may be resentful of being treated as an errant child. She is very patient with me. Even now, in spite of her failing memory, Mum reminds me that she would readily make a batch of her shortbread for me, if I needed it. Indeed she would. She was always there for me when needed. That is my mother.

Mum's pancakes had been her good, old, reliable standby, since the war years, on hand at a moments notice, ready for any visitor that turned up unexpectedly. Her successful recipe has been handed down to Neena and me and then on to our respective daughters.

A family get-together was planned by Neena's daughter Lisa, to celebrate Neena's 60th birthday in December 1998. This was held in the Botanical Gardens at Wollongong, bringing together as many of our family members as Lisa could contact. During the course of the day, Mum was sitting on a seat in the shade of a tree, a little distance away from the main family group. Lisa was standing just behind her, leaning over her shoulder, and spoke into her ear. 'It should gladden your heart, Annie Paterson, to know that when you look across at all those people standing there now, not one of them would be there without you.' There was a pause, then she said slowly and thoughtfully, in her characteristic Scottish brogue, 'Aye it does.'

Catherine's girls Karen, Sandra and Jeanette are all married with families of their own and still in the Illawarra area, close enough to visit Neena and me now and again, enabling us to share family news. Neena and Dianne, Catherine's two younger daughters, live in Sydney and we don't see them as often, but Lisa, who also lives in Sydney, is in touch with them and keeps us up to date with their welfare.

Mark, the youngest of Catherine's children, is working in Japan, teaching English. He came to my home with Sandra on her last visit and it was so good to see my late sister's children fairing so well, after such a rocky beginning. The three oldest girls and their husbands share a strong faith, and it is clearly evident in their little families. Witnessing this gives me great joy.

My brother Eddie had earlier left the army for a key position in the corporate sector. He had worked hard and long in the service, and at one stage was attached to Army Command Staff College in Victoria just before being promoted to major. He and Terri later lived in an army home behind the Royal Sydney Showgrounds. I found this to have been very convenient having a good place to leave the car when taking when attending the Royal Easter Show.

Eddie at one time was transferred to the US, then back to Queensland before moving on to Sydney. Their son Alex and daughter Jessica were born in Sydney. Both have now grown into fine young adults, no doubt making their parents real proud.

Children are a heritage from God.

THIRTY-ONE

Glenn's Dramas

'We can comfort others,
because God has comforted us'

For some time before Vic left the farm after our separation, he had concentrated his efforts on training the horses rather than driving, which he left mainly to Glenn. After he left, there were still horses in training that had to be worked. My contribution was helping with harnessing and training and feeding up, but I was not driving in races during this period. Glenn had been doing some of the training and most of the driving, but now it was all left to him. The total responsibility for the management of the property became Glenn's.

All at once Glenn found himself having to make major decisions as to how to manage the then 230 acres and all the animals in his care, without the ready assistance and experience of his father: how to adjust the grazing capacity of his paddocks to conserve the grass cover, in order to maintain his horses in peak condition; control and careful recording of his breeding stock; the weaning of progeny and their training; the trimming of hooves, worming and other necessary veterinary procedures.

Then of course, there were the mundane activities that went with running a horse training establishment, such as weed control, fertilizer and lime spreading, slashing and irrigation. Some of these activities may be seasonal, but considerable planning is necessary to be able to fit these procedures in with a *normal* day's training schedule.

Glenn now felt the pressure of management. Vic and I had the benefit of working together as a team and I believe that this was the secret of our success. Glenn did not have this benefit to the same degree. Toni, his wife, was untiring and very thorough with managing the administrative side of the business: controlling the finance associated with our shared investments, owners' prize money distribution, veterinary fees, transport fees to and from trialing and racing venues, and some stud management, as well as a wonderful talent for organisation. Toni was an excellent strapper but didn't participate in the training and driving of the horses.

In addition to the pressures he was already experiencing, Glenn and Toni's marriage had been 'rocky' for several years. On two occasions before I had left the farm, Glenn had come to live in my home for as long as three months, in an endeavour to reconcile their differences, while Toni remained in theirs, with the children.

Toni's attitude to their situation has not changed. She still works hard in the stables and continues to carry out her office duties as efficiently as ever. They share the children. Glenn has them over with him when Toni needs to be away and at other times when he is home. I love Toni and have a great admiration for her and for the position she has taken. The circumstances of my own separation and heartache give me an understanding of the painful dilemma in which she is placed.

Mother's bias aside, my son is good-looking and has been blessed with a bright, disarming smile and a most pleasant outgoing nature. This is evidenced by his many friends and his popularity among the harness racing fraternity. Unfortunately, these attributes are a two-edged sword.

Glenn's character not only helps him make friends easily, but makes him attractive to women, and of course like so many males, he has great difficulty in ignoring the attention. It seems apparent that Glenn is lost in the confusion, unable to make a decision which will resolve anything. He is a grown man and it is up to him to sort out his life, but I grieve for his children — my grandchildren.

The suggestion was made that Toni leave the farm and live in town, until Glenn could sort himself out, but she would not agree to this idea. She prefers to stay in their home, continue working as she does and seeing him every day. They act amicably to each other, going out together with the children to dinner occasionally, and sharing meals at each other's place. This at least gives the children some continuity of their joint company.

It gives me great pain to stand by and watch young Nicky and Andrew, subjected to what must be, to them, a most confusing situation. They seem happy enough and are told frequently that they are loved by each of their parents. But I can't help agonising over their position. How can they possibly differentiate between what they see and what they are told?

Glenn's approach to his work is a little more laid back than the course which Vic and I chose to follow. Many times we drove ourselves almost beyond our endurance. Glenn refuses to do this, learning from our mistakes, he says.

He takes a break each year, a short holiday away from the farm and from racing when he feels pressured, keeping him enthused and giving him a renewed sense of well-being, as well as the feeling of being on top of things again, on his return home.

Fishing has always been his preferred form of relaxation, but it was also responsible for his two very close encounters with death, the first encounter separated from the second only by a matter of weeks. Thankfully, I didn't know of the first brush with death until he was safely at home in Exeter.

During his many fishing trips to the Northern Territory, Glenn and his friends stayed at a little town called Borroloola, situated in the southeast area of the Gulf. Their accommodation was in a hotel in the town. On the first few occasions of their stay, the hotel was run by a married couple, George and Deborah, and Glenn grew to like them, enjoyed their company, and became a friend to each. On their later trips, the hotel was run by the wife, as the couple had separated. Glenn and his friends were always welcome and assured of being very well looked after during their stopover.

In the first week of November 1998, Glenn arranged a fishing trip to the Gulf with his friend Neil Arthur, who will be well known to many in harness racing in Victoria. Neil also owns and pilots a small aircraft. On other trips north, when Neil has accompanied Glenn, Neil has flown up from Victoria and picked him up from Mittagong airfield, then continued on up from there. This was when they went out in the publican's boat to do their deep-sea fishing.

On this occasion, however, Glenn decided to drive up to Borroloola in his Pajero four-wheel drive, hauling his recently acquired 16½-foot runabout, fitted with all the newfangled gadgetry. Neil and Glenn drove up together to Mount Isa, where they met Vic, who had flown across from Mooball, northern New South Wales, not far from Tweed Heads. From there, they continued on up to Borroloola.

The welcome at the Borroloola Hotel was just as friendly as it always was. Nothing appeared to be amiss on their arrival. Glenn, Vic and Neil went boating and fishing together for a few days, then Vic left early to go home. Glenn and Neil decided to stay on a little longer.

The sleeping quarters at the hotel consisted of small units made from corrugated iron and were spaced several feet apart. Their respective units were adjacent to each other and Glenn's Pajero was parked out behind Neil's. Glenn's unit was directly opposite the unit occupied by the friend of the lady proprietor of the hotel, their respective front doors facing each other across a cement walkway. Neil's unit was to the right of Glenn's, at the end of a 'T' section, his doorway facing up the walkway toward Glenn's.

They came home as usual, after a day's fishing, had their dinner, a few beers, swapped a few yarns, then tucked in for the night in preparation for the next day. This night was not to be like any other night that they had ever spent at Borroloola. At around 4am, Glenn and Neil were shocked from their sleep by the sound of a heavy thumping noise very close to their rooms.

Glenn said later that he thought the air-conditioning unit had fallen off the wall onto the floor, but changed his mind when the noise occurred more than once. There was yelling and scuffling coming from outside Glenn's unit, and very loud banging noises, sounding as if their wall was being hit heavily with something. They rushed outside to investigate the source of the noise, not guessing what they were rushing into. As they burst through their doors into the early morning light, what they saw stopped them in mid-stride; they were stunned, shocked to the core, left struggling to make sense of the dreadful sight before them.

The scene is seared into their minds forever.

There, lying in the doorway of the unit opposite Glenn's, was a woman, with blood streaming from her face. On the walkway in front of Neil's unit, a man was lying unconscious, with a badly injured face. Just above his head, on the ground, in two pieces, was a heavy calibre rifle, and standing over him was another man. The man standing was cursing and swearing, and now and again he would kick the prostrate form on the ground.

Neil and Glenn ran to the two men, firstly to prevent the man on the ground being injured further, secondly to restrain the other. The man standing was swearing and muttering, 'He's killed her! the #*@#*@ has killed her!'

What shall it profit a man if he gain the whole world and lose his own soul? Mark 8:36

It was only then that Glenn could run to the woman to give assistance, but she didn't seem to be breathing and appeared lifeless. The woman was the proprietor of the hotel, Glenn's friend and, as it turned out, the lover of the man standing.

There was nothing he could do for her, but her bloodied countenance awakened terrible memories. Memories that had been haunting him since the death of his brother: Glenn and Susan found Garry on the farm, after his accident, by the side of the water tank where he had fallen, covered with blood.

The man on the ground began to stir and show signs of regaining consciousness. The other man was in a state where he could easily do some serious injury, or worse, to the man on the ground. Glenn had the presence of mind to kick the pieces of the rifle out of the way, under the raised floor of Neil's unit, giving no opportunity for it to be used again.

Neil was leaning heavily on the man on the ground, preventing him from moving. Glenn had his hands full controlling the distraught man. Curbing his response gave them some very tense and anxious moments.

After what seemed an eternity, but was in actual fact only minutes, some sanity was restored. Two policemen arrived at the scene, in full anti-siege dress, in less than 15 minutes from the drama's commencement, much to the surprise of Glenn and Neil.

The police had been notified some time earlier by the hotel cook, who was aware of the impending tragedy, and because of the extreme danger of the situation, came prepared for the worst, dressed in their anti-siege suits, not knowing that the killer was already subdued.

Soon after, the facts leading up to the tragic chain of events were to emerge.

It appeared that the woman became involved with the man who ultimately shot her, after the separation from her husband. This liaison did not last for very long. It was then that she met her more recent friend, with whom she was in the unit opposite Glenn's, that fateful night.

The killer had come after they had all gone to bed and was sitting on the bonnet of Glenn's Pajero, drinking rum, waiting for someone to emerge from his ex-girlfriend's room. He was well under the influence of his drinking and well beyond reason by the time anyone was to step out of the unit he was watching. As it happened, the woman was to come out first, apparently going to check on her children.

The gunman, driven by his jealousy and the effects of the rum, fired two shots from the corner of Glenn's unit as she emerged, hitting her in the chest at close range. The woman fell, mortally wounded. Her friend was still inside their room.

The gunman went to their door, yelling that there was a bullet for him too, then he intended to shoot himself. As the rifle was pushed through the door and fired wildly, the man inside grabbed the barrel, endeavouring to wrest it free. The rifle discharged again, inflicting a bad powder burn along his forearm, the bullet grazing his side under his arm. The two men struggled together furiously. Outside now, between the units, they fought, random shots being fired as they struggled. It was the noise of the shots and their bodies banging against the wall of Glenn's unit that woke him.

The man holding the barrel of the rifle finally wrenched it free from the gunman's grasp and punched him to the ground, and it was thought that he hit the offender over the head with the rifle, causing it to break. It was at this point of the drama that Glenn and Neil blundered into the conflict. What would have happened had they come rushing out at the sound of the first shots, goodness only knows.

However, Glenn's experience less than a month later, on December 1st, makes this episode seem minor by comparison.

Returning home from my swimming exercise at Oak Flats pool, I took a message from my answering machine. It was Toni's voice, very agitated and with more than a touch of urgency about it. Straight away I picked up the phone and rang her; her phone was picked up and answered by our friend, Kevin Wells. He had gone to stay with Toni to support her in what I was to discover later, was a long and agonising wait.

Toni just could not talk to me, she was remembering, only too well, the last time she had been forced to speak to me in Perth, and break the news of Garry's death. This day had a real chance of following the same scenario, and after my reaction to her phone call on the Perth occasion, she was not willing to be the one to break the news to me this time.

The message I finally extricated from Kevin, with great diffi-

The greatest joy on Earth is the prospect of Heaven.

culty, was that Glenn and his good friend Geoff Howarth had gone fishing and were missing. Glenn's four-wheel drive with his boat trailer was found at the boat ramp at Jervis Bay, south of Sydney, where they had left it. Geoff and Glenn had left from the ramp at about 2 pm the day before and not returned.

Well! What conclusion could one draw, other than that the two men were still at sea, or worse, probably drowned.

'Oh no Lord! Not my other son!' was all I could gasp. I was trembling violently as I put the receiver down, 'Oh God no, please save my son. Please don't take him. Keep him safe. Please bring Glenn back to us.'

The trembling continued and I was crying as I prayed, 'Please God I just couldn't stand to lose my other son. I couldn't live if he should die. Please find him Lord and bring him back. If not, then please take me as well.'

Right now it seemed that there could be no hope for Glenn. He had been missing for over a day, somewhere in the vast ocean, and to me the odds of his survival were just too great. It looked hopeless; I could only think that he had drowned with his friend.

After I had composed myself a little, I phoned John at his work and his receptionist brought him to the phone for me, after I somehow got my message through to her. Through sobs, I tried to tell John what had happened. He coaxed me to calm down and said to wait until we had further information, before we accepted the worst outcome. He promised to pray for Glenn and Geoff with me, and to keep praying, which was so important to me then, as I felt the need of his support. Anne, his receptionist, had commenced praying immediately after my call.

John carefully and calmly pointed out some of the possibilities of this terrifying situation. He told me that, even though they had not returned to the car, they could be safe on an island somewhere, or had failure of the boat's engine and were waiting to be picked up. John said there were all kinds of possibilities and not to give up hope, which is what I had almost done. This had a calming effect on me, but still the next few hours were unbelievably long and most distressing.

Brett was away the day Glenn and Geoff went fishing. He had taken a few long-overdue days off from his work with the horses, to do some tiling jobs that he had arranged, to make some extra money. This left only Glenn and Geoff working the horses, and Toni and Susan helping with the harnessing and washing of the horses and gear after they had been worked. Glenn also had horses drawn to race at Harold Park that night, so it was out of the question for them not to return later in the afternoon of the previous day.

Even though it was clearly evident that something had to be wrong, because the boys were long overdue, it took a lot of persistence on the part of Toni before the police accepted that the men really were in danger and had not merely stayed later than originally planned. Toni had notified them that the men were missing at 7am the following day, when she first discovered Glenn had not come home, but the search did not commence until early that afternoon.

It was Geoff's birthday on the Tuesday, and Glenn decided to treat his best friend to a great day's fishing on Monday at Jervis Bay, in the flash new boat that Glenn had recently purchased. Geoff was just as keen a fisherman as Glenn and eagerly accepted the offer of the chance to wet a line and try the new boat.

They went fishing for yellow-fin tuna and set off from Murray's Beach, near the southern entrance to Jervis Bay, in the 5.1-metre boat, in a little choppy, but not the least dangerous, seas. Glenn logged in with the Shoalhaven Marine Rescue Association before they left, which is the custom with all fisherman going out to sea.

The weather forecast was good, so they headed out to the continental shelf, which is about 26km from shore, both in good spirits. Geoff pulled in the first tuna of the day, giving him the thrill of the first catch, an early birthday present.

Disaster struck at about 2.45pm, when a freak four-metre high wave suddenly rose out of the sea, taking them completely by surprise. As the huge wave rose in front of them, the surge of the rising water drew the boat into the oncoming swell, which was beginning to break.

They were trolling at the time and, because of the slow speed, Glenn could not do what he wanted quickly enough, which was to throttle up to top speed and drive with the wave, hoping the boat would surf with the wall of water until it petered out.

The wall of water was on them before they had time to position the boat, and the four-metre crest broke over them, capsizing the boat,

246   *We sow the seed, but God gives the harvest.*

leaving it upside down and half submerged. Glenn said he would have been okay with the giant swell if he had been 50 yards further away. The water had been reasonably calm, so they had not put on their life-jackets, because they felt restricted by them as they fished.

When they finally surfaced, after being hurled into the water, they were able to assess the situation, which they did as rapidly as possible. Glenn swam back to the boat, which was now partially submerged, dragging Geoff with him. The boat was lying upside down in the rough water, with the stern and motor exposed.

Geoff was able to hold onto the section of the boat clear of the water and Glenn was able to rest his feet on the ridge of the hull below the gunnel of the stem, which was under the water, and lie face down, along the hull toward the stern. They climbed as far as they could onto the hull, but the waves, all huge by now, were washing over them every 10 seconds or so.

When a situation appears to be humanly impossible to rectify, it is not so unreasonable to have one's thoughts turn to The Almighty. It was at this point that Glenn prayed. He prayed to a God whom he believes is a 'Good God', and he never doubted, from that time, that he would be saved and would see his children again.

Geoff, on the other hand, was sure that he would not make it and said that he would die. Geoff's nature was that of a worrier; he delayed going home from the stables frequently, until all the tasks that needed to be done were finished. He was never happy leaving a job until tomorrow if it could be done today. He had endured three heart attacks and a triple bypass in four years, and because of his weakened condition, he knew that if help did not arrive reasonably quickly, his chances of surviving in the water were not very good.

Geoff had been away from our stables, to work in a much less stressful job in Moss Vale, away from the horses, for about three years, but, as it was for me, stress or no stress he could not stay away. His addiction to the horses got the better of him. He had to come back.

Glenn had logged on with the Shoalhaven Voluntary Rescue Association and was sure that they would be looking for them, when it was discovered that they had not returned at the stipulated time. He thought, therefore, that they would have to stay with the boat and hang on for a few hours, contending as best they could with the large waves washing over them, until their rescue.

If this had not been the case, he may have tried to swim to shore, pulling Geoff with him, straight away, and not wait at the wreckage, but at the time it was much more sensible to hold onto what was in reach of the boat and to wait for the rescue boats.

While Glenn and Geoff lay together on the hull of the upturned boat, decisions had to be made to maximise their chances of survival. One such decision was to have Glenn salvage as much as he could from inside the submerged hull.

Glenn had to dive under the boat to retrieve life-jackets, flares, torches, an Esky that Glenn gave Geoff to use as a buoy, and any other items he could find during his search, limited to the extent of his ability to hold his breath.

In his first attempt, Glenn dived under and came up for air in the part of the boat that was protruding from the water. This was nearly his undoing, because the boat cavity was full of petrol fumes, and when Glenn drew a deep breath he almost lost consciousness. He just had enough strength and ability left to be able to dive back under the boat and come up outside, into the clean, fresh air where there weren't any petrol fumes. It took him quite a while to regain his strength and full consciousness.

Glenn retrieved one life-jacket, which he put on Geoff, who was not a strong swimmer, but was now also hampered by the state of his health. Many dives under the boat were needed before Glenn was satisfied that he had as many of the items as he could find, that would aid their rescue.

He retrieved some flares which he hoped he could use, should a passing boat come within range, close enough to see one. He put the next life-jacket he found on himself. The boat was beaten constantly by the two-metre swell and with each passing hour was sinking further and further below the surface.

Geoff was having great difficulty holding on and, on more than one occasion, Glenn had to swim out and pull him back to the wreckage, where he held onto him and the part of the boat that was within reach. The boat was below the surface of the water by now, and so far under that to hold the only piece of the rim that he could reach, Glenn's face was less than a foot (30cm) out of the water. He had to hold Geoff with the other hand, and every time a two-metre wave went over them, they felt as if they were never going to breathe again. The waves were rolling over them continuously and they could only catch their breath in short bursts, causing them to fatigue rapidly. The life-jackets, the very things their lives depended on, were becoming life threatening. When they were submerged beneath the wave passing over them, the buoyancy effect of the jackets would jerk them forcibly toward the surface.

Glenn's grip on the boat and on Geoff was sorely tested; his arms felt as if they were being reefed from their sockets with each passing wave. Geoff was affected badly by the buffeting of the waves and begged Glenn to let him go and let him drift; being held close to the boat was becoming unbearable for him.

Glenn agreed, but in a short space of time, he could see that his mate was being washed quickly out of reach and he swam out to him and brought him back. This occurred several more times, when Geoff begged to be let go.

They were managing as best they could in the water by the submerged boat, waiting, as they thought, for their rescue. At about 4.30pm or so, the situation was bad enough, but when one would think that their circumstance could not possibly get any worse, it did. A shark appeared in the water not far from where they were floating.

If there was anything good about this turn of events, it just so happened that Glenn had a fair working knowledge of sharks and he was able to discern this to be a Blue shark. Even if it was three metres in length, Blue sharks tend not to be a major threat. He was so relieved to find that the shark was not a dreaded Mako.

It was then that 'Murphy's Law' chimed in. In the late afternoon, not one, but two Mako sharks made their appearance. Knowing these creatures to be fierce and relentless predators and undoubted man-eaters, the two helpless men struggled to what they thought was the centre of the boat, beneath the water, hoping at least to prevent the sharks from coming up under them.

From the moment the sharks appeared and began to circle around them, both men knew the feeling of gut-wrenching fear. The sharks remained in the area until darkness fell; Glenn saw the last one at around 9.30pm and after that they could no longer be seen. He said he felt a nudge against his leg during the night and a stab of terror as he thought 'shark', but he choked back a scream to avoid frightening

Geoff any further.

The watch Glenn wore had a luminous dial, so he was able to determine what hour it was at any time through the night. If the sharks were still present during the night, Glenn believes it was the petrol fumes, and more than a little help from the Lord above, that kept them at bay.

It makes me shudder yet, when I think of them sharing the night with the man-eaters, apart from the ever-present threat of them being drowned with every wave that washed over them.

During the night, at about 10pm, Glenn caught sight of a boat passing by at a distance. He lit the last of the flares that he had managed to save. Some of the others were lit earlier, in an attempt to attract attention from the shore, or any other boat that may have been close by.

Sadly, the crew of the passing boat neither saw the glow of the flare, nor the men in the water. Glenn did not shout because he knew they would not be able to hear him. The craft sailed on into the night, totally oblivious of the desperate plight of the two men struggling in the water. This was a bitter disappointment to them both and was enough to give them some sneaking doubt as to their chance of survival.

About 3am the boat sank out of reach altogether, and they were left with no alternative but to try and swim to Point Perpendicular—about 22km away. Glenn and Geoff began the long, slow, energy-sapping swim toward the beacon, which they could see flashing out across the water through the darkness, off the Point.

They had held onto the hope that a rescue boat, which had failed to come during the night, would be launched at daybreak the next morning, and they would soon be saved.

Glenn used the lid of the Esky as a sail and Geoff held the Esky itself, as a float, and Glenn towed his friend for about 6km. Geoff gradually became so weak that he begged Glenn to leave him and to swim for shore, himself. Glenn was forced to accept the fact that his friend was close to death; he knew his only hope was to swim for help as quickly as he could. He grabbed Geoff on the shoulder and wished him Happy Birthday. Geoff did not panic or fret, he gave Glenn a smile and said, 'Thanks for taking me fishing for my birthday, mate.'

Glenn pleaded with Geoff to hold the Esky and not let go, to keep holding onto it no matter what, and said that he would be back with help as soon as he could. He then swam away, holding the Esky lid as a surfboard for assistance. The last he saw of his best friend was when he turned around to wave to him before he went out of sight, and Geoff waved back, still holding onto the Esky.

Glenn was never any better than just a good swimmer; he usually has to rest and tread water at the end of 100 metres, and yet, that day, he swam 18km, six of them pulling his mate, who was no lightweight.

As he swam, he kept saying to himself, 'God is a good God, I am going to see my kids again,' over and over. At other times, 'I have got to get there or Geoff will die, I've got to get there or Geoff will die.' These two affirmations kept him going. Glenn carried a firm belief that they would emerge from their ordeal safely, the whole time he was swimming.

We all have one or two Guardian Angels with us at all times, I believe, to guide and protect us, and Garry could be one of Glenn's by now, we don't know. We do know that he had some powerful help from some source that night.

Later, I asked the doctor at the hospital if it was possible for a human to do what my son had done. She said that they had been discussing this at the hospital and were all of the opinion that it was only a miracle that had saved Glenn.

'Not just a miracle, but also the power of God and prayers answered,' I said.

She replied, 'That was exactly the conclusion we came to.'

Glenn was only 3km from shore when the police helicopter saw him waving the Esky lid to attract their attention. Glenn said he could have cried when he heard that glorious sound from overhead, that characteristic whumping sound of a helicopter.

It was at this point, just when his rescue was so close, that Glenn said he experienced what strength he had left begin to drain out of him. Amazingly, even in his weakened state, he managed, with some difficulty, to climb into the life buoy floating in the water.

The helicopter rushed him to the Shoalhaven Hospital, which had been alerted and was ready for Glenn's arrival. The police emergency staff, whom I had phoned as soon as I became aware of the search in progress, were really kind and so helpful to me. As soon as

Glenn was rescued they rang to tell me that he was being flown directly to the hospital at Nowra, but were unable to give me any further information on his present condition. I thanked God that my son was alive and was given a fighting chance to survive.

There was still no sign of Geoff at this time. Toni and Elizabeth, Geoff's wife, were told only that one of the men had been rescued, however, they were not given any indication as to who it was.

What a dreadful situation for each wife to be in; to know that only one husband was found, and then left with the dilemma, which husband. They both felt those awful pangs of guilt, forced on them by the hope of it being their husband who had been saved and each praying desperately that it was.

We arrived at the hospital after what seemed to be an age, aggravated by the time it took to find a parking spot and then the emergency ward. Toni was there when I arrived. As I walked into the ward where Glenn lay, I could see the intensity of the strain in her face as she turned to greet me. A friend had driven her down from Exeter earlier and Toni insisted on remaining the night. Even though they were still separated, it was patently obvious that she still loved Glenn and it was such a strain for her, not being free to show her true feelings.

At last, I was with Glenn, and even though he looked a fright, I felt the sensation of a great weight being lifted off my shoulders and an extreme joy at seeing him alive.

He was suffering with hypothermia, as a result of his being submerged for so long in the freezing water. He was wrapped in thermal blankets up to his neck, in order to bring his body core temperature slowly back to normal. There was a risk that if they didn't get the temperature normalised in time, he could lose any of his extremities (hands, feet or both).

His face was severely sunburnt and he was evidently in pain, as a consequence of back and muscle strain caused by holding on to his friend and swimming for so long. As I hugged him, I told him how much I loved him, and thanked God that he was here with me once again.

Despite the dreadful discomfort he was enduring from his sunburnt face, his aching back and the raw, burning sensation of his throat, caused by having swallowed so much salt water, Glenn needed to

Above all you must be loving, for love is the link of the perfect life. Col. 3:14

talk and I was a willing listener. Whatever he had to say, I wanted to hear; I needed to know what had happened to them, but as his story unfolded, I found it difficult to grasp the magnitude of their ordeal.

It was nothing short of miraculous him having survived as long as he did, in such conditions, and then having Glenn here in front of me, telling me all about it. If I did not have the faith that I have now, I would have most certainly taken a different view of his survival.

My mother has always loved Glenn and the following morning, I asked her if she would like to visit him. Now that she has great difficulty with remembering anything as recent as an hour or so, I was acutely aware that the trip to Nowra would be a long and some-what frustrating one, but, as we had arranged, I went to pick her up from the nursing home at 8am, hoping she would be ready.

One of the staff met me at the front door and informed me that Mum was a little shaken this morning. She had overslept and a nurse was sent to bring her up for breakfast, and that was where she was now. This was very unusual because Mum has always been an early riser, being up and about by 6am most days.

Using the lift to reach the second floor where the dining hall was situated, I went in to her table where she was sitting, just finish-ing her large plate of porridge. My mother has always said that a plate of porridge, which she has eaten for breakfast all her life, stands by you all day. She said, 'I'm so dizzy, I have had a bad dream, I can't get over it. I am still shaking.'

Hoping she could remember it, I asked her to tell me about the dream and, knowing my Mum, should not have been surprised by her answer. She had dreamed that she had been thrown out of a boat and had been clinging onto something for hours. She said there was some-one else with her that she could not help. She said it was very deep water and she was very frightened, because she could not help the other man.

Mum had seemingly picked up on the accident that Glenn and Geoff had, and was reliving it herself. That peculiar and amazing talent of hers was in evidence again.

It is my firm belief that Mum could not have imagined those events or fabricated them, because she had already forgotten where we were going that morning, and why. Everything I had told her about the accident was gone from her mind.

Mum is 85 now and is healthy apart from her dementia and I knew she would want to see her favourite grandson and give him a spiritual healing in her own quiet way. Every time that Glenn or Geoff was mentioned, or anything about the accident, I had to explain in detail each time; her short-term memory has failed.

Toni and the two children arrived just after Mum and I and it was very emotional to watch father, son and daughter greet one another.

Glenn must have had some doubts at times during his long vigil, that he may never see them again; it brought tears to his eyes, when he hugged them and held on as if he never wanted to let them go. It was more than I could stand, as I stood and watched them holding on tightly to one another. I reached for my handkerchief.

A television crew arrived about the same time and caught much of that poignant and emotional scene on camera, but no-one seemed to be aware of their presence; they were lost in the intensity of the moment. That was to be the first of many magazine and television interviews that Glenn was to be subjected to.

When Glenn was discharged from hospital the next day, the family went home together. After all the heartbreak and fear, Glenn and Toni decided to try to make their marriage work once again. Toni was content to just give Glenn some tender loving care and be patient with a still grieving husband. She was inundated by numerous phone calls over the next two to three weeks after the rescue. The aching of his back, the pain of his sunburnt face and the raw burning throat soon healed, but none of these approached the pain of the loss of his friend, which still remains.

My son was the strong one of the family when we lost Garry; he continued to drive the horses when neither Vic nor I could, and he supported Susan as well. I have always felt that he never let himself grieve fully for his brother, and I believe that since then, he has been living his life as hard and fast as he can. To experience as much as he is able at every opportunity, since there is no guarantee for the quality or quantity of one's life.

A probable explanation for the many dangerous things he has done in his short life is that he seems to have little fear of anything. He believes that our lives are planned and what will be, will be.

The view from my back door out across Lake Illawarra gives

Hardening of the heart is more serious than hardening of the arteries.

me a real sense of tranquillity. I would be lying if I said I never worried about my family's future, or mine, but those times are becoming rare. When it does happen, I take a cup of tea onto the back porch and sip it slowly while watching the activities on the water. I stay awhile and let the peace of God seep into my soul. It doesn't take long and I am soon on top of things again, and—back at the computer. Now though, I experience a comforting presence with me, making fear and doubt infrequent visitors.

At least this son believes that he is going to have a long life and not a short one, as Garry had. After all that has happened, it is my expectation and my prayer that he will, and I trust that he considers carefully any action that may put him in harm's way.

Glenn and Toni are receiving bible classes from Wayne Tilsley, the Anglican minister from Bundanoon, who goes out to their home once a week for this purpose. He was so supportive, ringing and going out to see them often, during the days following the disaster. The Rev. Peter McDonough, the Australian Director of Capernwray Bible Colleges, stationed at the Moss Vale branch, went out at my request, to speak with Glenn during the first week he was home. Peter's visit proved to be fruitful to both Toni and Glenn and he offered to come again, any time they felt the need. The staff and pupils at the College continually prayed for all of us and proved to be powerful in support of Peter's visit and in our time of great need.

The reconciliation did not last long. Within a month Glenn moved back over to the main family home, which has been vacant since my departure to Oak Flats. Vic and I realise that it seems to give him an open invitation to leave his marital home, whenever he wants a break from his marriage.

We are now considering our options as to what to do with the house. As parents, we want the best for our children, even when they are grown and parents themselves. It is so hard when you love them, to stand by and watch them suffer the agonies of their decisions. But as adults, it is entirely up to them as to how they manage their lives. We as parents stand aside, being available for advice, but only if asked.

It will take a long time for Glenn's memory of the tragedy to soften. The memory of that terrible night spent with Geoff in the water; the sight of Geoff waving to him as he looked back and now knowing that was the last time he was seen alive, will remain.

Glenn was quick to set up a trust fund for Geoff's three children. He had promised his friend that should he survive their ordeal, he would personally help take care of the children.

In June of 1999, Glenn arranged to hold a dinner and auction at Harold Park, similar to an idea I had organised for charity a few years earlier. This had been called 'Spots Before Your Eyes', a name Janet Greason had suggested, which was most appropriate since Westburn Grant was to be paraded during that evening, being walked right into the function room at the course.

Naturally, Glenn enlisted the aid of his mother, no doubt due to my enthusiasm to work for charity. Many, many hours were spent finding sponsors for some of the races and organising donations to auction. Thank God for computer faxes. I made extensive use of mine. I expected it to begin blowing smoke! This was a time when I did feel more than a little stressed, because I was virtually doing two things at the same time. I was nearing the conclusion of my writing about this time and had set a tentative deadline for publishing, and time was fast running out, but the time needed for the organising of the trust fund night was running out faster.

With just a week to go before the night of the trust fund auction, Glenn phoned me in a state of desperation, pressing me for a little extra effort, to encourage more people to attend and support the auction, because up until then, the bookings were very disappointing. When he hung up, I was in a quandary, left wondering 'What on earth could I do?' My visits to Harold Park were infrequent and, because I was no longer driving, I was fast losing contact with many of the racing identities. As I sat with head in hands staring out across the lake from my back door, I was thinking, 'What I need now is definitely not a coffee, but a miracle.'

On an impulse, I rang Rod Fuller at 2KY and Ryan Phelan at SKY channel. They were both wonderful and did an excellent job for me. They not only did the advertising for the night themselves, but arranged for the news presenters to continue with the advertising through the week, for me as well. John and I arrived at the function room early. There was still some last-minute preparation to be done and, as I looked around the room, there were a few familiar faces, but the room was far from full. I must confess, I was more than a little apprehensive. This feeling soon evaporated, much to my delight. By

I will never leave you nor forsake you.   Hebrew.13:5

the time the evening was due to begin the room was full, filled by many familiar faces and others associated with racing.

Darren Beadman was the guest of honour and proved very popular with all in attendance. Darren donated many of his favourite trophies, which were eagerly sought when presented for auction. My contribution was a framed set of my racing colours. The night was a tremendous success, and the outcome was certainly worth the time and the effort. The Howarth children received quite a substantial legacy to be invested for them, once again demonstrating the willingness of the racing people to support a worthy cause, and their open-handed generosity.

Worthy charities for which I felt strongly have long held by interest and enthusiasm. I have on numerous occasions been overwhelmed by the support of the people in harness racing. Most of the time when they would see me coming with tickets in my hand they would just hand me their money, or say 'How much, Margaret?'

The first large charity event I was involved with was back in 1985. This was the building of a Cardiac Assessment Unit at the Bowral Hospital. It was a vital need for our area; people who needed heart scans or tests were taken to hospitals in Sydney because there were no facilities for their treatment in our local hospital. I volunteered to hold an Open Day on our property.

Vic and I were then both at the top of our profession, and our horse Glenn's Thunder was at his peak and creating a lot of interest. The program took months of organizing with a committee that we had formed for the purpose. On the day of the event it rained. I just felt like hiding myself in the house and not venturing outside. My nerves were frazzled, I was strung out, I thought I was about to bear witness to an abysmal failure. But! In spite of the early rain, which soon dispersed, and to my immense relief, about 5000 people turned up. We had cars and buses parked in our lucerne paddock, a sight worth seeing.

Some of the leading harness racing drivers willingly brought their horses to the farm for displays of racing on our track. Vic drove Glenn's Thunder around the track, while I gave a running commentary, by loudspeaker, on the technique of horse training. Of course Vic did an excellent and patient job of answering the many questions asked later by his interested audience. There were many forms of entertainment arranged for the day, but one in which I had a particular interest and would have enjoyed watching was the tennis exhibition.

Several well-known Australian tennis players, John Alexander, Phil Dent and his wife Betty Anne, Bob Giltinan and a few others, came and gave a display on our court. The reason I was unable to watch even for a minute was that someone had placed a walkie talkie in my hand and said 'Hold this'.

A race was organised with little Shetland ponies, which a friend had brought down from Sydney especially for the purpose. The drivers were some of the local doctors from Bowral Hospital, and the tennis players. It was hard to say who enjoyed it the most, the drivers or the spectators. The sight of the tiny ponies with some of the drivers, who were over six foot tall, scrunched up in the little sulkies, all struggling for positions, was hilarious and a sight to remember. The event was won by our local specialist, Dr Ken Mayman.

There have been several occasions when my family and I have required the professional services of doctor Ken. During one of my last visits to his surgery, I happened to mention his winning the pony race, and what great entertainment it gave to the crowd watching. Ken looked at me with a little smile on his face, then he informed me that the other doctors had conspired to let an older driver win, and asked him to join the conspiracy. 'I agreed,' he said, 'but I didn't know how to pull the thing up.' Ken's use of the phase, 'pull the thing up', made me chuckle, because this is one of harness racing's slang phases. A term with which no race driver ever wishes to be associated. Definitely not popular with the stewards.

There was a skillful display of horsemanship by Vince Sylvestro, where he demonstrated his ability to stand in the sulky behind his horse, this being difficult on its own, at a very fast speed, holding the reins in his teeth. This man became well known for his stunt displays, and quite often gave exhibitions of his skill with his horses on our metropolitan tracks. Vince's reputation subsequently spread to America, where he was invited to perform before their racing enthusiasts.

There were other trick horses and handlers there and a variety of other events to amuse and entertain the public. Even our blacksmith was recruited to show his expertise, and explain the art of shoeing. Many people were keenly interested in his work, because he told us afterwards that he had fun fielding the many questions that were

When life gets you down, keep looking up.

asked of him. Considering how I felt, with my confidence in my boots when the day began, and then as I watched its progress as the weather changed for the better, I can only say that the day not only met my expectations, but surpassed them.

The local Lions, Apex, Rotary, and Quota clubs, CREST, CSW, the RSL Club, as well as some of our local commercial houses, offered their services and supplied food for the day, and Carlton United supplied some beverage.

My mother, who was in her seventies at the time, made 500 apple pies and a lot of mince tarts for the occasion. A few friends and I landed the job of peeling and cooking the apples for the pies. What a job! We were bumping elbows with one another in the kitchen and walking on each other's feet. There were apples and skins everywhere, not to mention that, by the time I had peeled my last apple, I think I had a band-aid on every finger of my left hand. All the work involved in the preparation, the cooking, freezing and thawing of the pies was worth the effort. Every pie was sold. There was a large marquee erected especially as a cake stall. The women excelled themselves by the number and quality of the cakes presented and, just as it was with Mum's apple pies, not one remained at the end of the day. Other stalls, such as our plant stall, met the same fate. Empty at the end of the day.

When the day finally drew to a close, approximately $25,000 dollars had been raised, and we now have a cardiac unit in Bowral Hospital. The management and staff were most grateful. They honoured all those who were donors or who were involved with the financing, by including their names in a booklet that was published about the unit. The reward that really mattered was the fact that now we had a cardiac unit in our own hospital, and that emergencies could now be taken care of, quickly and efficiently, in our own area.

A driver was critically injured in a race fall one night and, tragically, he died in hospital later. I went to see the family there, and while with them, learned of their financial position. I began an appeal for the family and went again to the people of the trotting industry. Once again the appeal was supported generously and by many. Apart from the generosity of the racing folk, and the considerable sum that was donated to the grieving family, the warm and overwhelming support from so many was a comfort to the family as well.

Even the 'battlers' (and there are some in the racing game) gave as much as they could spare; not one refused me.

Unfortunately, due to my eyesight, I was later forced to relinquish my participation in the one charity that was very dear to my heart: Ronald McDonald House, a home away from home for terminally ill children and their families. Two dear friends, Janet and Ron Greason, who then lived in Bundanoon, a village about five miles from Exeter, first introduced me to this home. For a long time, Ron helped in the stables and with the horses. He has dragged bales of hay and cut winter firewood for us as well. When it came to volunteering to assist with the organisation of functions, or cooking for them, Janet was first in line. Janet and Ron were a tower of strength to Vic and me, particularly after Garry's death. They were tireless workers for the home, since the loss of their son, Robert, from leukemia 20 years ago, and know the agony of the parents and suffering of the child. Janet and Ron have since moved to Sussex Inlet and have been forced to retire from helping the home, by ill health and distance.

There was an urgent need for a minibus for the home, to take the residents to and from hospital and to other places necessary for their children's treatment. I came up with what I thought was a brilliant idea. I thought of having a dinner and auction in the function room at Harold Park. I needed at least 100 people to attend, and a large number of items available for auction—items that people would want to buy, and valuable enough to give a reasonable return.

At times I have been astonished at the notoriety I have gained from my selling tickets of one kind or another. Once I had a get-well card that I wished to send to a dear man, the late Eddie Simms, a fellow trotting driver who was very sick. I was taking it around the stables at the Park for the other drivers to sign. As soon as they saw me coming with a pen in my hand they would start putting their hands in their pockets and say 'How much, Margaret?' They were so used to me selling raffle tickets that they took it for granted that was what I was doing again. I have a very great admiration and affection for this crowd and have always have felt so at ease with them.

To be asked to stand in front of a crowd, or even to address a small group, was stressful. I have found myself more nervous having to talk to groups, such as Rotary Club members and others, than having to stand out in front of a large race crowd and address them. With

Cast your cares on the Lord and He will sustain you.   Psalm 55:22

the racing fraternity, I was one with them, I could be totally me and they knew me, we used the same vocabulary.

Glenn has also done much and achieved much in this regard, sometimes putting others before his own immediate interests. There have been times his own family has suffered as a consequence. It is often late before he can give his children the time they need, the time to play the games that they enjoy sharing together, and as a result, because they both go to school, Nicki and Andrew find it hard to wake up in the mornings.

Glenn did not win many races in the first few months of 1999 after the accident, but he is battling to change this situation. A few good horses to race would be a blessing to him right now, as most of his team are on their marks and, as all trainers know, it is almost impossible to win races when this happens. Brett and Glenn are breaking in some of Westburn Grant's progeny and one colt in particular is showing some promise. It is only a slim chance at this stage, but the knowledge of owning a good horse would give their flagging spirits a big lift, which is very much what they need right now.

The Frost family knows what it feels like to own and race a champion. It is not an experience that comes to all owners, or owner-drivers, but once having had the elation that goes with the experience, the search for the next champion goes on. Maybe it will be the next horse that is bought, or the next foal, that becomes our elusive champion.

It would give me the greatest pleasure for Glenn to acquire a horse of outstanding promise, to train and race in the family colours, so that he and the family may experience for themselves the wonders of owning and racing a champion, as Vic and I had done. Hopefully, now that Brett has his trainer's licence also, he may one day train a champion for me as well.

These days, my interest in racing and training is kept up mostly from a distance. Glenn and Brett keep me well informed of any developments taking place at Glen-Garry Lodge. I still have part ownership of several horses and keep a keen eye on their performance, even though none of them have been any more than mediocre. Once a horse person, always a horse person. I can no longer train or drive horses, but I still have an interest in them and I don't expect this ever to change.

It is difficult to remain away from the farm for long; it was my life. My children and grandchildren live there. My grandchildren are unable to visit me except on school holidays and of course the holidays aren't frequent enough for me. I love them so much and want to have some influence on their little lives; I want them to grow up knowing that they are loved just for themselves, a grandmother's specialty. As much as I enjoy living on the lake, I cannot leave the farm without a lump in my throat.

Sadness, physical and emotional pain still make their presence felt, and I have prayed to my Lord in tears at times, when made more aware of the frailty and perishable nature of my human condition. But I give Him thanks for bringing me this far and for revealing a new spiritual dimension to me. My faith is my strength.

John wrote a poem about my grief for Garry and, because of the effect it has on me, I wish to share it.

Missing Him

She was leaning on the railing,
Looking out across the sea.
I could hear her whisper softly,
'I can feel him here with me.'

The stars were twinkling brightly,
In the dark and moonless skies,
And their shimmering in the water,
Was reflected in her eyes.

She stood there in the darkness,
Her thoughts were far away.
Her memories took her back
To those of another day.

She didn't speak for quite some time,
As her memories flooded in.
What pain was welling in her breast,
Who would dare begin?

In the silence of the evening,
I could hear the waves upon the sand,
She reached up, gently wiping
A tear away with her hand.

'Yes, I'll be all right now,
I just needed time to be.
These precious moments that I've had
Have left me feeling free.

'He is here—I know it!
my toils and troubles cease.
The faith and strength of knowing—
His Presence gives me Peace.'

When my mother migrated to Australia after World War 2, other members of the family were not all that came with her. She brought with her the family's almost famous recipe for pancakes that had been handed down from mother to daughter in our family for goodness only knows how long.

MUM'S PANCAKES

2 Cups of SR Flour
2 Tablespoons of sugar (syrup)
Pinch of Cream of Tarter, and bi-carb
2 eggs
2 Cups of Milk
Adding a tablespoon of melted butter is optional

The syrup makes lovely flavoured dark brown pancakes, with the syrup needed to be heated enough (with butter) to mix easily.

• Sift flour into bowl, add dry ingredients, then beaten eggs, milk and melted butter

• Mix well and put tablespoons of mixture onto hot griddle or fry-pan, lightly greased with copha, and cook until small bubbles appear

• Turn and cook until light brown

• Wrap in tea-towel after taking from fry-pan

MUM'S APPLE SPONGE

6-8 cooking apples
1 cup of sugar (to suit taste)
4oz butter or margarine
1 egg
1 cup SR Flour
Enough milk to make firm, but not runny.

• Cook apples with sugar and place in Pyrex bowl

• Cream butter or margarine with sugar, then add egg and beat well

• Fold in SR Flour, and if too dry, add milk

• Smooth on top of apples and cook in medium oven foe about 20 minutes

• Serve with ice-cream or custard